W✟FEWORK

WHAT MARRIAGE **REALLY** MEANS FOR WOMEN

SUSAN MAUSHART

BLOOMSBURY

Published by Bloomsbury, New York and London
Distributed to the trade by Holtzbrinck Publishers

Library of Congress Cataloging in Publication Data

    Maushart, Susan, 1958-
      Wifework: what marriage really means for women/ Susan Maushart
        p. cm.
    Includes bibliographical references ([254]-266) and index.
    ISBN 1-58234-202-4
    1. Wives. 2. Marriage. 3. Divorce. I. Title.

    HQ759 M3944 2002
    306.872--dc21

                                 2001052662

First published in Australia by The Text Publishing Company, Melbourne, in 2001

First U.S. Edition 2002

10 9 8 7 6 5 4 3 2 1

Typeset by Palimpsest Book Production Limited, Polmont, Stirlingshire
Printed in the United States of America by R.R. Donnelley & Sons Company, Harrisonbury, Virginia

for Karen

'Only she who says
She did not choose, is the loser in the end.'
Adrienne Rich

contents

wifework: the job description

'Wife: 1. a. A woman: formerly in general sense; in
later use restricted to a woman of humble rank or "of
low employment".' *Oxford English Dictionary*

In many languages, there is a single word for 'wife' and 'woman'.
Perhaps we should be thankful that English is no longer one of them.
Somewhere in the last quarter-century, the term 'wife' has lost its
neutrality. Once a simple descriptor of a woman's marital status, the
word today evidently means a whole lot more—and a whole lot less—
than it did a generation or two ago. Even sociologists and demographers
speak of 'married women' or 'female partners', as if 'wife' were a four-
letter word best left unspoken in polite company.

Many married women today actually shun the designation 'wife'.
They fantasise about acquiring a wife, not becoming one. 'Well, I'd have
another wedding,' one divorced woman explained, 'but next time around
I'd make sure I married someone who didn't want a wife.' I'd wager that
99 per cent of ever-married women know exactly what she means—and
that a similar proportion of ever-married men wouldn't have a clue.

Wives, it seems, have gone the way of patterned lino, fondue pots
and ironed sheets—a cultural collectable now viewed with amused
disdain. 'Take my wife...please!' went the old gag. It used to make

husbands laugh until they were weak. Yet somewhere in the last few decades, it seems somebody *has* taken her.

We hear a lot these days about the breakdown of the family. We've been hearing it for a long time now. In the US, the divorce rate now exceeds 50 per cent; in the UK it is only slightly under that figure. Even in conservative Australia, 43 per cent of all marriages end in divorce. In raw figures, that's 50,000 divorces a year—carrying an estimated price tag of six billion dollars in court, health and social security costs.[1] Young people are especially divorce-prone, with most break-ups occurring after two to four years of marriage.[2] In the UK, it is estimated that a third of couples marrying right now will be divorced within fifteen years.[3] In the US, reflecting trends throughout the English-speaking world, approximately one child in four now lives with a single parent—no surprise when you realise that roughly two-thirds of all American marriages that end in divorce involve children.[4] So-called 'traditional' families—two parents plus dependent children—now constitute only a quarter of all US households, and the profile is similar throughout the industrialised world.[5]

And yet social researchers, with apparent seriousness of purpose, continue to struggle with the question of whether marriage still 'works'. Maybe it's just habit. Books with titles like *The Future of Marriage* or (more ominously) *The End of Marriage* have been pouring from both academic and popular presses for decades. They all seem to conclude the same way: acknowledging that there are 'difficulties', yet ultimately promising 'real change'.

Such faith is touching. It is also a little puzzling. As social critic Dalma Heyn observes in her book *Marriage Shock*, any other social institution with a track record this dismal would have been dismantled long ago. Imagine a public-school system in which half the students dropped out. Or a justice system in which a third of law-breakers could be counted on to re-offend—or in which a third of juries handed down demonstrably false verdicts. Imagine a health-care system that disabled four in ten of its users, or an institution of higher learning rendering half of its graduates unemployable for life. For a society to tolerate such obvious inefficiencies and ineptitudes would seem unthinkable. Yet when it comes to marriage, we are willing, even eager, to make exceptions. Why?

Why do we remain agnostic on the question of whether we 'believe in' marriage? Why, despite an avalanche of evidence for the prosecution, do we remain reluctant to convict?

The reason, I have become convinced, is quite simple. As everybody knows, marriage works for some people, but not for others. It follows logically that we can't really analyse 'marriage' until we know *whose* marriage we're talking about. Yet by that I do not mean the Smiths' marriage versus the Joneses', or the Finkelsteins' versus the Fongs', or a 'good' marriage versus a 'bad' one.

I mean His marriage versus Her marriage. The husband's marriage versus the wife's.

We can't make up our minds about marriage because we have not yet acknowledged that these two versions of the one relationship are fundamentally and perhaps irreconcilably divergent. And, more to the point, we have not yet acknowledged—perhaps not even to ourselves—that His marriage still works. And Hers doesn't.

It was the noted American sociologist Jessie Bernard who first articulated the concept of the two marriages. 'Anyone...discussing the future of marriage has to specify whose marriage he is talking about: the husband's or the wife's,' she observed. 'For there is by now a very considerable body of well authenticated research to show that there really are two marriages in every marital union, and that they do not always coincide.'[6] Bernard wrote those words almost thirty years ago. Today, of course, we live in a different world. Today, they almost never coincide.

Ironically, our belief that the two marriages should coincide, indeed that they must do so, has grown ever stronger. Our new egalitarian convictions have made it even harder to penetrate beyond the veil, as it were. Both males and females in our society publicly profess their dedication to the ideal of what social researchers call 'companionate marriage'—a covenant between two equally loving and nurturant partners, in which the divisions of labour and leisure are negotiated rationally, equitably and, above all, without reference to gender.

But when a woman marries, what she sees is not what she gets. The exterior architecture of the contemporary marriage emphasises fluidity, simplicity and light. No wonder it's got such fantastic street appeal. Venture inside, however, and you're in for a nasty shock. Notwithstanding the tastefully renovated facade, the interior of today's marriages remains as dusty, cramped and overelaborated as a Victorian drawing-room. It looks awful. And it feels worse. Is it really so surprising that so many of us eventually pack up and leave that house—even if it renders us literally homeless to do so?

Look closely at the facts surrounding so-called family breakdown and a surprising pattern emerges. The edifice that's crumbling is not really 'marriage' at all. Being married is not the problem. Nor is being a parent, or at least not in the same way. The problem is being a wife.

Everyone knows the divorce rate in our society has skyrocketed, but few realise that two-thirds to three-quarters of those divorces are initiated by women. The inescapable conclusion is that women are more dissatisfied within marriage than men. Perhaps even more telling, the vast majority of divorced women—more than eight in ten, according to Australian Institute of Family Studies researchers Irene Wolcott and Jody Hughes—report having no regrets about their choice.[7] They are also nearly twice as likely as divorced men to describe themselves as being happy. No wonder ex-wives are so much slower to remarry than ex-husbands. Married women who imagine they might be better off single often find, upon divorce, that they really *are* better off single. Not financially—divorce typically lowers a woman's standard of living by 73 per cent and raises a man's by 42 per cent—but emotionally.[8] Psychologically. Spiritually. Even physically.

In a review of studies of adult well-being conducted over a period of three decades, sociologist Janice Steil found that married women consistently fare worse on every measure—including feelings of loneliness, anxiety and depression—than their husbands. Unemployed wives are the most disadvantaged of all females. These women consistently report the greatest number of psychiatric symptoms and experience the highest incidence of depression.[9]

Indeed, for females, depression and marriage go together like the proverbial horse and carriage. Wives report levels of depression two to three times higher than unmarried women, and, if they are unhappily married, three times higher than that of their husbands.[10] (Bizarrely, the depression rate for women in 'happy marriages' is higher still![11]) As Dalma Heyn has observed, compared to single women, wives suffer 'more nervous breakdowns, inertia, loneliness, unhappiness with their looks; more insomnia, heart palpitations, nervousness, and nightmares; more phobias; more feelings of incompetence, guilt, shame, and low self-esteem'.[12] 'Many problems brought to individual psychotherapy are really relationship problems,' notes Howard Markman, head of the Center for Marital and Family Studies at the University of Denver. 'First and foremost is depression among women. Our studies show a co-variation of depression and marital problems.'[13]

It's not that marriage is bad for women. On most well-being indicators, in fact, married women score slightly higher than their single sisters. But what sociologists call the 'protective effect' of marriage is far weaker for women than it is for men. 'Marriage is pretty good for the goose most of the time, but golden for the gander practically all the time,' notes Pulitzer-prize-winning journalist Natalie Angier, author of *Woman: An Intimate Geography*. That's a fair summation of the research. But it also begs a number of questions. Questions like, 'pretty good' compared to what? And 'Is "pretty good" good enough for a woman to stake her life on?'[14]

Studies of adult well-being do show that married women edge out their single sisters—often narrowly—on many indicators. But for women, there are some significant holes in the marital ozone layer. Women gain from marriage, no question. But the ratio of benefits to costs is nowhere near as advantageous to wives as it is to husbands.

Women who tell themselves that marriage is 'just a piece of paper', that 'it won't make any difference to our relationship at all', are kidding themselves. If you are female, marriage will make a huge difference— and a surprising proportion of that difference will be negative. Becoming a wife will erode your mental health, reduce your leisure, decimate your libido, and increase the odds that you will be physically assaulted or murdered in your own home. Is it any wonder that increasing numbers of single women are happy to stay that way? Although three-quarters of all people who divorce will eventually re-marry, men are three times more likely to do so than women.[15] In the US, the number of unmarried couples has nearly doubled in the 1990s, from 3.2 to 5.5 million. In 2000, for the first time ever, the number of Americans living alone—26 per cent of all households—surpassed the number of married-couple households with children. Families headed by women who have children grew nearly five times faster in the 1990s than did two-parent nuclear families.[16] Demographers are now predicting that, among Australian women thirty-five and younger, up to 45 per cent will never marry at all. In the UK, out of 3.8 million women in their thirties, almost a million are single or divorced. The British Office for National Statistics forecasts that a quarter of all women will be single by the year 2020.

One can only speculate how many among this growing number will remain 'never-married' by choice. The evidence, however, strongly suggests that single women are increasingly cynical about their marriage prospects. Data from the 1993 US General Social Survey showed that three in four never-married men under the age of thirty described getting married as important for their lives—compared with only two-thirds of young women.[17] From one point of view, of course, both are absurd underestimates. Marriage profoundly affects *all* of us, 100 per cent, male and female alike. Whether we ever personally undertake it, whether we even choose to 'believe' in it, marriage remains the basic building block of our social structure, the very touchstone of adult identity.

Monogamy is supposed to be 'a compromise offering something for everyone', argues evolutionary anthropologist Sarah Blaffer Hrdy. Evidently, what it's offering women today is simply not enough.[18]

The research shows that His marriage feels better the more closely it approaches the traditional nuclear template. Her marriage feels better the further it retreats from that ideal. Wives experience the highest levels of physical and psychological well-being in marriages where there are few or no young children, where the gap between their own and their husbands' incomes is relatively small, and where they continuously pursue a full-time career that predates the marriage. As researchers have been quick to point out, these factors all increase a woman's power in the relationship, and empowered women—surprise, surprise!—are happier with their lives and therefore happier as wives.[19]

One would think this would make for stronger, more successful marriages. One would be wrong.

It doesn't take a PhD in sociology to observe that the better women fare in the workforce the worse they (and their partners) seem to fare in marriage. Indeed, a look at the figures reveals a clear inverse relationship between marriage dissolution and women's improving socio-economic status. Some researchers have suggested that for high-earning women, the 'opportunity costs' of marriage may simply prove exorbitant. Without doubt, what the sociological establishment still euphemistically calls 'status inconsistency' has become a big risk factor for marital instability—but only when the wife's professional rank exceeds her husband's. When his status is higher, the inconsistency, it seems, is, well, consistent. A woman's educational attainments are also inversely linked to marital stability. As her qualifications increase, so does the likelihood that her marriage will come unstuck.[20]

What's more—and more disturbing—is that the greater a wife's earnings relative to her husband, the worse she says she feels about herself as a spouse. For men, it's exactly the opposite. It seems that, despite the worst fears of most males, if women had their way in marriage they would no more seek to dominate men than they would seek to weave themselves into doormats. So what *do* women want? The answer, the research suggests, is something far more elusive. Researchers call it 'equality'. You and I might call it 'justice'.

Men want equality in marriage, too, of course. The difference is, they think they already have it. If we accept that 'equal' has become a kind of code word for 'unproblematic'—and I am convinced it has—then this perception becomes a great deal more explicable.

Marriage is not only unproblematic for men, it is positively and empirically life-enhancing. Men do not initiate divorce for one very simple reason: they like being married. For men, marriage not only still feels good. It *is* good. And the more traditional that marriage is, the better it gets. What gets better? Just about everything, if the research is to be believed. In the words of University of Virginia sociologist Steven Nock, 'Men reap greater gains than women for virtually every outcome affected by marriage'.[21] Marriage increases men's wages. It reduces substance abuse, drinking and other unhealthy behaviours. Married men see their relatives more often, attend church more regularly, go to the pub less, and have greater involvement in community organisations. They are also more philanthropic (he may be less likely to help out a friend, but a married man is more likely to assist a relative or make a public donation). Married men live longer, in part because they are less likely to be murdered than unmarried men. Marriage enhances men's mental health, providing a particular bulwark against depression. For men, it is not marriage, but divorce, that poses the greatest risk for depression. Divorced men are not only more depressed than married men, they are more depressed than *anybody*, of any marital status.[22]

Marriage may or may not increase a woman's vulnerability, depending on the quality of the relationship. For men, it's different. Becoming a husband is like putting on a suit of armour. Social scientists are still puzzling over the reasons for what they call the 'protective effects of marriage' for men—effects which remain consistent across all socio-economic strata and which persist in troubled and even deeply unhappy marriages.

One conclusion researchers have drawn from all this is that marriage and masculinity are tightly interwoven. 'In their marriages, and by their marriages,' Steven Nock reminds us, 'men define and display them-selves as masculine.'[23] The relationship between a woman's femininity and her role as wife, by contrast, is of a different order of magnitude. Significant, certainly. But definitive, hardly. In this sense—as in many others—women just don't seem to need marriage as much as men do.

For middle-class women of the baby-boomer generation—women who grew up within a traditional family structure yet came of age socially, sexually and intellectually during feminism's second stage—the experi-ence of marriage has proven particularly fraught. To some extent, these women are history's hybrids, grafted imperfectly from ancient rootstock to produce new and often unpredictable varieties of growth. Their failure to thrive in the role of wife is perhaps to be expected. Yet it is no less painful for all that.

We have matured into a public culture in which gender no longer matters, or matters very much. In the US, women who work full time for pay earn only 76 per cent of male wages.[24] In the UK, the figure is 82 per cent.[25] But today, at least, such statistics make headlines. Legally, educationally, professionally, sexually, in just about every way imagin-able, women demand equal rights, are guaranteed equal rights, and most of the time—even if it's grudgingly—are granted those rights. This is true for every institution in our society, with one exception. Marriage.

Beyond the lip service paid to 'equal marriage' by both men and women, the contemporary family remains primarily, and profoundly, organised around gender. Beneath the veneer of its sleek post-feminist contours, the divisions of labour within the family remain rigidly gender-specific. Females within marriage are strenuously, over-whelmingly, outrageously responsible for the physical and emotional caretaking of males and offspring. Whether they're working for pay part-time or full-time. Whether they or their partners profess egalitarian ideals in public, in private or only in their dreams. Whether husbands appreciate it, acknowledge it or even know it. Or whether women themselves do.

Research conducted throughout the English-speaking world continues to show that wives, whether employed or unemployed, perform 70 to 80 per cent of the upaid labour within families. And husbands whose wives work full-time for pay do no more domestic labour than husbands of women who are not in paid employment at all.[26] What such dreary and familiar statistics conceal, however, is that wives also contribute 100 per cent of the husband care—the myriad tasks of physical and emotional nurture that I call 'wifework'.

By anybody's reckoning—if only somebody *would* reckon it—wife-work is a time-consuming, energy-draining and emotionally exorbitant enterprise. Centred primarily on the care and maintenance of men's bodies, minds and egos, wifework is a job that violates every principle of equal-opportunity employment—often, chillingly, in the name of 'love'. For there is no counterpart to wifework, no reciprocal 'husband-work' driving males to provide caregiving to their female partners at the expense of their own well-being. There are plenty of onerous and unfair expectations of males within marriage, too, of course. But, as we shall see, they are very different expectations, and they tell a very different story.

Wifework includes:

Performing a hugely disproportionate share of unpaid household labour (by conservative estimates, at least two-thirds to three-quarters of it, irrespective of Her occupational status—or His, for that matter).

Assuming total responsibility for His emotional caretaking (from organising His underwear drawer to arranging His social life).

Managing His intimacy needs at the expense of Hers (including relating sexually in a way that responds to His libidinal timetable and otherwise privileges His preferences).

Taking full responsibility for child-care drudgework (laundry, meals, tidying, homework supervision, shopping) so that He can enjoy quality time (games, sport, watching television with the kids).

Monitoring His physical well-being (providing a healthy diet, encouraging and supporting fitness activities, organising medical treatment, etc.).

Preparing meals tailored specifically to His taste, appetite and schedule.

Deferring to His agenda in day-to-day conversation (women initiate more topics, but men choose which ones will be pursued, demonstrating their conversational dominance by completing women's sentences, interrupting and withdrawing attention when it's the woman's turn to speak).[27]

Maintaining His extended family relationships (ringing, buying presents, sending thank-you notes, staging and catering family gatherings—and, most important of all, allocating the mental space to *remember* all of the foregoing).

Laughing at His jokes. (I'm serious. People have studied this.)

Wifework includes what Virginia Woolf called 'reflecting a man at twice his normal size'. Why, one wonders, would anyone want to do such a thing—and for a grown-up, no less? Dale Spender quotes one ex-wife, a speaker at a recent women-in-management conference, who asked the same question and, like so many other women, failed to come up with a good-enough answer. 'It just got to be too tiresome,' she told the audience. 'I woke up one day and decided I'd rather keep my money for myself. I had a good job, I really reared the kids...I did all the house-work. For God's sake, I even mowed the lawns. And I just decided that the husband had to go. There wasn't any advantage in keeping him.' According to Spender, the all-female audience 'nodded their heads in empathy and agreement'.[28]

Yet perhaps the most startling fact of all is not how unequal our marriages remain—but how, despite all the 'empathy and agreement', women have continued to collude in keeping them that way. And make no mistake about it. We do collude.

Recent research shows a remarkable degree of congruity between men's estimates of the disproportionate unpaid burden their wives bear and women's own estimates. The cynical among us will not be surprised to learn that the majority of husbands describe this hugely asymmetrical state of affairs as 'fair'. The real shocker is that their wives do too. There is a veritable social research industry dedicated to figuring out why. Yet until ordinary women begin to ask themselves the same question, the answers must remain academic in every sense of the word.

On the one hand, both men and women agree that they want to pursue relationships characterised by 'equal sharing'. Yet both reject—or say they do—that this sharing should be divided along traditional gender faultlines. 'We'll each do the things we're good at,' young couples maintain. If she likes to chop wood, fine. Let her chop wood. If he likes to cook, or mop the floor, he'll do it. Problem is, he never does like to mop the floor. And although he may genuinely enjoy preparing meals, the cooking, the planning, shopping, serving and cleaning up are another matter altogether. So she ends up chopping the wood, all right. (He doesn't have a problem with that.) She ends up not only changing the sheets and the baby's nappies but the oil and the light globes as well. In her zeal to show that she can do anything, she finds herself doing everything. Suddenly, the traditional division of labour along gender lines doesn't look so bad. 'Just tell me what to do and I'll do it,' he protests. But, as far as she's concerned, this only underscores the frustration. Which is that the joint enterprise of marriage is really her problem. He's just a volunteer.

Parenting works out much the same. Couples start out talking about co-parenting and fifty-fifty sharing, yet over time—usually a very short time—something happens to those good intentions. New mothers and fathers emerge from the haze of baby-shock to find themselves behaving like something out of a 1950s sitcom. Suddenly, he goes to work and brings home the bacon. She stays at home, frying it and feeding it to junior. 'It's only temporary,' they tell each other. Yet by the time she's ready to rejoin the workforce, the pattern has been set in concrete. Sure, he still talks about sharing the load. But, assuming he's like 70 per cent of fathers in a recent US study, he doesn't simply assume few child-care responsibilities. He assumes none at all, if by 'responsibilities' we mean not simply following orders but taking charge. Doing the mental work of parenting, if you will, as well as the physical work.[29]

To imagine a genderless marriage—a marriage in which roles and responsibilities are determined irrespective of gender considerations—is to imagine a paradox. Since time immemorial, and up to and including this morning at 11.30 a.m. (the time of writing), the very meaning of marriage has had gender at its core. To a great degree, marriage makes sense only to the extent that it involves two parties who acknowledge their mutual incompleteness. Marriage without dependency or, to use the trendier and slightly less scary term, interdependency, is therefore hardly recognisable as marriage at all.

Traditionally, the dependence of the female in marriage has had an economic or material base, and that of the male a biological and psychological base. Money or the promise of 'security'—whether that means protection from brute force, or simply the goods and services whose exchange value money represents—has always and everywhere bought men love, or at least purchased their progeny.

Evolutionary anthropologists agree that the institution of marriage arose as a means of preventing males from accidentally tipping their precious resources into somebody else's gene pool. Sexual exclusivity, in other words, was not some primitive romantic ideal but a blunt instrument for determining whose kid was whose, a neolithic 'gentle-man's agreement' trading off reproductive quantity for quality. It was an evolutionary gamble that paid off. By limiting a male's sexual options, monogamy produced many fewer offspring. But those who were produced enjoyed an unbeatable survival advantage: two parents devoted more or less single-mindedly to their nurturance and protection.

All organisms, whether male or female, respond to the evolutionary imperative to reproduce in order that their own DNA (and not some other bastard's) will 'live to see another day'. As can be readily seen, this places males at a serious structural disadvantage. Imagine a female exam-ining her newly born baby in an effort to determine if he is 'really hers'. Sexual exclusivity remains at the core of marriage not because men neces-sarily wish to repress women, but because they wish to know who their children are. The control of women's sexuality is simply a by-product of this wish—a bonus, if you will.

The monogamy gamble pays particular dividends to non-dominant males who, under a more laissez-faire mating system, might never get the chance to breed at all. Females, for their part, sacrifice variety and freedom of choice for the protection of a male against other males. In monogamous societies girls have less fun, but they live longer. The biggest winners in the monogamy stakes are the offspring. In evolu-tionary terms, at least, parents are a lot like heads, or Tim Tams. Two are better than one. For this reason it is probably more accurate to speak of three marriages, His, Hers and The Kids'.

It is my belief that marriages without children constitute another sort of entity altogether which, despite the profound importance it has for its participants, has only negligible social consequences. From the point of view of a social researcher, there is a very real sense in which, as one observer pithily explained to researcher Judith Wallerstein, 'Marriage needs children. That's what makes it a marriage. Otherwise it's just a date.'[30]

From a historical or biological perspective, marriage without chil-dren is an oxymoron, a construct as problematic as a meal without food.

It is no exaggeration to say that marriage is *about* children. It always has been—although we in the industrialised west have in the last hundred years or so persuaded ourselves otherwise. Marriage, we now insist, is primarily about romantic love. The couple, and their feelings one towards another, form the bedrock upon which the edifice of marriage is built—and to which, like a second-storey extension, offspring may or may not be added. In the past half-century, these convictions about the dispensability of children to marriage and marriage to children, utterly unprecedented in human history, have become a standard feature of our assumptive world. It is now a truism that having a child will not 'save' a marriage; and the whole concept of 'staying together for the sake of the kids' seems as antiquated as the dictum to 'love, honour and obey'.

Our collective denial that there exists such a thing as Their marriage, the Children's marriage—our refusal to reckon with the stubborn biological fact that monogamy is more than the sum of the emotional parts of its adult participants—lies at the heart of our confusion about the future of marriage. However we may feel personally or politically about the matter, the exclusion of offspring from our reckoning of what marriage means represents a daring attempt to cut the institution off at its roots. No wonder it is dying on the vine.

Trying to understand how marriage works without reference to its three stakeholders—wives, husbands and children—is like trying to understand bread without reference to flour, yeast and water. It's illogical, impossibly abstract and doomed to failure—yet we persistently do so anyway. Possibly this explains why we can't quite make up our minds whether we 'believe' in marriage, or whether the contemporary family is 'breaking down' (or simply breaking through).

Of course, it was not always like this. The lopsidedness of contemporary marriage is not essential to the institution. It is rather a set of adaptations to a particular environment, shaped by biological imperatives on the one hand, and by socio-historical forces gaining momentum over the course of several centuries on the other. The fact that these adaptations are proving to be increasingly unworkable and inefficient is both the bad news and the good news. It's bad because it underscores how perilously marriage is now sagging under the weight of our extravagant and contradictory expectations. Yet to see marriage from an evolutionary perspective also reminds us that we are not doomed to beat our heads against this particular brick wall—or not indefinitely anyway. It reminds us that adaptations that don't work are eventually abandoned in favour of those that do.

We are not there yet, though. The adaptations that have rendered marriage such a lopsided institution continue to perform a decent job of work for two out of three of its stakeholders. The result is a role structure which benefits men enormously, children adequately and women insufficiently. That seems unfair. That *is* unfair.

And that's where the evolutionary parallel ends. A social institution, even a social institution that fulfils a vital biological function, as marriage does, is never simply a means to an end. It is also an idea. Unlike the mechanisms of 'nature red in tooth and claw'—the various means which guarantee the survival of the fittest—human institutions are answerable to a set of pesky moral imperatives, justice among them. The research on the experience of men and women in marriage, however fascinating and enlightening it may be, seems to have missed a fundamental insight with great explanatory power: men get one thing from marriage that women never do. They get wives.

One wonders how this salient fact eluded everybody—except wives!— from psychologists and social researchers to cultural critics and the guardians of our public morality. It's so incredibly obvious. It explains so much. Indeed, it explains almost everything. Why marriage confers protection on men, yet fails to do so for women. Why marriage increases women's physical and emotional workload, and creates more leisure time for men. Why women initiate so many divorces, and are happy to stay single, while the majority of their exes 're-offend' within a year. Why most men describe their wives as their best friend, yet most wives describe their husbands as 'another child' and experience true emotional intimacy primarily with other women.[31]

The jokes about women needing wives, too, have been around since the dawning of feminism's second stage. 'I want a wife who will take care of my physical needs,' 'radical' feminist Judy Syfer confessed more than a quarter of a century ago. 'I want a wife who will keep my house clean. A wife who will pick up after my children, a wife who will pick up after me…I want a wife who is sensitive to my sexual needs, a wife who makes love passionately and eagerly when I feel like it, a wife who makes sure that I am satisfied.'[32] For middle-class women today, such sentiments are about as radical as 'equal pay for equal work'. We *know* that. But knowing, it seems, ain't gettin'.

It's supposed to be different now. In the bad old days, Germaine Greer reminds us in *The Whole Woman*, 'Men could have both a marriage and a profession, but not women, because being a wife, unlike being a husband, was a fulltime job'.[33] Tsk, tsk, we reflect. So much has changed since then. The problem is, so much has also remained the same. Much, much more than we are comfortable admitting to ourselves. Much, much more than we ever read about in the press, or watch on television. (The media, never forget, is change-driven, focusing always and everywhere on what's new and improved—or new and debased, it doesn't really matter—at the expense of what persists.) Our rhetoric about marriage remains revolutionary, particularly when we've had a couple of champagnes with the girls. But for the vast majority of us, the real picture—beginning with the fact that being a wife is *still* a full-time job—remains sepia-tinted. For the vast majority of us, marriage remains a matter of dancing to somebody else's tune—till death, or divorce, turns down the volume for good.

The steps to that dance are what I call 'wifework'. If you're married, and a female, you already know what they are. Whether you secretly love wifework (and, frankly, that would put you in a tiny minority), secretly loathe it or, like most of us, can't seem to make up your mind from one day to the next, one thing is certain. You know the choreography by heart. You know exactly what to do, and when and how. What you might not know is why you do it—or whether it's possible to start doing it differently. 'Wifework' is a shorthand for what I think of as the unwritten contract into which a woman enters upon marriage. The job description most of us were determined would never apply to us.

# of marriage, metamorphosis and rotten eggs

'Marriage is an institution. And I ain't ready for an institution yet.' Mae West

At the time of my first marriage back in the mid-eighties—sorry, but you're going to have to keep reading if you want to find out how many more there were—I was no blushing bride, believe me. Aged twenty-seven, I'd had two long-term monogamous partners, one of whom I'd lived with for two years, in addition to the usual assortment of more casual boyfriends. I had been financially independent for almost ten years, in which time I'd completed a BA, MA and PhD. Like most native New Yorkers, I thought of myself as fearless—and, if my habit of riding the subways unaccompanied and unflappable at 4 a.m. is any indication, I suppose I was.

The privileged daughter of a middle-class nuclear family, complete with full-time homemaker Mum and sole-breadwinner Dad, I naturally became an ardent feminist. So did almost everybody else I knew in graduate school. When I became engaged, my girlfriends thought it was the kitschest thing they'd ever heard of. Those older than I were, almost by definition, already divorced. Those my age and younger seemed to regard marriage as a prospect almost as distant as preparing a last will and testament—and about as appealing. Or that was the rhetoric, anyway.

Like students everywhere, perhaps, we were convinced that we could remake the world. Indeed, we were convinced that we already had. And this very much included marriage and family life. I no more dreamed that I would one day have a marriage like my mother's than I dreamed I'd have her wardrobe or hair-do or (heaven forbid!) her taste in music.

Clearly, the world had moved on from the kind of marriage my parents made in the deep dark recesses of the early fifties. Girls were now educated exactly as boys were (I believed). They competed equally in the workplace (I believed). Thanks to the Pill (I believed), young women were as free as young men to explore and express their sexuality. Having children was now clearly a choice (I believed) and, if you made that choice, you and your partner shared equally in the benefits and consequences. Marriage was a piece of paper (I believed) that changed nothing, with the possible exception of the willingness of relatives to provide kitchen appliances. As far as gender roles in marriage were concerned, they were about as relevant (I believed) as a glory box full of embroidered linen napkins.

I believed all that. And yet, from the moment I said 'I do', my behaviour belied those beliefs. And my husband's did too. In the two years of our courtship, I'd never once inquired into his beliefs—even the conscious ones—about marriage. It seems never to have occurred to me that the fact that he was Australian, ten years older and a male might in some way colour his view of things. I remember being surprised when he requested, rather firmly, that I refrain from smoking during our outdoor wedding reception. As a heavy pipe-smoker he was hardly in a position to get all holier than thou on me. 'But why now?' I wanted to know. 'My cigarettes have never bothered you before. And everybody else will be smoking.' (Remember that this was Manhattan in the mid-eighties.) 'I'd just prefer that you didn't,' he replied evenly.

And that was the end of it. I didn't smoke. Not until the last guest had departed—at which point I lit up and promptly burned a big black hole in my beautiful veil. Maybe it was an omen.

We spent our honeymoon night in a swank uptown hotel where, when I wasn't otherwise occupied, I puffed away to my heart's content. The next afternoon we returned to what had been his apartment and was now, for the very first time, ours. I remember how I kept stealing glances at my ring during that cab ride. 'I'm married now,' I tried to get myself to believe. 'I'm somebody's wife.' Somehow or other, I just couldn't get it to sink in. Not counting the relief I felt that the wedding was mercifully over, and my mother and I had managed to avoid a public brawl, I felt exactly the same as I'd felt the day before. So why was I acting so strangely? Why, when I got 'home', did I proceed directly to the bathroom—*the bathroom*—and scrub it from top to bottom? I still wonder. Was this some weird way of marking female territory? A reverse form of weeing in every corner? All I knew for sure was that scrubbing that bathroom felt good. Wifely, even. I don't even remember what he was doing. Something husbandly, probably, like reading the paper.

But wait. It gets better.

By the time I'd sprayed, scoured, polished, rinsed and flushed away my temporary identity crisis, it was time to have dinner. Nothing earth-shattering about that. After all, we'd been having dinner together most nights for over two years. Like many graduate students, we mostly ate takeaways or grabbed a cheap meal at one of the many cafes around the university. If we ate in, and we were at my place, I cooked. If we were at his place, he did. Frankly, I don't even remember who did the dishes, or whether we even used dishes. Preparing meals wasn't something either of us ever really thought about.

And then we got married.

'I suppose I really ought to cook dinner,' I remember thinking to myself rather uncertainly. I checked the fridge. It was the usual collection of bachelor stuff: a few bottles of beer, some wizened tomatoes, a carton of milk. Undaunted, I reached for a cookbook. It was *Betty Crocker*, a shower present from an elderly aunt. Only a few weeks earlier, it had seemed faintly comic, lying on my desk on top of a pile of research monographs and journals. Now I studied it with rapt attention. After what seemed like hours I produced a macaroni and cheese casserole (!) every bit as bland and gluggy as my mother's own. It is a testament to his feelings for me that he ate two portions. It is a testament to my feelings about being a wife that I felt compelled to prepare it in the first place.

No one told me to scrub the bathroom and prepare an evening meal. If anyone had, I would have laughed long and hard. 'Excuse me,' I would have said between gasps, 'but this is 1985, not 1955. I'm a PhD student, not a Barbie doll.' I had the feminist script down perfectly. And I wasn't just parroting sentiments I'd heard others express. I sincerely believed every word. My consciousness was raised, all right. But my subconscious was still dragging along the ground. My behaviour simply didn't accord with my convictions at all. At first, I didn't even notice the contradiction. Like many young people starting off in marriage, I was too much in love (trans: too dazed by sex) to notice. Later on, I noticed it with a vengeance. Indeed, the more my awareness grew, the more puzzled and resentful I felt. Yet when I forced myself to 'walk the talk', as I eventually did, it felt even worse. Instead of experiencing empowerment, I experienced guilt.

We soon settled into a routine that was riddled with what I had learned in college to identify as 'sex-role stereotypes'. Within a few months we had both finished our doctorates—in my case, thanks largely to my husband's intervention. For another mysterious effect of marriage was my sudden and almost overpowering lack of interest in finishing my thesis. Vainly, I tried to convince him that it was imperative that I get a job. At the time, I tried to pass this off as a practical necessity. This was not entirely spurious since we had no income beyond a couple of measly stipends and our wedding loot. In order to return to Australia to take up a new position, he was working to a very tight deadline. In my case there was no urgency at all ('now that I was married' I might have added—but of course I didn't). 'Take as long as you want to finish,' he finally told me. 'But you're not leaving New York without the degree.' I was terribly offended by this. But in the end—in time-honoured wifely fashion—I did as I was told. Now I think of that saga as a classic post-feminist parable: once upon a time, there was a wife who got her advanced qualification…because her husband told her to!

The funny thing is, if anybody had asked me whether I regarded our marriage as 'equal', or our decision-making as 'shared', I would have honestly answered *yes, of course*. That *was* how I saw it.

I've since learned that the sociologists have a word for this particular delusion: pseudomutuality. A state of affairs in which both parties profess egalitarian ideals, and pretend that they are sharing equally, while still conducting their married lives according to more or less rigid gender-typed roles. Pseudomutuality is not simply a public pretence—not just a 'front' married people adopt to impress researchers or friends or neighbours. It is, rather, a front we adopt to impress ourselves, to convince each other that our marriages are fundamentally different from our parents' marriages, that what seem to be enormous contradictions between thought and action aren't, really. If that makes pseudomutuality sound like a form of denial, it *is* a form of denial, according to Australian sociologists Michael Bittman and Jocelyn Pixley. And they should know. They coined the term in their 1997 book *The Double Life of the Family*.

Bittman and Pixley argue that we take refuge in pseudomutuality— where we say we're equal, but act as if we're not—for exactly the same reason we seek out other forms of denial. We are (a) scared. And we are (b) confused. Denial is a way we keep up the illusion of control in the face of overwhelming evidence to the contrary. Denial makes us feel more comfortable—at least over the short term—by reducing the unbearable tension of collapsed boundaries, or shuffled priorities, or any other formerly stable structure in our lives that has begun to sway, buckle or disintegrate. We are most vulnerable to denial, in other words, whenever we are most caught up in change. Whenever the demand to adapt to a new set of conditions either outstrips our capacity to do so fully, or compromises our ability to do so without pain or awkwardness.

Denial, or what my mother used to call 'making nice', is no respecter of gender, even if men and women have different ways of doing it. Pseudomutuality is not just a matter of men paying lip service to an ideal they have no intention of attaining—although there are plenty of men who do this. More significant, and more interesting by far, pseudomutuality is a stance adopted by both men *and* women, most often (and most insidiously) as an unconscious way to protect consciously and genuinely held beliefs. If those beliefs—beliefs about justice, equity, intimacy, sharing—were not important to us, we wouldn't need to bother about subterfuge. The incongruities wouldn't get to us.

Some commentators have suggested that pseudomutuality is, for women, an admission of defeat. They contend that women may be pretending their marriages are 'really' fair, or that they are 'really' lucky to have the husbands they do, because they have lost all hope of attaining anything better. These observers may have a point. 'When desired outcomes, to which one feels entitled, are perceived as unattainable,' one 1998 study observed, 'a frequent response is to define the situation to redefine the injustice'.[1] Or, as Orwell might have put it, it's not that husbands and wives aren't equal. It's just that husbands are more equal than wives. As Bittman and Pixley point out, this is 'a characteristically "modern" form of the exercise of domestic power'.[2]

Pseudomutuality, I now know, is not some bizarre aberration that afflicts people too young or too silly to know better. On the contrary, pseudomutuality is not an aberrant pattern at all. Indeed, I would argue that in our society, at the present moment, it is a typical one—probably *the* typical one among middle-class men and women over the age of twenty-five.

My first marriage was a textbook case of pseudomutuality in action. On a personal level, we had all the usual good intentions without any of the requisite skills or insights. On a historical level, we were part of what some social scientists have called the 'sandwich generation', caught between the traditional families in which we were incubated and the equal-opportunity world into which we hatched, wide-eyed and expectant. Structurally, our so-called equal relationship was farcically asymmetrical from the time of our first date. He was older, taller, stronger, and earned more money in a higher prestige job. And, far from eroding with time, the differences simply grew more pronounced the longer we were together, an effect that, if we'd had a child together, would have accelerated exponentially. Eventually—inevitably—the tension of living a pseudo-life together was more than we could stand. Or, perhaps I should say, more than I could stand.

Don't get me wrong. From my husband's point of view, our married life was hardly a bed of roses. Then again, it was no bed of nails either. Without doubt, he felt neglected and unsupported. In a vague sort of way he could never really articulate, he felt disappointed. Let down. As if marriage had, for him, made more promises than it could deliver. On the other hand, I was beginning to realise that his expectations of the relationship were very different from my own. In some ways, those expectations were much higher. He certainly expected a level of physical care and nurture far beyond anything I'd ever even contemplated for myself. The first time he grumbled about a lack of clean jocks in his underwear drawer, I honestly thought it was a joke. The day I started lying to him about line-drying his shirts (in fact, I threw them in the dryer as soon as he left for work), I knew it had gotten way beyond a joke.

In the wake of the macaroni-and-cheese incident, it will hardly come as a surprise to learn that I continued to do most of the cooking. 'I do the washing up, though,' he used to tell everyone. Technically, this was true. He did wash the dishes. What he didn't do was dry them or put them away. He also didn't wipe down the table, stove or benchtop, sweep the kitchen floor, or clear away the leftovers. He washed up. Period. His approach to laundry was similar. 'I did three loads of washing today' meant he had dumped clothes into the washing machine, added soap powder and turned it on, and that he had done this three times in a row.

Early on in the piece, we'd had a series of conflicts about how we spent Saturday morning. The way I saw it, the problem was that he played golf and I cleaned and did the shopping. The way he saw it, I was depriving him of something approaching husbandright. Although he did work longer hours for pay than I did, I still couldn't quite get myself to believe that such a division of leisure time was equitable. 'If you need help with the housework, just tell me what to do and I'll do it,' he used to maintain. Initially, I found this very reassuring. Then it dawned on me how much I hated 'asking', how much it always came out sounding more like 'nagging'. It would be years before the choice of the verb *help* would register as significant. In the end, we solved the problem—as do so many other dual-earning couples—by what today we call 'outsourcing'. Then, we called it hiring a cleaning lady.

Emotionally, his concerns—professional, intellectual, spiritual, whatever—were expected to be my concerns too. My concerns, on the other hand, were…well, my concerns. Like many wives, I found myself turning more and more to my women friends when I felt the need to talk things over and be heard.

So many times in the three years we lived as 'man and wife' he would announce, after yet another bitter and fruitless fight, that 'the marriage was over'. Yet when I finally called his bluff, and agreed—adding if he hadn't packed up and moved out by week's end that I would—he was shattered. In shock. I felt stifled, numb, middle-aged, way before my time. Yet neither of us could say exactly why.

When a marriage breaks up, not even the most dedicated social researcher can see herself as 'representative' or 'part of a trend'. But I know now that I was, anyway. This is not to say that our experience of marriage was not unique. Of course it was. And its nuances and complexities could never be captured by sociological analysis. Be that as it may, the fact remains that my husband and I were living out a social reality that would be duplicated—and still *is* being duplicated—in countless other marriages in similar circumstances around the English-speaking world. Our expectations, our disillusionments, our concerns and confusions were of course highly personal and intensely private; at the same time, they reflected a public, political reality of which we were not even dimly aware.

We thought we were making it all up as we went along. Improvising freely, wildly—perhaps badly at times. As a wife, I often felt awkward and unconvincing. I never realised that I was acting from a script. That my 'role' as a married woman was crafted far, far below the level of my own consciousness, impelling me to behave in ways I neither understood nor approved of.

I do recall that the break-up of that marriage was like waking up from one of those unsettling dreams which you explain by saying, 'Well, I was me, but I wasn't me, if you know what I mean.' I felt an enormous sense of relief that, as a single woman, I became 'myself' again. Yet within a couple of years, I was right back where I'd started from. With a new man, a new baby, in a new marriage, yet still playing out the same old script. There were lots of new episodes this time—some of them exciting, others truly terrifying—but the basic outline remained remarkably intact. I was right back in role (only this time with the added vengeance that comes of combining wifework with motherhood), alternately resenting it, revelling in it, and feeling guilty about it.

Two more kids and two more years later that marriage ended as well. And let me say before I go any further that there is nothing in the least typical about *that*. Marrying and divorcing twice in a decade is not exactly a Guinness record, but it hardly constitutes a trend either, thank God. Yet I do maintain that these peculiar circumstances allowed me to experience marriage in an unusually concentrated, potentially nearly lethal dose. Despite the rigours of single-handedly parenting three kids under the age of five, it was in the aftermath of my second marriage that the outlines of wifework first became clear to me.

One of the first things I noticed about life as a single parent was how much free time I seemed to have. Again, given the ages of my children, this hardly seemed possible. But there was no getting away from the fact that, in strictly relative terms, I had a great deal less work to do without a husband than with one. I was beginning to grasp the truth that, as Australian sociologist Anthony McMahon has observed, 'the help that husbands provide does not even cover the amount of work they create'.[3]

Even more shocking than rediscovering the concept of 'free time'—something I dimly recalled from my life before children—was the rediscovery of what I sometimes think of as 'free space'. Until I lived alone with my children, I'd never realised how much *space* a man takes up. When my husband left, it was as if a whole tribe had vacated. And all the big stuff seemed to go with him. The big antiques, the ones I'd always secretly considered rather ominous. The big sofas. The big stereo. The big car. It was weird at first. But as we started to downsize, I felt—to my surprise—less and less diminished, and more and more in control. The day we moved house, to a weatherboard cottage a third the size of the nuptial home, I felt like Alice who drinks the right potion at last.

Our circumstances were 'reduced' in every sense of the word, but I'd never felt less claustrophobic in my life. Why, even the fridge seemed spacious. So did our food budget—which I found myself quite effortlessly chopping in half. At first, every time I went grocery shopping, I marvelled at how economical I seemed to have become. Then it occurred to me I wasn't buying much meat any more, apart from the occasional sausage or meat pie. In fact, I'd pretty much stopped shopping for 'dinner' altogether. No surprise, really, when you consider that I also stopped cooking it! I still prepared the same sort of simple tea I'd always cooked for the children, feeding them as usual around five o'clock. The difference was I was no longer bothering to do the 'grown-ups' meal— the one that featured meat or fish, sauces or gravies, rice or pasta or potatoes, cooked vegies or salad. That, it suddenly dawned on me, was a man's meal. And now that I didn't have one of those anymore, I could eat what I liked—more often than not a sandwich, or a bowl of soup, or just the kids' leftovers. When they were in bed, I'd relax with a cup of tea and a couple of biscuits. It was bliss. (It was also remarkably slimming.)

Without a husband, life, just like my pre-pregnancy jeans, felt infinitely more spacious. It wasn't just the fridge. Even my mind seemed so much less cluttered than it had before. I still had plenty of other people's needs to anticipate and attend to—three totally dependent children, for starters. But this seemed like child's play after several years of dealing with a complex, overworked, emotionally immature, middle-aged professional every night. I had begun to realise that the unequal division of household labour in marriage is as nothing compared to the unequal division of emotional labour. It was only much later that I would start to examine the ease with which I had bought into this particularly arduous aspect of wifework—to consider which of my own needs were being met by allowing my husband's more obvious 'neediness' to take centre stage.

'You may know men who are emotionally self-sufficient. You may be such a man yourself,' Stephanie Dowrick observes in *Intimacy and Solitude*. 'Nevertheless, men's willingness to be cared for, and women's eagerness to collude, is worth consideration.'[4] In the years that have followed, I have considered it very closely indeed.

Then there was the matter of parenting. To be honest, I was less surprised at how little difference the absence of a father seemed to make, on an hour-to-hour, day-to-day basis, than I was by almost anything else in my post-divorce experience. I *knew* how little time he spent interacting with the children, let alone taking care of needs like feeding, toileting and comforting. Like the wives of many successful professional men, I'd already learned the hard way—from within the marriage—what being a single parent was all about. Compared to being a wife, being a single parent was easy. Yet the impact on my kids, which seemed so negligible at the start, was another story. It would take me years to discover, or perhaps admit, the difference between 'my divorce' and 'their divorce'.

Another unexpected change was the way my commitment to my own career shifted with my marital status. Like many women of my generation, I had struggled with the loss of financial independence that seemed an inescapable part of having children in your thirties. After the birth of my first child, I tried every possible permutation of full-time, part-time and casual work until resigning myself, as it were, to full-time motherhood when my second came along. It was no longer a financial necessity to work for pay, and I was grateful that I had that option. I sincerely felt I was doing the right thing for my children, who were then both under the age of three. At the same time, however, I felt guilty about what my husband called 'not contributing'. I worried too about the loss of professional identity. Finally, there were times when I was just plain jealous of my employed girlfriends who had another life to escape into: a professional, public life where they got to do stuff like wear stockings, and complete tasks, and talk to grown-ups. Pregnant with my third child, I half-heartedly applied for a small research grant. I was dumbfounded by my own excitement when I received it six months later. Maybe I wasn't as ambivalent as I thought I was. Still, I was so anxious about 'doing the right thing'—so impossibly indecisive about either pursuing my research or not pursuing it—that I remained stalled, both intellectually and practically.

And then my marriage broke up. And all the decisions that had seemed so hard became easy.

Becoming a single mother meant that I had 'permission' not to work for pay—or so I believed. Now that I was officially on my own as a parent, instead of technically part of a couple, staying home was easy to justify. After all, my youngest was only five months, my eldest only four years. Suddenly, it seemed obvious that my 'professional identity' (whatever that was) could wait. Financial worries that had vexed me as half of a high-earning couple evaporated overnight. What was the big deal? Now that I was eligible for the single parents' pension, and could count on receiving regular child support, I no longer worried about money.

I didn't have much, but I knew exactly when and where it was coming from. That was enough.

Then a funny thing happened. Within six months I became unquenchably interested in working again. It wasn't so much the money, although that was part of it. I realised I didn't actually like being supported by the state, although I was incredibly grateful that I had that option. It was better than being supported by my husband, mind you. But it still made me feel 'kept', I suppose you might say. I still wanted to spend most of my time at home with my children. But equally keenly I wanted to feel that I was participating in some way in the great world outside our cottage door. Well, why shouldn't I? Somehow, this yearning—which in the past had seemed deviant, or irresponsible, or just selfish—I now recognised as entirely right and natural. Of *course* I needed to do work in the world. I was not just a mother. I was a grown-up.

So I went back to work, very much on my own terms. Perhaps because I'd finally figured out that I didn't have to do anything, I found I could happily do almost everything. I was fortunate in having one or two opportunities fall into my lap, crowded though my lap was. More to the point, though, for the first time in my professional life I took risks. And the risks paid off. I wrote a book proposal, and found an agent (miraculously) to try to sell it for me. Even more miraculously, she succeeded. I started writing articles about parenting for a local newspaper, and before long I was offered a regular column. The day my earnings squeaked over the means test for Social Security was one of the proudest of my life. 'You're a writer, are you?' asked the usual case worker behind the counter when I handed her the documents. I think it was the first time she'd ever looked at me. I wouldn't have traded that moment for winning Lotto ten times over.

OK, OK. Enough already. So what am I saying? That busting up your marriage is the way to health and happiness and financial security? Of course not. And yet, I would be lying if I said there wasn't a grain of truth in that—and, in my case, perhaps even a small silo of it. My experience was not typical. Maybe no one's is. I now know that my marriage was not just difficult, but really peculiarly awful: chaotic, emotionally abusive and full of openly expressed hostility. There was almost nothing at all in that marriage which I could miss, let alone mourn. And this was a personal tragedy. Yet having had such a dreadful marriage, about which no one could possibly be sentimental, conferred some surprising benefits. It enabled me to view the role structure within marriage with unusual clarity—although doubtless some will call it cynicism, or cold-bloodedness.

You don't need to eat an egg to know that it's rotten. For that matter, you don't have to read the relevant research to know when one is rotten either. But it sure helps eliminate uncertainty if you do. I ought to know, because I've spent many years doing both. And no, I do not think marriage is rotten. And I do not think men are rotten, either. What I do think is that the way we typically divide up the business—and the pleasure, too—of our adult relationships is inefficient, maladaptive and unfair.

I also think we've been kidding ourselves about how much marriage has changed, and how differently we approach the role of wife from the way our mothers and grandmothers did. Things *have* changed, and we *do* approach the role differently. But not nearly as much as we're comfortable admitting. What have changed enormously are not the role structures, or the divisions of labour, but the expectations we bring to marriage. The mismatch between our words and our deeds, the rhetoric we profess and the reality we construct, is acute. And the confusion this engenders, I am convinced, does not simply contribute to our spiralling divorce rate. It explains it. The resulting pain and disruption for women, for men and—in my opinion, most importantly of all—for children makes this one of the most pressing ethical concerns of our age.

meet the wife: the origins of wifework

'I come from a big family. Mammals.' Gabriel Moran

Wifework is neither a natural nor inevitable feature of the relationship between men and women. Yet, because its basic features are as old as the species itself, it has come to seem 'second nature'—an inheritance so fully assimilated we have a hard time even discerning its outlines. Wifework is not natural, but until very, very recently in human history it has probably been necessary. This chapter will explore the biological origins of monogamy, and the 'service mentality' that is a central feature of its role structure. (Feel free to skip ahead if you've never wondered why marriage compels you to do things that make no sense at all. Like putting your own needs last, for instance.) But before we get down to the biology of wifework, we need first to address love its psychology. In particular, the question of what—if anything—love has got to do with it.

In my opinion, love isn't blind. It just provides exceptional camouflage. And this is probably why it has taken social scientists so long to 'discover' wifework in the first place. Where 'love' rushes in, analysis fears to tread. Particularly when we confuse a universal way of feeling with a universal, or normative, way of behaving—which seems to be all the time. Love is supposed to lie at the heart of marriage, and these days it usually does. Yet love doesn't begin to explain how we construct ourselves as husbands and wives. Hell, it hasn't even heard the question.

Love may be a many-splendoured thing, but it's surprisingly mono-variate. What is immensely diverse and changeable is not love per se, but the ways we translate it into action. To argue, therefore, that women perform wifework—that they take care of men physically and emotionally without being taken care of in these ways in return—because they 'love' their husbands is to confuse chronicity with causality. Women may love their husbands, and they may also perform wifework: but the connection is purely incidental. Wifework is a behavioural repertoire that may or may not be associated with a feeling state called love. Indeed, some of the most conscientious performers of wifework are those who regard their partners with a feeling state more closely resembling contempt. This should be obvious. I am certain that for most of us, male and female, it is not. And so I press the point.

Performing services for men has become a conventionalised way in which women show their love for them. Yet the connection between the inner state called love and outward and visible signs like the nightly preparation of a 'proper meal', or ironed shirts, or regular sex on demand is no more intrinsic than is the connection between, let us say, genuine commitment and the arrangement of carbon molecules we call a diamond. A diamond does not equal a commitment. Rather, a diamond can be said to 'stand for' commitment because of its beauty, its durability, its capacity to reflect light, its rarity and, of course, its price. Although commitments and diamonds share a number of interesting qualities, no one would argue that they are interchangeable (even though, upon acceptance of an engagement ring, a good many of us carry on that way!). The relationship is a conventionalised one because it depends on a shared agreement about meaning. In another cultural context, where that shared agreement is absent, a diamond may be feared or worshipped or discarded as a worthless rock—but it certainly doesn't mean it's time to call in the caterers and hire the hall.

There is no doubt that 'doing things for people' is one way we show how much we care. The question is, what things? And for which people?

The possible list of things to do is infinite. So why is the list of things included in the job description for wifework so short? And, more to the point, why does it remain so strikingly gender-specific? Is there a husband alive who shows how much he cares by steam-pleating his wife's skirts, or making sure she always has enough bras in her underwear drawer? Does a man in love feel guilty about falling behind in the dusting? Does he assume 94 per cent of all child care tasks, refusing to use day care because 'he didn't become a father to let somebody else look after his kids'? Does a truly devoted family man feel terminally conflicted about juggling paid and unpaid work commitments? And will he ever in a billion trillion years cop flak if he forgets his mother-in-law's birthday?

What's love got to do with any of this? Does the fact that men do not express their love for women by performing such services mean they do not 'really' care? The very idea is absurd. Yet this is precisely the sort of logic women use to defend and rationalise the status quo in which they find themselves mired.

But surely it's different for girls. I mean, isn't it? Are women not the nurturing gender? The gender for whom caregiving comes as naturally as drawing breath? The gender that finds *fulfilment* in meeting the needs of others? Well, yes—some of the time. Females do 'naturally' offer care to their young (although when survival prospects for those offspring are dim, animal mothers—including human ones—have a chilling capacity to turn a blind eye). Yet whether the so-called nurture instinct in human mothers extends 'naturally' to caring for adults is a highly questionable proposition. Observation suggests that the majority of women are extra-ordinarily inept at self-nurture, for example. If we are such experts at caretaking, how come we're so bad at looking after ourselves? And why do women channel so much energy into providing care to their male partners at the expense of, say, their mothers or fathers, their friends or neighbours? Even if we accept that nurturing comes more naturally to women than it does to men—and I am not saying for a moment that in any literal sense I do believe this—we would still need to explain why women place so many of their caregiving eggs in their husbands' baskets.

I would argue instead that there is, in fact, nothing 'natural' about the performance of wifework. There is nothing foreordained in our nature that makes the servicing of males by females either desirable or necessary—although there is much foreordained in our society that makes it convenient. Wifework is, in other words, an artefact of culture—a behavioural adaptation that arose, as do all adaptations, as a way to enhance survival. In this case, the survival of females and their offspring.

In all likelihood, wifework evolved as a form of barter between males and females. Well, all right. A bribe. The provision of a wide range of caretaking services was how females persuaded males to stick around, to share resources and to provide protection to offspring—generally, from the marauding of other males. This remains, albeit in different form, a primary benefit of monogamy for women. Evolutionary anthropologist Sarah Hrdy cites approvingly Alison Lurie's observation in *The War Between the Tates* that all women need men sometimes, 'if only to protect us from other men'.[1]

Anthropologists now believe that, in early human groups, the male's protective function may have been more important over the long haul than his 'economic' function. In hunter-gatherer societies, it is females, the gatherers, who are the primary breadwinners. The exclusively male hunters' role, by contrast, is largely symbolic and ceremonial. According to one current view, men did not hunt big game to put meat on the table, as it were, but to increase their sexual attractiveness. As the !Kung explain, rather coyly, 'Women like meat.' Anthropologists call this the Show-off Theory of the division of gender by labour.[2]

Problem is, even the most fantastically fit hunter-gatherer female slows down a bit—to be honest, quite a bit—during pregnancy, childbirth and lactation. Among other things, this helps explain the direct and inextricable connection between monogamy and reproductive responsibility. It may also explain why modern marriage, while terrifically difficult to sustain when young children are present, is even harder to sustain without them. Researchers have pointed out that the 'option' of having children within marriage remains something of a myth. For example, US figures indicate that, at present, only 11 per cent of ever-married women are still childless by age forty-four. That figure is even more astounding when you consider that the overall rate of unexplained infertility is about 8 per cent. Hardly surprising, then, that 'the question of whether a married couple would have children is rarely asked. Rather the question is *when* a married couple will begin having children,' as Steven Nock has noted.[3]

In evolutionary terms, the question 'What do women want out of marriage, anyway?' is easy to answer. What women want is a mate to protect and provision them and their offspring—at least until those offspring are off their hands. Exactly when this point is reached will of course vary wildly depending on physical and cultural context. Irrespective of context, though, and compared to any other primate species, it's going to be an awfully long time indeed. Human babies are born incredibly needy and incomplete. In this respect, every newborn is a premature baby—especially when compared to those of most other species which emerge capable of walking, clinging, foraging and practically doing their times tables. Our babies have to learn to do *everything*, and that takes time. More to the point it also takes energy. Calories. Food. As mothers, we need sustenance not only to perform the demanding mental and physical work of rearing our exquisitely dependent young, but also to fuel the extraordinary biological production line called lactation.

For all these reasons, parenthood in our species is very much a joint enterprise. From a biological point of view, males are absolutely essential to the system. This is not because of the direct child care they provide. On the contrary, in almost all human groups, dedicated 'fathering time' is minimal, sometimes to the point of non-existence. Men's real business within the family is to feather the nest, not sit in it—to maintain a safe haven within which offspring can grow to maturity, to defend mother and offspring against possible predators (including sexual predators) and to provide supplementary nourishment as needed, particularly for the female during lactation.

'For monogamy to benefit a mother,' Sarah Hrdy has observed, 'her mate must be in a position to protect her or to reliably provision her'— and to do so to a higher standard than she could hope to attain without his assistance.[4] In other words, to provide a better lifestyle, and with it a greater chance for more viable offspring. That's the pay-off for females, and it's a big one. It needs to be. Because the security monogamy offers doesn't come cheap. It requires females to sacrifice their sexual autonomy, and often to sever or curtail their kin relationships and to relinquish solidarity with other females. Primates do not make such sacrifices out of the goodness of their hearts. We make them for one reason and one reason only: to give our DNA a better chance in life.

Human females are not alone in this evolutionary obsession, sometimes called the Selfish Gene Theory, to preserve our genetic inheritance by producing progeny which can be counted on to do the same. Our DNA, according to this now widely accepted theory, is like an inter-generational chain-letter we are condemned to keep up with through all eternity. At the highest level, players in this game are engaged in a contest to determine the winning species (the famous 'survival of the fittest'). To this end, reproduction is a non-zero-sum game for its male and female players. When offspring survive and reproduce, mother and father are equal winners. When offspring fail to do so, they are equally disadvantaged.

At another level of the Selfish Gene game, it's every male and female for him or herself. They must still devise mutually advantageous strategies for reproductive co-operation; yet each also acts out of a highly individualised notion of enlightened self-interest. At this level, the 'team' is not an entire species, but a family line. To a female player, a male is simply a vehicle that makes possible the transmission of *her* genes to *her* offspring. Her investment is not in him; it's in what he can do to further her own evolutionary progress. Not consciously, but instinctively, we are all the worst kind of users.

Male behaviour is driven by identical biological imperatives. Males have no choice but to co-operate with their female team members 'for the good of the species'. United they stand, divided they become extinct. At the same time, however, males of the species are in indirect competition with those same females. (With males, on the other hand, they are in direct competition.) Females with whom they do not mate are an implicit threat. By remaining available to mate with the 'enemy'—any other male—their very existence blunts a bloke's competitive edge. It's not for nothing that males in our society refer to sexual intercourse as 'scoring'. But females with whom a male does mate are also a worry. It's always a toss-up whether to put all one's seed in the one basket, as it were, or to continue to spread it around, a question of quality versus quantity. And for males—who are the sex who have been given the option—the decision between consolidating and diversifying is a tough biological choice.

From a species-wide perspective, male human sexuality is very much a hit-and-run affair. Theoretically, a man is capable of inseminating thousands of women in his lifetime and producing veritable legions of offspring—and still not be left holding a single baby. (In modern times, the official record for offspring from a single father is a staggering 899.[5]) In the reproductive war of the sexes, that's a serious advantage. Among other things, it makes sex an incredibly low-risk investment. Is it any wonder most men regard any opportunity for sex as an offer they can't refuse? For women, it's just the opposite. Women have to be more fussy about sex than men because the consequences are so enormous. If that sounds suspiciously like what your mother was telling you back in Year 10, don't blame me. Or her, for that matter. Blame biology. In some species—egg-layers, for example—reproduction doesn't much cramp a girl's style. For *Homo sapiens* females, on the other hand, carrying, bearing and nursing an infant takes a huge physical and psychic toll. Until recently, scientists believed that females were for this reason 'naturally' monogamous and males 'naturally' promiscuous.

Nineteenth-century psychologist William James summed the whole thing up in a clever and justly famous jingle:

> Hogamous, higamous, men are polygamous.
> Higamous, hogamous, women monogamous.

Translation: men are inherently promiscuous and commitment-phobic; women are by nature 'good girls', which is to say, sexually unadventurous. And this, until the last several decades, has been more or less the received wisdom on the subject. There are sociobiologists today who still believe this fable, though in dwindling numbers. To an extent, one can even understand why they believe. Compared to women, men do solicit more sexual partners. What's more, their standards for these partners seem rather low. Science has now explained why. It's because their standards *are* rather low. In two field studies conducted across different decades, for instance, researchers have found that 'most men, but almost no women, agreed to a sexual offer made by a complete stranger of the opposite sex', regardless of the attractiveness of the stranger.[6]

Nevertheless, monogamy is by definition a two-way street. Zoologically, it can be applied only to couples, not to individuals. A species cannot be 'half monogamous'—i.e., the female half! The ethnographic record is very clear that the vast majority of human groups live monogamously. Only a very small scattering practise polygamy, and even then only elites ever get to play. Polyandry, or family systems based on multiple husbands, is even rarer. If men really are polygamous by nature, that's a mighty unnatural state of affairs.

Evolutionary biologists now recognise that in nature, as in certain sectors of the Roman Catholic Church, sexuality is first and foremost a matter of reproductive strategy. It is never simply an end in itself. For all creatures, including humans, sexual desire is our way of panting after posterity. That's a truth so obvious only a human could forget it. Sex is, quite literally, a matter of life and death—whether of a particular gene pool, or family, or of an entire species. Reproduction, in other words, is not a by-product of sexual desire, but quite the other way about. The rage to reproduce is our deepest and most urgent instinct. And in this sense, all of us, males and females alike, live for sex. We just have different ways of going about it.

The most basic asymmetry between the genders—indeed, perhaps the only basic asymmetry—is the one that discussions of 'equal opportunity' are most likely to ignore. I refer, of course, to the fact that females give birth and males don't. From this single anatomical acorn has grown the mighty oak of patriarchy: a social structure that systematically privileges males and all things masculine, while controlling and constraining females and all things feminine. In this sense anatomy really is destiny. Among other things, it destines females to hold disproportionate reproductive power over males—and it destines males to do whatever they can to even up the score. Biologically, females have the upper hand. But under patriarchy—the macrocosm, of which marriage is the microcosm—males are compensated by social and economic advantages so enormous, and so deeply entrenched, that most of the time we forget they are constructions at all.

It's important to recognise that patriarchy is not simply one social structure among many that human groups may adopt. It is *the* social structure that human groups adopt. Societies in which females dominate males are not rare. They are unknown. Societies in which males dominate females are not simply common. They are universal.

Why then do I say that females' reproductive power is 'superior' to, and not simply 'different' from, that of males? In what sense is the ability to bear young really an advantage? Men can 'have' children on the cheap, for the cost of a single ejaculation. And they can keep on doing so for as long as they are able to find (or coerce) female partners, evading any responsibility for child support, whether biological, social or economic.

If anybody's in the catbird seat, reproductively speaking, surely it's males?

If it were all just a numbers game, males would have the advantage hands down. Then again, if it were all just a numbers game, our species wouldn't be monogamous in the first place. We'd be like deer or sheep or the family cat: the 'one-night stand' mammals that mate and go their separate ways, leaving legions of single Mums to get on with things in the enviably efficient style to which nature has accustomed them. Monogamous species—of which there is a surprising multitude in nature—have taken a different path, and for a very good reason: it gets them to the finish line faster. In nature, remember, it's not how you play the game that matters, it's whether you win or lose. Inseminating 100 females is all well and good. But producing a single infant who survives to maturity counts for a great deal more. And, in the case of humans, the odds of succeeding in this effort are lengthened immeasurably by the presence of a live-in Dad.

In many species, where offspring are born hardier and reach maturity quicker, paternal investment is neither necessary nor advisable. It would be a waste of time. It's different for humans. In our case, a male's best chance of ensuring that his genes get passed on is to stick around and help out. (How long is long enough? In evolutionary terms, that's negotiable.) But to make *that* kind of sacrifice worth a guy's while, he's got to be sure of one thing. That the kid is his. In fact, he can never be sure; it'll always be a matter of playing the odds. Monogamy dramatically increases those odds.

No matter how recklessly males sow their wild oats, in the end they pay a steep evolutionary price for the privilege. The male may scatter his seed to the four winds (if that's his idea of a good time), but to the female belongs the harvest. In the end, it is she and she alone who is left holding the baby. The drawbacks to this are many. There is, however, one enormous advantage to belonging to the sex that does the birthing, an advantage so obvious we generally forget all about it. Mothers worry about almost everything, but the 'maternity' of their offspring is not one of them. Not even the most anxious first-time mother has ever beheld her freshly delivered baby, still umbilically attached, and wondered whether it was really hers. A woman's baby is as much 'hers' as her own right arm, and disputes about ownership about as likely.

Which is not to say that every baby does not equally belong to a male as well. The question is, which one? In evolutionary terms, that uncertainty is, quite simply, the tie that binds. Monogamy is the price males pay for knowing whose kid is whose.

Reproductive power, it turns out, is like any other kind of power. It derives primarily not from force, but from knowledge. Or, to quote my own little jingle,

> Man's greatest infirmity?
> Uncertain paternity.
> Through all of eternity
> We've been sure of maternity.

Monogamy, and the human institution of marriage to which it gave rise, constrains the sexuality of both sexes 'for the sake of the children'. At another level, males choose monogamy because it's the next best thing to having a womb of one's own. Of course, not even a female can count her chickens until they're hatched; without monogamy, males have no hope of counting them ever. Monogamy, which demands sexual exclusivity (or near to it) for both partners, reduces that biological anxiety. Monogamous males inevitably invest more heavily in their offspring, because they have maximised their chances of figuring out who their offspring are. (And this explains, too, why 'maternal instinct' is so much stronger than its paternal counterpart. A female who expends energy nurturing her offspring is making a bluechip biological investment. For a male, parental investment is always an iffier proposition. For males, monogamy is like a certificate of ownership. For females—who already know what belongs to them—it's more like contents insurance.)

Ultimately, what men can look forward to from monogamy are more and better carriers of the family genome into the next generation. In evolutionary terms, it doesn't get any better than that. In the shorter term, however, the benefits of monogamy for males are a good deal less compelling. Supporting a family requires enormous altruism. It means working harder and longer for less reward. It means sacrificing sexual variety. It means choosing to take on very definite immediate responsibilities in return for indefinite future privileges.

Monogamy is indeed 'a compromise offering something for everyone'. Yet, from a purely biological perspective, it probably offers a slightly better deal for females and their offspring than it does for males. In part, this is because mothering a child is a potentially risky business in a way that fathering a child isn't. Indeed, a male's survival prospects are not affected in the slightest by his reproductive participation. Almost by definition, a breeding female is more 'needy' than a breeding male. Specifically, her needs for protection and provisioning are considerably more pressing than his need for establishing ownership. Which is not to say that she, or her offspring, couldn't survive without him. They might survive very well. Then again, they might not. The participation of the paternal male does not guarantee survival, but it does increase the odds. And in evolutionary terms, even the slightest tipping of the scales can pay disproportionately huge dividends.

Do females lose anything at all in the monogamy compromise? As it turns out, they do, and big time—although it is only in the past ten years or so that evolutionary anthropologists have even thought to ask the question, let alone to answer it. Like males, monogamous females sacrifice sexual autonomy and freedom of choice. Among other things, this means forgoing opportunities to mate with potentially higher calibre males than one's partner—a temptation every bit as strong as any felt by the stereotypic philandering male. Sociobiological research into the so-called trophy-wife phenomenon suggests that fertile young females are every bit as sexually predatory as the wealthy older males who 'collect' them. Exactly who is the trophy for whom depends very much on the eye of the beholder. Monogamy may also mean severing links with other females—especially female kin—who might otherwise serve as important means of support, particularly for co-operative child care.

Clearly, the presence of a protective male partner is invaluable to a female during the acute biological crises of pregnancy, childbirth and lactation. What's easy to forget, however, is that for nearly all of human history, the life of an average adult female was an unbroken succession of such crises. Pregnancy and lactation were not isolated experiences, but pretty much the sum total of a woman's lot in life. So too were extraordinarily high rates of infant mortality. This meant that a female might need to bear ten or twelve children in order to produce one or two survivors. The female's relative biological vulnerability—relative, that is, to that of a male or a non-breeding female—was the source of her dependence, the tie that bound her to a male partner for her life.

Yet monogamy without *interdependency* is as unworkable as a chair with three legs. As we have seen, males suffer from a different sort of biological vulnerability—the anxiety of the wombless—and monogamy solved this problem as well. Although monogamy presented a better reproductive strategy for males than its alternatives, the advantage was only marginal (particularly in the case of 'high quality,' dominant males, who would have excelled as sexual hunters and gatherers). How, then, to balance the scales? How to re-jig the interdependencies so that male and female come out roughly equal?

Monogamy offered males plenty over the long haul of their reproductive destiny. But if the compromise was ever to prove viable, it also had to dangle some carrots that could be enjoyed in the here and now—a spoonful of sugar to make the medicine of monogamy go down. And this, I argue, was the evolutionary origin of wifework: the complex of services—sexual, social, emotional and physical—by which females have provisioned and protected males within the context of monogamous marriage.

chapter 4

the monogamy trade-off

'Human nature, Mr Allnut, is what we were
put on this earth to rise above.'
Miss Rose Sayer, *The African Queen*

When we explore the origins of wifework, we are really exploring the origins of patriarchy itself. We are tracing the evolutionary logic behind the gender-role structures of female submissiveness and male dominance. The monogamous unit—a female, her offspring, and a male—is the building block of human society. In marriage we see the entire sexual politics of our species writ small, as an intricate series of biological and social trade-offs.

In the broadest sense, the social or constructed superiority of males can be seen to have evolved as a compensation for their natural, repro-ductive inferiority. (Freud, who believed babies functioned symbolically as a penis substitute for their mothers, had it back to front. Phallocentrism, the worship of all things male, is a baby substitute.) That is the original 'gender balance', and its evolutionary advantages are clear to see. Because nature gave women something men wanted (offspring), culture needed to give men something women wanted (social power and personal autonomy). Any other division of the spoils would have led to a sexual imbalance so extreme as to make co-operation impossible, either within the microcosm of the family or the macrocosm of the group at large. Females who both bred *and* held power in the public domain would have upset the applecart of monogamy entirely, and rendered patriarchy just another in an infinite line of evolutionary paths not taken. This did not happen, not because it would have been 'unfair' to men—nature is indifferent to gender equity, or any other kind of equity for that matter—but because obtaining male co-operation in the female business of procreation was biologically non-negotiable. Under the conditions of a hunter-gatherer society, without access to any but the most rudimentary technologies, the people who need people are pretty much all of them female. And, yes, the ability to procreate does make women the luckiest people in the world. It also makes us the neediest.

The reproductive power of the female is purchased at the price of a corresponding biological vulnerability. At one level, pregnancy and child-birth are a miracle of female creative power. At another, they create a debilitating set of new dependencies. Breeding females need more food, yet have less energy for foraging or other productive labour. They are also heavier and slower. This makes them less able to defend themselves without assistance. Human mothers are temporarily weakened even further by the rigours of a uniquely traumatic childbirth (one problem evolution has not yet solved is what obstetricians call cephalo-pelvic disproportion, and the rest of us call agony).

Once their babies are born, lactation will place further heavy demands on an already compromised system. Unlike other primate species, human infants have lost the instinct to cling—only the vestigial 'startle reflex' or Moro response survives—and must be carried everywhere. For these and other reasons, infant care will consume an extraordinary number of extra calories. And it will eat up mother's mental space, as well. Being exquisitely tuned into the needs of her offspring means being tuned out to much else in the environment. What's more, even the healthiest human baby will be born so helpless that, in a crisis, it will need every ounce of the protection *two* adults can give.

To put it bluntly, our species is biologically ill-equipped for single motherhood. All other things being equal—and, under pre-technological conditions, they generally are—women need men more than men need women. Where females can only look forward to continuous pregnancy and lactation throughout their adult life-span, snaring a steady man is not just a feather in a girl's cap, but a matter of life or death. Evening up the interdependency score between males and females has been an evolutionary sine qua non for our species, because equal need yields equal commitment, and equal commitment guarantees co-operation, and it is only through co-operation that the needs of our offspring will be met.

Wifework evolved, I propose, as a way of redressing the imbalance between the dependency needs of males and females. On the one hand, it reinforced the dominance of the monogamous male vis-a-vis his female partner. At the same time, however, wifework would have succeeded in making males vulnerable, seducing them into a way of life that, for all its privileges, would ultimately serve the needs of females first and best. It may not be going too far to say that wifework became a useful strategy for cultivating a learned helplessness in males that mimicked the innate helplessness of breeding females. The resulting balance of interdependencies created a symbiosis powerful enough to bind a couple for life.

From an evolutionary point of view, wifework arose as an enticement for male participation in family life, a diversionary subterfuge that hooked males into monogamous arrangements from which they might otherwise have received little immediate benefit—and, once hooked, kept them securely on the line with an ingenious variety of reinforcements. Wifework, you might say, has been man's bonus for 'doing the right thing' by his offspring, their mother, and the species at large. It is the female saying cunningly to the male, 'If you will but serve me and the children slavishly, I will make you monarch of all you survey.' It is the male saying belligerently to the female, as my seven-year-old says to anyone lower down on the playground pecking order, 'I'll play—but only if I'm the boss.'

Wifework ensures that males are cocooned from the more taxing and tedious aspects of nuclear family life, while ensuring a steady, sexual soporific. The result is a style of monogamy that seduces males with the offer of an extraordinary level of attentiveness and care from their female partners. As the beneficiaries of wifework, monogamous males enjoy a special status, not only relative to females, but relative to non-monogamous males. The legacy of this special, protected status cannot be overestimated. For monogamy did not simply make partici-pating males feel good, although this it most assuredly did; it made males live longer and more productively. In Darwinian terms, monogamy enhanced male survival, just as modern marriage continues to do today.

Monogamy works to the extent that it makes each gender an offer it can't refuse, or at least one that does not seriously compromise its own well-being and that of its offspring. And the reverse is also true. Where the consequences of refusing the offer of monogamy are minimal for one gender or the other, the 'tie that binds' will loosen and eventually wither away.

In this regard, it is helpful to remember that the institution of monogamy (which in its elaborated form we call marriage) is not really an institution at all, but one strategy among many for playing the game of reproductive roulette. The winner of this game, as we have seen, is not necessarily the player who scores the most offspring, but the player who finishes with the 'fittest' offspring: the ones most likely to survive to reproductive maturity, and keep the game going into the next round. As we know from our observation of other species, this same game can be played singly, in pairs (which is what monogamy is) or as a team (for instance, in a beehive, ant colony or harem). There is no 'correct' config-uration for family structure. There are only strategies that conduce to offspring survival under a given set of environmental constraints, and strategies that don't.

If there is one thing evolution has taught us, it is this: either an inef-ficient reproductive strategy becomes extinct, or the species does. There's no third way, and—survival not being at all like a game of horseshoes—there's no such thing as coming close, either.

From an evolutionary perspective, William James was wrong twice. Males are not polygamous by nature at all. Nor are females really monogamous. Rather, both genders are sexually strategic by nature. Like a canny shopper, or an astute investor, both male and female are always trying to get that little bit extra for their reproductive dollar. Throughout our history as a species, monogamy has proved a pretty fair gamble for both of us, offering the best compromise available for minimising reproductive risks and maximising reproductive advantages. Throughout our biological history, in other words, the pluses associated with monogamy have more or less outweighed its minuses. And this has been true in roughly equal proportion for males and females.

Up to now, that is.

Somewhere in the eye blink in evolutionary time called the twentieth century, something happened to upset this ancient balance, to unravel the delicate web of interdependencies upon which monogamy rests. We see the resulting confusion all around us: more people divorcing, or choosing to remain single; more women pursuing motherhood outside of marriage; more children whose day-to-day care and support is left to one parent, not two; more men evading parental privileges and parental responsibilities. (According to the US Department of Health and Human Services, men are more likely to meet financial obligations for their automobiles than for their offspring.[1])

It's not that we've entirely given up on monogamy. But somewhere along the line we started to veer away from the lifelong variety ('matrimony') in favour of a more abbreviated, less binding style. Although the term 'serial monogamy' still sounds more like a criminal offence than a lifestyle choice, a bit like describing remarriage as a form of recidivism, the fact is it's an increasingly accurate description of the way we live our lives. Colloquially, a 'long-term relationship' can refer to any affectionate tie that endures past the first couple of dates.

'It's a different world,' we hear our parents and our grandparents say sadly. We may even be saying it ourselves. Or thinking it, at any rate.

And it *is* a different world. The changes in the past century—hell, in the past half-century—have been enormous and rapid. We know that. We ought to know it. Because we never stop hearing about it, never stop talking about it. Far from being oblivious to such change, our post-industrial society is obsessed with it. We are compulsive trend-spotters, practised forecasters. Yet our readiness to observe how much things have changed has obscured our capacity to see how much they have remained the same.

Every once in while, the really big news is not what's happened. It's what *hasn't* happened. And marriage, I would argue, is a perfect case in point.

This is why an evolutionary perspective is so vital: it places the emphasis on the constraints within which organisms must operate, constraints imposed jointly by biology and environment. It shows us what we're stuck with. And it reminds us that lasting change—as opposed to ephemeral blips in the system—is always in the direction of increasing adaptiveness. Which in turn reminds us to keep looking for a kind of collective coherence, even when it seems that all of the personal sort may be gone. We may make self-defeating individual choices, but as a species we cannot help but seek the most efficient possible means by which to compete, survive and ultimately prevail.

So what, exactly, has changed? And what has remained the same?

Recent advances in cloning and IVF techniques notwithstanding, females still give birth to babies, and males don't. The difference now is that females can choose when, and even whether, they will do so. Our reproductive biology hasn't changed one iota, in other words, but our capacity to control it has increased beyond imagining. Effective contraception and safe abortion on demand have seen to that. Together, and over the course of a mere five decades, they have redefined maternity, once every female's immutable biological destiny, as an optional extra. Granted, it's an option an overwhelming majority of women still choose to exercise. But the real choice contraception has given women is not whether to have children. It's whether to spend our entire adult lives having them, and having almost nothing else besides.

At other times and in other places, women managed to keep family sizes within survivable limits, of course. But the price was hideously high. Heartbreaking rates of infant mortality and socially sanctioned infanticide took care of the problem of excess mouths to feed. Because lactation suppresses ovulation, the spacing of offspring could also be engineered to some extent by continuing to feed until well past infancy. (In traditional societies, weaning rarely occurs before age three or four.) Such 'methods' of family planning took pressure off family groupings and the wider community. They did nothing, however, to alleviate the biological toll of continuous reproduction on women's bodies. Family sizes were kept within environmental limits, in other words, but at the *expense* of mothers' well-being.

Modern forms of contraception, by contrast, keep family sizes to within environmental limits while enhancing women's well-being. They have transformed the mixed biological blessing of belonging to the childbearing sex into an unambiguous source of power and prestige. By making it possible for women to choose motherhood without choosing a lifetime of vulnerability and dependence, access to effective contraception has redefined what it means to be adult and female. At the same time, in a definitional domino effect, it has wrought equally dramatic changes for male identity, and for the nature of the relations possible between men and women.

It's important to remember that it's not simply having babies that makes females structurally dependent on males. It's having babies all the time. Breeding as a way of life rather than a phase of life is a classic case of too much of a good thing, a sorceress's apprentice scenario that dooms females to exist in symbiosis with males and offspring—or not at all. Like it or not, 'barefoot and pregnant' is exactly what nature intended for females. Thankfully (or sadly, I suppose, depending on your point of view), technology has intervened to allow us to subvert that intent.

The result is not merely more empowering and convenient for women, it is highly adaptive for the species. It allows females to concentrate their reproductive energies by producing a handful of offspring with excellent chances for survival, rather than large numbers with poor chances. Having fewer babies is not only good news for the babies themselves—who get proportionally more food, shelter, clothing and care. It's good for their mothers too. For females, the number of offspring is inversely related to most physical and mental health indicators. And we don't need Darwin to tell us that healthier, happier, more rested mothers are more effective caregivers.

Theoretically, the ability of females to control their own reproductive destinies should have been good news all around—all other things being equal, even for males, the ones who masterminded it in the first place. The Pill was going to give males undreamt-of sexual access, both inside and outside marriage. By removing the major obstacle to female receptiveness, or what males thought was the major obstacle—the fear of unwanted pregnancy—the Pill was supposed to transform sexual relating into a win-win situation for all parties. For a little while it looked as if this vision, a sort of technological wet dream, might even come true. The 'if it feels good, do it' school certainly attracted a huge number of enrolments, particularly among the unattached young. Yet over the longer term, when it was much too late to do anything about it, males found the sweet smell of sexual success turning sour. The revolution in contraceptive technology just kept on firing. The Pill, which began by freeing sexual enjoyment from the spectre of unwanted pregnancy, ended up demolishing the biological bedrock of our entire social order.

Call it an unanticipated side effect.

Being female, post-Pill, means we are not who we were, who we have always been 'by nature'. Our anatomy is still a good part of our destiny, but the twentieth century taught all of us that technology is destiny, too—especially when it enables us to exercise significant control over our bodies. It is almost impossible to imagine a biotechnology analogous to the contraceptive pill in its power to change our individual and collective destinies. (A tablet that enables us to store food energy, as camels do, in humps on our backs? A chemical means of stimulating the 90 per cent of our brain's capacity that presently lies dormant? A communications medium that allows us to digitise one another through space and time?) Females who are able to control their fertility reduce their biological deficits drastically, while retaining all their former reproductive assets. Females who are able to control their fertility, in other words, tip the ages-old balance of gender interdependencies. Overnight (as it were) they need men a whole lot less than ever before. Eventually, and inevitably, they will need men a whole lot less than men need them. And when that happens, monogamy will tumble…cradle and all. Which is exactly what is beginning to happen.

Access to contraceptives has given females unprecedented power to break the endless reproductive cycling which has heretofore been their lot in life—and ultimately to disrupt the biological substrate from which patriarchy itself has grown. It's important to keep in mind, however, that being female does not per se mean 'weakness' relative to males. It only does so in a species like our own—in which the processes of pregnancy, childbirth and lactation are so peculiarly depleting and in which newborns are so peculiarly helpless for such a long time. Contrast this situation, for a moment, with that of your family cat. She is neither 'weaker' than her male consort, nor subservient to him. Why? Could it have something to do with the fact that she can give birth to five offspring in a matter of minutes, eat her own placentas for dinner, and go back to work full-time at six to eight weeks with the kids totally off her hands for life? Why on earth, you may well wonder, would a woman who could do all *that* bother with a man? The answer is, she wouldn't. And she doesn't.

Now that women are freed of the biological constraints of continuous fertility, they are no longer getting a solid deal out of the monogamy compromise. Indeed, many are paying through the nose for it. In the present circumstances, lifetime monogamy means females end up doing *more* provisioning, not less, assuming greater responsibility for the well-being of their mates than their mates do for them. Marriage asks women to spend the rest of their lives paying back a 'debt' that—thanks to contraception, formula feeding, child care and other key changes to the environment—no longer exists, or exists only to a trivial degree.

On the one hand, women are still behaving as if they have something to be grateful for. On the other, they know for a fact that they are getting less out of this deal called marriage than they are putting in, and they resent that. A sizeable minority of wives resent it enough to call it quits and break up their marriages. Even among those who don't, who still feel they—or, perhaps more commonly, their children—are getting enough return to justify the level of investment, many experience a simmering level of frustration, a pervasive sense of injustice, a demoralising degree of resignation.

The crisis in marriage we face today, I am convinced, arises directly out of these basic biological facts.

We have had patriarchy for as long as we have, not because it was ever 'just' in any abstract sense, but because it worked. Females who still perform wifework, who continue to be submissive in marriage in deed, even if they are highly conflicted about it in thought and word—which is to say, almost all of us—would probably be shocked to hear themselves described as the last outposts of patriarchy. But that is exactly what we are. We are so enormously conflicted about our marriages, and our roles within those marriages, because at some level we have grasped that marriage itself is on a collision course with the wider culture. Monogamous marriage—the gendered institution par excellence—fits a social order dedicated to genderlessness as neatly as a glove fits a foot. Which is exactly the way women raised in a feminist spirit, who have always taken equal opportunity for granted, fit the role of wife.

Those of us who have enjoyed the questionable privilege of growing up in a post-industrial world know for a fact that patriarchy is dead—or dying, anyway. We know it, and we're glad. We celebrate its passing—or, if we are male and powerful, we pretend we do. The irony, however, is that we still expect monogamous marriage, the very building block of patriarchy, to be alive and kicking. Why else do we feel bewildered by the 'breakdown of the family', appalled at the rise of single-parent families, maybe even nostalgic for the good old days when Mum stayed home, baked brownies and swallowed tranquillisers? Why else does even the most rabid neo-traditionalist deplore the faintest whiff of gender discrimination on the job or in the community—yet happily go home to the most male-dominated institution the world has ever known? How is it we do not perceive the contradiction between the equal opportunity we insist upon in the public sphere, as professionals, and the ultimate pink-collar ghetto to which we persistently and placidly submit in private, as wives?

why do we do it to ourselves?

'It is better to marry than to burn.' St Paul

In 1999, the Australian Institute of Family Studies conducted a large-scale inquiry into the reasons couples divorce. Similar studies are being conducted every day by social scientists throughout the English-speaking world. It's not hard to understand why. If divorce is to be prevented we need to understand why people are doing it.

Wouldn't it also be a good idea to work out why people are *not* doing it? What drives men and women to marriage in the first place? And, once having arrived at this outlandish decision, what on earth is keeping us there? Always remember that, give or take a few per cent, roughly half of all marriages *do* survive. Questions about why people continue to marry, despite everything, have remained virtually unasked within the research community. Perhaps, like the rest of us, social scientists tended to regard the answers as self-evident. And, once upon a time, they probably were.

Today, those certainties are crumbling, as the very ground on which marriage rests has shifted. Yet a few preliminary observations are possible. The first is that women's ideas about marriage have changed faster than men's. The second is that women's ideas about marriage have changed faster than the capacity of men to respond to those changes. And the third is that women's ideas about marriage have changed faster than women's own capacity to respond to those changes.

As one of the authors of the AIFS study, senior research fellow Irene Wolcott, told the *Australian Financial Review*, 'The real question is no longer "why wouldn't a woman get married?" so much as why would she?' Why, indeed. (Tellingly, Wolcott betrayed no equivalent curiosity about why a man would want to marry.) 'The fact that we even ask that tells us how much life has changed for women and men,' she concluded.[1] In this, I am convinced, Wolcott is absolutely correct. Yet the fact remains that she is one of the very few social researchers who *has* asked the question. I'm certainly not aware of any who have attempted to answer it.

So why do women want to marry? Why, in this day and age (as my mother would say), do we even bother?

Marriage is a contract. But no marriage is purely a legal agreement, or reducible to a set of religious prescriptions. Nor is marriage simply a covenant between two people—although in our romanticism we often tend to forget this. To us, it seems natural to imagine marriage as a highly individual enterprise and family life as something that, as we say, 'goes on behind closed doors'. In fact, nothing could be further from the truth.

Marriage is first and foremost a *social* contract, whose terms and conditions are determined neither individually, nor formally (that is, laid down by legal or secular laws), but collectively, within the context of culture. The most important sub-clauses of the marriage contract are unwritten and implicit. They are also surprisingly inflexible. You can bring your own agenda to marriage—and heaven knows, all of us do—but, in the end, the institution will exert its own imperatives. Some of these are as old as humanity itself; others are of much more recent provenance. Taken together, they ensure that marriage is quite literally bigger than both of you. It's also stronger, older and incomparably uglier.

At one level, every adult person in our society 'knows' what marriage entails. On another, most would be hard pressed to 'tell' what they know.

All of this helps to explain how a person—you, say—could start off with one set of ideas about how marriage was going to operate, and what your role was going to be like within it, and end up doing something entirely different. It helps explain why wifework persists. Why, even in a society that likes to think of itself as being gender-neutral, wives remain to an astonishing degree exactly what St Paul suggested they should be two thousand years ago: namely, subject to their husbands. Even though they don't want to be. Even though most of their *partners* don't want them to be. (Not consciously, anyway.)

This chapter will explore the expectations women bring to marriage today, both conscious and subconscious. We will be looking at how their ideas have changed over time. But we will also be examining how they have failed to change, or resisted change—and why. What do women today expect from marriage and family life, and what do they expect to offer in return? Perhaps most importantly of all, how do their expectations about married life match up to reality?

As members of a putatively post-feminist society, we should have long since radically reconstructed the role of 'wife'—and by extension the role of 'husband' too. But have we? To what extent, if at all, have our feminist-inspired expectations about public life spilled over into our private lives? What about in our marriages and in our roles as parents? Are our homes equal-opportunity workplaces? Do we even want them to be?

Women may be more disenchanted with marriage than ever before. They may even bristle at the very label 'wife', with all its fifties overtones. I have one friend who managed to alienate an entire set of brand-new in-laws the day one of them casually introduced her as 'Tony's wife' at a family gathering. 'I have no problem about being married,' she snapped. 'But I'm damned if I'll be anybody's wife.' The fact is, however, women continue to pursue marriage almost as aggressively as they now pursue divorce. Notwithstanding our increasing scepticism about labels, becoming a wife remains for most young women a consummation devoutly, and at times even obsessively, to be wished.

In some ways, this is strange. After all, there is no longer a stigma attached to cohabitation—or so everyone tells us. So why bother 'making it legal' in the first place? And if all the rhetoric is true, and marriage really is 'just a piece of paper', why is it a piece of paper so many people—particularly women—want so badly?

To what extent have women moved on from marriage—or at least the kinds of marriages built on the fossilised rock of rigidly defined gender roles? Which traditional assumptions, if any, have survived feminism's second stage—and which have been supplanted? Have we all changed as much as we thought we were going to? Have we changed as fast as the media tell us we have, or travelled as far as we think we ought to?

In the past, human society was constructed in such a way that females desperately *needed* to marry. Over many millennia, a social system evolved that institutionalised the dependency of females, investing males with hugely disproportionate power to control and direct resources. Under such a system, any woman who wants to survive, let alone to reproduce, has no choice but to marry. Not only to marry, but to stay married. Which is why 'spinster' is as much a socio-economic category as a socio-sexual one. Until well into the nineteenth century, any woman who managed to live outside of marriage, or outside of service to a male-headed family, was by definition a woman of means. It is a sociological truism that unmarried males represent the dregs of society, and unmarried females the cream.

Conservatives who thunder that feminism has pulled the rug out from under family life are in many respects completely accurate. The fact is, what we are accustomed to call 'family life'—a monogamous unit designed to ensure the survival of offspring—has been predicated primarily on female enfeeblement, both biologically based and socially cultivated. Or, to put it even more bluntly, what keeps marriages together are wives who have no choice but to keep them together. What puts marriages asunder are wives with access to other options.

No one wants to hear this. Not because it's too complicated to understand but, on the contrary, because it may be a truth too brutishly simple to bear. Many feminists don't want to be caught dead making such an argument. It makes the whole platform sound positively anti-family. Problem is, to the extent that the whole feminist platform centres on empowering women, it *is* anti-family—or at the very least anti-what-we've-always-defined-as-the-family. Female subservience to the needs of men and offspring is not incidental to 'family life'; it is the very ground on which we have constructed family life. To refuse to admit this, I believe, does not make one pro-family, but anti-reality. As a feminist, I am more interested to discover possible alternative foundations for family life—ones that might serve the purpose equally well or even better.

Women seek marriage today for many of the same reasons that they have always done. In order to raise children, in order to obtain economic security, in order to establish adult identity in the community, and in order to experience love and companionship. These four needs—reproductive, economic, social and psycho-sexual—can be thought of as the pillars on which the institution of marriage rests. All of them are ancient (though some are older than others). Despite this, each of them continues to bear a surprising amount of institutional weight. In this connection, it is interesting to speculate that what makes marriage strong is weakness—or, to be more specific, the balancing and counterbalancing of the weaknesses, or needs, of its participants. Without interdependence, in other words, marriage is if not logically impossible then at least logically implausible. Almost by definition, 'the man who has everything' is an unlikely marital prospect. The 'woman who has everything' is even less so.

The nature of our reproductive, economic, social and psycho-sexual needs has remained more or less constant. What has changed, at times dramatically, is how we prioritise those needs—which ones we tend to enshrine or celebrate and which ones we downplay or deny. Our needs are the same as ever. How we choose to assign meaning to them is not.

What have also changed, especially in very recent times, are the alternatives available for getting those needs met. From the hunter-gatherer societies in which human culture first evolved and the agrarian civilisations which succeeded them, right up until the modern, industrialised age of the mid-to-late twentieth century, marriage was not just one way for a woman to get her basic needs met. It was the only way. Today, all that has changed. Marriage is still the most obvious route to the same destination. But many other socially acceptable options also exist. According to Census Bureau figures, the decline in the proportion of married-couple households with children is 'the most noticeable trend' in population shift in the US today—from 40 per cent of all households in 1970 to 24 per cent in 2000.[2] Although a slim majority of American adults—56 per cent—were married and living with their spouses in 1998, more than one third of those aged twenty-five to thirty-four had never been married at all.[3] In Australia, current projections show that 29 per cent of men and 23 per cent of women are expected to remain single for life.[4] Projections are similar throughout the English-speaking world. Add those figures to the huge numbers who will divorce, and marriage begins to look downright counter-cultural.

Traditionally, marriage presented the only option for a woman wishing to bear so-called legitimate children—in both the legal and social sense of that word. Today, the era of the 'shotgun wedding' has well and truly fired its last round. In the US in 1960, for example, 60 per cent of pregnant teenagers would marry before the birth of their child. Three decades later, the figure had dropped to a mere 15 per cent.[5] The idea that a pregnant woman *has to* marry has gone the way of glory boxes and hand-embroidered aprons.

Nevertheless, the idea that it would be preferable for her to do so remains. As a former single mother, I know exactly whereof I speak. I'll never forget the call I had from the Western Australian Registry of Births, Deaths and Marriages a few weeks after my daughter's father and I married. 'I'm pleased to tell you we will now be able to issue your child

with a new birth certificate!' gushed the male clerk. 'She is now legitimate!' In the pause that followed, I didn't know whether to laugh, cry
or press charges. I think I just hung up. When my daughter reached the
age of about seven or eight, she started questioning me closely about
her origins. We had certainly never made a secret of any of it—indeed,
she is featured prominently in most of the wedding photos—but it was
only at this age that the sequencing suddenly struck her. 'You mean you
weren't married when I was born?' she demanded, almost accusingly. I
answered as matter-of-factly as I could. 'I didn't even know you could
do that,' she later admitted.

To be honest, I was shaken by her concern. I thought we—not just
she and I and the wider family, but everybody, the whole society—were
beyond that. I was wrong, I think, about all of us. While it's true that we
of the middle-class no longer openly stigmatise single mothers, we do
not really accept them as the social equals of partnered mothers. Even
a child knows this. It's the same with our attitude towards cohabitation.
We see it as a sort of B-grade alternative to marriage, certainly not an
equivalent.

Maybe we haven't gone the full 180 degrees on the subject of single
motherhood—probably we never will. The fact remains that we have
covered an immense distance in the course of a mere generation. Thirty
years ago, when I was in high school, a girl who was pregnant and
unmarried was ipso facto a social outcast. Marriage was not simply the
most desirable option. It was the only one. Those who failed to take it
up were forced either to give up their babies or their 'standing in the
community' (i.e., their future marriageability)—and usually both. Today,
although I would argue that our attitude towards sole parents remains
deeply conflicted, we increasingly ascribe to the notion that motherhood is the right of every female, whether married or unmarried. In the
context of the history of human groups, a more revolutionary notion is
impossible to imagine.

Legal history is clear that, as Blackwell puts it, 'the interests of husband and wife are one—and that one is the husband'. This very much included children, who were, until well into the nineteenth century, regarded as the property or chattels of their father. (Remember that we are talking of a time in the west in which children's labour was routinely exploited for economic gain.) Under English common law, males enjoyed 'an absolute right to ownership and control over their children—as if they held title', writes legal professor Martha Albertson Fineman. In the US, the situation was much the same. The mother was regarded as the legally inferior parent even within marriage, and 'it was a battle getting her established in law as a potential contender for custody of her children at divorce'.[6] The assumption of automatic paternal right was not eroded until the mid-nineteenth century, with the gradual development of a judicial standard acknowledging that children had rights too, and that those rights should be regarded as of paramount concern. The rights of mothers, interestingly, were never asserted in law at all, let alone protected by it. It was only indirectly, through the doctrine of 'the best interests of the child', that mothers became legally favoured as the custodians of their own offspring.

The notion that females have a superior claim to children they have carried in their bodies, borne and suckled, makes intuitive sense to almost all mothers, as well as to many fathers. Technically, however, the privileging of biological motherhood over biological fatherhood remains almost totally without legal foundation. In practice, of course, decision-making in today's family courts is very much undergirded by the principle of 'mother right'—to the intense and sometimes violent resentment of many non-custodial fathers. The number of fathers' rights organisations dedicated to challenging the so-called 'anti-male' bias in the family courts continues to grow—including the National Association for Child Support Action in the UK, the publisher of a 'Book of the Dead' chronicling fifty-five cases of self-inflicted death attributed to adverse family-court judgements. In Australia, recent revisions to the Family Law Act have been specifically designed to prevent such 'bias', and to strengthen what are now asserted as the 'equal rights' of fathers. In the US, family-court decisions regarding custody are increasingly based on a gender-neutral Parenting Evaluation process, a formal investigation that attempts to assess the level of each partner's parenting skills. Ironically and inaccurately, we now describe as 'traditional' those judges who persist in reflexively granting custody to mothers.

Without getting into the moral debate, it is plain that what psychologists call the 'mother-child dyad' has become widely accepted as a viable social unit in today's post-feminist world. In most circles in western society, a woman who decides to bear and raise children as a single mother, independently of the economic or other support of a biological father, is probably still regarded as aberrant, or at least unwise; but she is no longer persecuted as a social deviant. The fact that we now *debate* the issue of, for example, making IVF technology available to single and lesbian women is evidence of a seismic shift in public perception about women's entitlement to offspring. There is as yet no legally protected 'right to mother'; nevertheless, the notion of such a right has taken definitive root within our public consciousness. A 1993 survey released by the Family Research Council, for example, found that 70 per cent of Americans between the ages of eighteen and thirty-four supported the idea that a 'woman should be able to have a child out of wedlock without anyone passing judgment'.[7]

The gradual untethering of motherhood from marriage—and, by extension, of child care from wifework—is probably the single most explosive issue in the debate about the future of the family. It is a concept that has become even remotely thinkable only in the last thirty years or so, thanks to a convergence of technological innovation and economic upheaval. There is no doubt that the emergence of a concept of reproductive rights for women represents a profound cognitive leap—although whether forward or backward is still very much open to dispute. To take single motherhood seriously is the social equivalent of a Copernican revolution, dethroning marriage from its central place in our social galaxy. To have babies without strings—i.e., men—attached is not simply a new lifestyle option. It is an almost unimaginably radical act of cultural subversion.

And it's happening more and more every day. In the US, 53 per cent of first births that occurred between 1990 and 1994 to women fifteen to twenty-nine years old were either born out of wedlock or conceived before the women's first marriage. About sixty years ago, the figure was one in six.[8] In the UK, the situation is much the same. In the early 1970s, for example, more than 90 per cent of births were within marriage. Currently, around two out of every five births are outside marriage. Having said all that, though, it would be a mistake to anticipate a huge rush towards single motherhood by choice. Demographers are quick to point out that most out-of-wedlock births are to cohabiting couples— or to intact ones, anyway. In the UK, for example, only seven to eight per cent of births to so-called single mothers are registered by the mother alone. What's more, half of the women who were single at their first birth were married by their second.[9] 'True' single motherhood— undertaken wholly independently of a monogamous relationship with a male—remains in practice a distinctly minority experience. Yet the mere existence of the option packs a disproportionate symbolic wallop. In this respect, single motherhood is a bit like atomic capability. Whether you have any real intention of taking up the option is almost beside the point. What changes everything is just knowing it's there.

The knowledge that women no longer *need* to be wives in order to become mothers—even if most of them are still choosing to do it that way—threatens to topple the last major power imbalance on which patriarchy still teeters. It is enabling women, for the first time in the history of our species, to stand back from monogamy and ask, 'What's in this for *me*?' To stand back from prospective mates and ask 'Will you make my life *better*?' rather than 'Will you make my life *begin*?'

That said, the desire to reproduce remains an important reason women continue to choose marriage. In the US, for example, although

26 per cent of children now live with only one parent, the flip-side of that much-quoted statistic is that three-quarters live with two parents.[10] Similarly, one in five dependent children in Great Britain currently live in one-parent families, but 80 per cent don't.[11] Sure, there are other ways of doing it now. But raising a family within a stable, monogamous relationship remains by far the most popular 'first choice'. Partly, this is because marriage still makes motherhood easier. Yes, we are liberated now. But the constraints of motherhood remind us that we remain mammals. When the rhetoric about a woman's inalienable reproductive rights is all said and done, the fact remains that having sole material and emotional responsibility for a child is gruelling and, in many cases, un-relenting work. Life with father may not be a day in the park, either. But, assuming that the father is willing to be regarded as such, that he acknowledges a long-term commitment to the mother, and provides a modicum of support (financial and/or otherwise), most young mothers will bend over backwards to keep him. While other sources of support are imaginable—collectives of female friends or kin, for example—they cannot spring into being overnight, as needed. Networks that really do work need to be knitted together painstakingly, over time. And their ground rules need to be invented from scratch, which takes more time and patience—luxuries that most women making the transition to motherhood can only dream about.

Where the male is willing and able to provide protection and provi-sioning—especially during the crisis years of early child-rearing—he remains the obvious answer to a still-pressing set of socio-biological questions. Where his capacity to protect and provision is threatened, however, or where it has been equalled or outstripped by other sources—the state, or the woman herself—pursuing legal marriage in order to mother will begin to seem a dubious bargain. And this, of course, is precisely what has begun to happen, particularly among underclass populations characterised by widespread male unemployment. Among Australia's Aboriginal population, eight out of ten births occur outside of marriage, compared to the national rate of less than three out of ten.[12] In the US, the ratio of ex-nuptial births to African-American women compared to those of the female population at large is similarly skewed. In the UK, the situation is similar, and lone mothers are more likely to come from less advantaged backgrounds than mothers with partners, as well as to come from lone-parent households themselves.[13]

Women who desire children also seek to become wives because they believe it will make life better for their children. I would venture to say that most of us still believe that children need fathers. Yet our conviction on this point has been rather violently shaken in the past thirty years. Australian Sex Discrimination Commissioner Susan Halliday, for example, told journalists in 2000 that the notion that children had a right to fathers was 'out of step with community beliefs'.[14] If Australians are following in the ideological footsteps of their American cousins, she may be right. More than ten years ago, three-quarters of respondents in one US survey agreed with the statement that 'a family is a group of people who love and care for one another', while only 22 per cent insisted that families needed to be related 'by blood, marriage or adoption'.[15] In the UK, a study bluntly titled *What Good Are Dads?* Was released for Father's Day 2001 by four charities, two of them government-backed. According to the *Independent*, 'the survey has found that dads are good for quite a number of reasons'. Hardly the stuff of headlines, one would have thought. Obviously, one would be wrong.[16]

Conservative US critic Barbara Dafoe Whitehead, who deplores the concept of the detachable Dad, documents the rise of what she calls the 'Love Family' ideology, in which 'the love bonds between parent and child (or any caregiver and child) are idealized as ungendered love…there is no mother love or father love—simply love'.[17] When it comes to family-making, reproductive technologies have not only rendered sex expendable, they've rendered fatherhood expendable too. At least theoretically, a father need be nothing more than—as one advice manual for solo Mums suggests—'a nice man who wanted to help me become your mother'.[18] Another author, US therapist Jane Mattes, advises single mothers to keep the story of their children's biological fathers to the barest minimum: something along the lines of 'My father's name is Dave…He's in Vermont'.[19]

More recently, we have seen a backlash in the popular press, with books like Steve Biddulph's *Raising Boys* attempting to resuscitate fatherhood from the post-feminist malaise into which it has been allowed to slip. Traditionally, the notion that children need fathers was about as controversial as the idea that plants need water, or that babies need milk. Today, it is the stuff of bestsellerdom. 'An Ordinary, Decent Father Can Make a World of Difference' announces a typical plaintive headline.[20] Obviously, such reports are attempting to redress a very recent imbalance. Forty years ago, father still knew best. Today, we wrestle with the question whether he knows anything at all—or anything worth hearing.

According to a 1998 *New York Times* report titled 'Daddy Dearest: Do You Really Matter?', fatherhood is now, after decades of neglect, 'the hottest stop on the social science circuit'. In many ways, the new wave of family research into fatherhood is unabashedly neo-traditionalist—a salvage operation. But the assumption that father is an indispensable member of functional family life remains oddly unsupported by the evidence.

Consider, for example, the exhaustive eleven-year study of traditional, two-parent families that found 'the influence of fathers is relatively minor' for adolescents. Researcher Frank Furstenberg, a sociologist at the University of Pennsylvania with more than twenty years' experience in the field, is the first to admit that such findings 'run in the face of common sense and conventional wisdom'. 'My own theory,' he adds, 'is that once you have one good parent in place, having another parent in place doesn't have a huge effect.'[21] Other cutting-edge research has tended to support this view—again, perhaps counter-intuitively. A study by sociologist Kathryn Edin and public health researcher Jennifer Culhane, for example, has found that children may have a more positive impact on fathers than fathers do on children. In August 2000, psychologist Dr Lisbeth Pike told a conference of the Australian Institute of Family Studies that the children of sole-parent families did just as well at school as those from traditional families. At the same conference, keynote speaker Professor Carol Smart exhorted the family-studies research community to stop its 'hand wringing'.[22]

As *New York Times* journalist Patricia Cohen notes, 'It seems self-evident to just about anyone who has ever had a father that a caring, involved Dad is good for a child. But try proving it.'[23] Many other commentators disagree, of course—including such big guns as Whitehead, family studies doyenne Judith Wallerstein and men's movement guru Robert Bly. One recent study of 800 six-year-olds, for example, showed that those whose fathers were present were better learners, had higher self-esteem and fewer symptoms of depression than fatherless kids.[24] According to the authors of *Boy Troubles*, a study conducted by the Centre for Independent Studies, single motherhood is the greatest cause of boys' social and educational woes.[25] These observers maintain that the myth of the expendable father is just that, a myth. And, according to the more cynical among them, a convenient myth at that, reducing parental guilt and responsibility to bearable levels within the divorce culture.

Cherry Norton, Social Affairs Editor of the *Independent*, argues that in the UK 'fatherhood has been transformed in the past 30 years'. Part of that transformation has been an emphasis on the importance of the father's role in children's lives, Norton continues. Yet the change in status of fathers, one can't help suspecting, may be largely ceremonial. Certainly fewer and fewer British men are experiencing traditional fatherhood. In the 1960s, six out of ten men were living with dependent children. Today, the latest figures from the Office for National Statistics show that only 35 per cent do.[26]

Under the 1999 Employment Act, UK fathers are entitled to thirteen weeks of unpaid paternal leave (though the British press wasn't slow to notice that Prime Minister and new Dad Tony Blair was not among the takers for the new entitlement.[27] 'Improving fatherhood services' has been a declared aim of the present government.[28] In the press, reports of Dads being socially excluded from 'feminised' day-care centres and playgroups are commonplace, while organisations like Working with Men are churning out research with topics like 'What makes a good father?' (answer: love and responsibility top of the list, breadwinning at the bottom).[29] Another group, Fathers Direct, has lobbied employers to institute a Father's Day 'Dads Go Free' package—offering a day's pay to men who take the holiday off to be with their children.[30] At the same time, maternity units across England are gearing up to provide better facilities for fathers under a hundred million pound plan to modernise reproductive health-care.[31]

All this is welcome, and yet the emphasis on the New Fatherhood, UK-style, has been very much on the rights of fathers, rather than on the rights (let alone needs) of children. Questions of access and entitlement centre on raising Dad's claims to a level equal of Mum's claims. One survey published in 2000 by the National Childbirth Trust, for example, found that new fathers overwhelmingly wished to have more involvement in pregnancy and birth, as well as more leave to care for their babies after they were born.[32] Prominence has also been given to research showing that 'fathers who live with young children work harder, get better jobs, are more sociable and attend church more frequently' than other men.[33]

Again, it's very much a question of what children can do for Dads, rather than what dads can or should be doing for children. It's an interesting change of tack.

The question of whether fathers matter so terribly much after all—particularly after controlling for the crucial variable of economic contribution—remains unanswered. In a sense, it hardly matters. True, false, or unanswerable, the notion has profoundly infiltrated our public consciousness anyway. And in doing so it has dislodged yet another plank in the foundation of monogamy as an essential social institution. Women still seek husbands, whether prospectively or retrospectively, in order to provide fathers for their children. But, rightly or wrongly, they are doing so with significantly reduced urgency, and acutely heightened ambivalence. Most of us probably still believe that having some sort of Dad is better than having none at all. We just don't believe it absolutely anymore.

rising expectations and diminishing returns

'Blessed is the [wo]man who expects nothing, for [s]he
shall never be disappointed.' Alexander Pope

In theory, social change happens slowly and in orderly increments. In reality, however, the social order appears to experience sudden growth spurts, intermittently streaking ahead of our ability to track it. The participation of women in the paid workforce, and particularly of women with children, is a striking instance of this. The feminist movement, whatever else it has or hasn't achieved, has effectively dismantled the economic basis of patriarchy throughout the English-speaking world.

Needless to say, women in the workforce have still got a long, long way to go to achieve parity with male workers. Gender discrimination remains embarrassingly rife, and large discrepancies persist between men's and women's wages, in some cases by up to 50 per cent.[1] The earnings gap can be statistically neutralised by controlling for exactly those variables (types of jobs worked, amount of overtime, bonuses and benefits, career interruptions due to child-rearing) that account for gender-based workplace discrimination in the first place. But by any methodological reckoning, we're still looking at a dismayingly stacked deck. In the US in 1998, the gap between the earnings of men and women who work full time still hovered around 25 per cent.[2] In the UK, the gross annual earnings gap in 1999 was more than 40 per cent, according to the Office for National Statistics.[3] In 1998, the average full-time female worker in Australia, for example, earned only 80 per cent of the average male wage.[4] This is partly because Australian women remain disgracefully under-represented in high paying jobs. As of May 1998, one in five male employees earned $1000 a week or more, compared with only one in twenty females.[5] There is still plenty of inequity out there. Nevertheless, the gains in women's participation in the paid workforce in the past thirty years have been indisputably impressive. Indeed, they constitute feminism's greatest success story.

It's hard for us to get our minds around the fact that, as recently as the 1960s, married women were actively *barred* from employment in many industries and openly discouraged and discriminated against in many others. Even in the teaching profession, Dale Spender recalls, 'women who became wives were expected to resign from their jobs—and to resign themselves to financial dependence on their husbands'.[6] In the US, for example, it is only in the last century or so that married women have acquired rights to own property in their own name.[7] 'Don't you think a man is the most important thing in the world?' asked Debbie Reynolds, presumably rhetorically, in the 1955 movie *The Tender Trap*. 'A woman isn't a woman until she's been married and had children.' Publisher Katharine Graham, who in the 1960s became one of the most powerful women in America, would have agreed. 'Once married,' Graham recalls in her memoir *Personal History*, 'we were confined to running houses, providing a smooth atmosphere, dealing with children, supporting our husbands.' It was only when Graham's husband died that she reluctantly took over the reins at the family-owned *Washington Post*, a decision 'so singularly surprising' it threw the organisation into turmoil.[8] Young girls were expected to enter the workforce—but only as long as it took to catch a husband. 'Most girls are interested—naturally—in the marriage prospects offered by various careers,' observed the *Australian Women's Weekly* in 1959 in an article aimed at school-leavers. 'If your object is matrimony, it is logical to take a job where you'll meet men.'[9] A few years earlier, when Australia's Marjorie Jackson, the fastest woman runner in the world, returned home from the Empire Games, a journalist asked her husband, 'But how is she with a broom?' The *Australian Women's Weekly* approvingly reported Jackson's retirement from sport to become a 'full time wife'.[10] As late as 1984, academics like John Mirowsky and Catherine Ross of the University of Illinois observed that self-esteem was the 'central problem' for the husbands of working wives. They identified 'embarrassment, guilt and apprehension associated with the wife's employment' as major marital stressors.[11]

Over the course of a single generation, the transformation in 'women's work' has been astounding. Today, marital status has almost no effect at all on women's labour-force participation. According to 1998 figures, 50 per cent of all American women in the prime working ages (twenty-four to fifty-four) were employed full time year round. Among married women in this age category, the figure was 46 per cent—only 4 percentage points lower.[12] This small discrepancy is almost certainly the effect of child-rearing rather than of marriage itself. In 1913, the year in which the US Department of Labor first started compiling statistics, only 2 to 3 per cent of married women were in the job market *at all*.[13] The idea that a woman would give up work upon marriage—the assumption being that wifehood is a full-time job—now seems as quaint as ironing tea towels, or beating rugs with a stick.

Most married women no longer expect to work for 'pin money'—most of us wouldn't know what to do with pins once we bought them—but for a living, just as adult men do. In the US, in fact, more than a quarter of employed wives earn more than their husbands do.[14] There, as in Australia, precious few prospective wives expect to be 'kept' by their husbands. Again, the magnitude of this change in one generation is enormous—a spectacular violation of the rule that 'real' social change happens slowly. According to US figures, fully a quarter of the mothers of the baby boom performed no work for pay at all between ages twenty-two and thirty-one; for their daughters, that figure has decreased to a mere 5 per cent.[15] This is not to suggest that we feel no residual nostalgia for the good old days when husbands went out to work and wives stayed home, doing whatever it was that wives were supposed to do. Many women resent having to work for pay (although not nearly as many, I suspect, as men). Still, in most circles, the very idea of a wife being financially dependent on her husband is seen as retrograde, if not humiliating.

Interestingly, the only exceptions to this rule are found at either extreme of the socio-economic spectrum: among immigrant and working-class communities on the one hand, and the upper-middle-class on the other. In the early 1990s, my girlfriend Kim, for example, was encouraged by her Sicilian fiance to work long hours to help pay for their wedding. She was in her early twenties, and Vince was about ten years older. Once married, however, Vince put his foot down. No wife of his was going to go to work, he insisted. For years, Kim was the only woman I knew who did no work at all for pay—until I moved to an upscale, beachside suburb populated by high-salaried professionals and their families. (In our family we refer to ourselves, wryly but accurately, as the local 'white trash'.)

Meeting other mothers at the local school, I discovered that I'd not only moved neighbourhoods, I'd entered a virtual time warp. Almost no one was doing paid work, and they regarded those who did with a mixture of awe and pity. Many women spent their time exactly as their own mothers would have done: shopping, gardening, lunching, organising the household help (cleaners, nannies, ironers, etc.) and doing occasional volunteer or community work. Whether coincidentally or not, I found that divorced mothers were almost as rare as working mothers in this new social setting. In our previous working- to middle-class neighbourhood, intact families were a distinct minority, and all but one of my nine-year-old's friends lived in single-parent or blended families. Somehow or other, I doubted very much that the privileged women in my new neighbourhood would identify themselves as 'financially dependent'. The sheer quantity of resources at their disposal changes the equation. So too does the knowledge, however implicit, that in the event of divorce the Family Court would see to it that they got their fair share, plus top-dollar child support.

These extremes aside, few middle-class women enter marriage expecting to be 'supported' for life. Even fewer perceive any conflict between the roles of wife and paid worker. Which is not to suggest that financial considerations now play no part at all in spouse selection. On the contrary, the evidence suggests that, wherever possible, women continue to seek to 'marry up'—that is, to choose mates who are not only slightly taller, slightly older and slightly better educated than themselves, but also slightly richer. High-earning females are no exception to this seemingly iron law of human mating behaviour. They simply seek out even higher-earning males. As we shall see, the persistence of 'marrying up'—a practice which anthropologists call 'hypergamy'—is one of the most serious obstacles to achieving genuine equality within marriage today. In a sense, hypergamy guarantees that wives will start out behind the eight-ball in the game of marital power politics—and ensures that they remain there for the life of the marriage.

With our mammalian brains, human females still seek mates who will 'provide', for the benefit of our families and ourselves. The idea of marrying 'for money' or security, however, fills most of us with a kind of romantic indignation—even more so, perhaps, than does the suggestion of marrying in order to procreate more efficiently. Indeed, the very idea of marrying out of 'need' of any kind seems at best dated, and at worst neurotic. To cite one very personal example, my first husband's proposal speech stressed that he believed he *could* live without me, but would rather not. I wasn't quite sure how to take this at time. Nearly twenty years later, I'm still not.

Ours is the first society in the history of human civilisation in which marriage is pursued not out of need, but out of want—and which predicates family life not on the solid rock of reproductive necessity but on the gossamer wings of sentimental preference. Marriage, we insist, does not lend itself to spreadsheet-style accounting of assets and liabilities, whether economic, social or biological. Even in the age of the pre-nup— a practice still confined to a tiny minority of high-earners—the foundation of marriage remains a feeling state, which we yearn to believe exists independently of any crudely material consideration. We call that feeling state 'love'. Love has much to do with erotic passion; yet we insist it is more than just sex. Exactly how much more we are far less certain, although we would agree it includes communication, compatibility and commitment.

What do we believe we are committed *to*? Biologically, marriage commits its participants to co-operation and compromise for the sake of the offspring. Yet, as we have seen, we now reject that notion too. We reject it both implicitly, in our modern insistence that children are optional extras within marriage, and explicitly, in our derision of the notion that an unhappy marriage may be a better compromise than no marriage at all. Tellingly, we are as interested in the impact of children on our marriages as we are on the impact of marriage on our children. Whatever else it may or may not signify, marriage is no longer 'about' raising a family.

The ideal of love-based marriage is hardly a natural feature of human society. On the contrary, historians regard it as a culturally peculiar development that arose in northwestern Europe no more than two centuries ago. Historian Edward Shorter has dubbed marrying for love 'the first sexual revolution'.[16] In the ancient world, the practice was rare. Plato, for instance, discusses marriage primarily as a means of mating. 'Romance', in the sense of sexual passion united with sentiment, was largely reserved for the homoerotic love of older Greek men for boys.

Prior to the industrial revolution, the vast majority of human societies (and a sizeable number even today) were far too concerned with simple survival to think romantically about marriage, or anything else, for that matter. In *The End of Marriage*, psychiatrist Julian Hafner observes that 'matters of appearance and personality were over-shadowed by the vital struggle to preserve or increase economic status'—and, I would add, by the parallel struggle to preserve and enhance one's genetic endowment, through the production of viable offspring.[17] From this point of view, the success of arranged marriages is no longer so puzzling. As Hafner explains, when 'people did not expect much emotional or sexual fulfilment from marriage, they were not greatly disappointed when these failed to eventuate'.[18]

It's not what we get from marriage that's the decisive factor; it's what we *expect* to get versus what we actually do get, the ratio of hope to reality. And until very, very recently, both men and women hoped for very little indeed.

Our expectations regarding the emotional rewards of marriage rose precipitously with the advent of the industrial revolution, when escalating standards of living made the ideal of romantic love an affordable luxury for middle-class consumption. Despite the growing allegiance to this ideal, however, the business of spouse selection remained in practice more or less that: a business. Pragmatic considerations were particularly central for women. In many ways, the pursuit of marital happiness through 'love' was strictly a male prerogative. Hafner, for one, goes so far as to suggest that romantic love was 'invented' by males as a way of preserving the convenient—for men—split between 'wives and mothers, who were virtuous and asexual, and other women, who were mere objects for sexual gratification'.[19] As the biologically more vulnerable gender, females needed to be more hard-headed—or their families did on their behalf. Making 'a brilliant match' was far too important to be left to chance, and the education of girls (such as it was) was devoted almost entirely to the art of entrapment. Those who, like Emma Bovary, bought into the myth of conjugal romance were the least likely candidates to succeed in the wifely role.

Emma discovers what every other female who has ever been married discovers: that romantic love and marriage are not simply difficult to sustain, but virtually impossible. Why? Because, to put it bluntly, the role structures within marriage could not be more inimical to erotic love. Wives are not sexy. Wives are safe, and safe is the opposite of sexy. Ironically, this is both an important reason women seek out the role of wife—to take themselves off the open market, as it were—and an important reason women reject it.

To some extent, we all know this is true. We make jokes about it, even. ('Marriage,' reads the fifties-style postcard someone sent me recently. 'The end of a perfectly good sex life!') But at the same time we cling to the myth that sexual love is the only acceptable basis for modern marriage. Germaine Greer believes the pressure to be sexually active within marriage has actually replaced the primordial rage to reproduce. The result of all this, she points out, 'places unmated women in jeopardy, and fills them with anxiety and the sense of failure'.[20] I would argue further that it has the same effect on so-called mated women. If it is true, as Michael Bittman and Jocelyn Pixley argue, that 'the sexual life of married couples is assumed to be a litmus test of the health of the marriage', no wonder we feel nervous.[21]

We start out believing that to marry for pragmatic reasons—for financial or social security, say, or to raise a family more efficiently—is hopelessly crass. Yet we end up discovering that to marry for 'love' or, to use the current buzzword, 'intimacy' is hopelessly unrealistic, especially if what we mean is a lifetime of erotic fulfilment.

Erotic love, we are discovering, is not necessarily any more enduring within marriage than it is outside of marriage. Sexual desire fades, and it fades fast. And it fades faster still under conditions that are relatively predictable, secure and danger-free, and where partners enjoy unlimited and unfettered access to one another. And those are exactly the conditions created by any 'good' marriage. Depressing? Sure. But true nonetheless. It's easy to keep the sexual flame alight almost indefinitely in an extra-marital affair, a long-distance relationship or a virtual romance. In a conventional, cohabiting marriage, most of us are looking at eighteen months to two years. Tops. In these days of heightened erotic expectations, anyone who gets to the seven-year mark before experiencing the 'itch' is either extremely lucky, deeply in denial or quite possibly both.

Women who expect that marriage will fulfil what Bittman and Pixley call 'The Dream of Intimacy' are almost certain to be bitterly disappointed. And that means most of us. Obviously, though, intimacy means something more than mere sex. Unless you happen to be male, that is, in which case it may not be obvious at all. Or even true, in many cases. This is not to suggest that men necessarily equate intimacy with good sex. On the contrary. Most of the time, they equate it with any sex at all.

On the basis of a massive review of the relevant literature, sociologist Janice Steil concluded that men really do appear to 'need' less intimacy than women. Specifically, the evidence shows that on the whole husbands describe themselves as satisfied with the level of intimacy within their marriages; they are also more likely to describe themselves as sexually satisfied than are their single counterparts. Indeed, one researcher has observed that 'the high level of married men's physical satisfaction with their sex lives contradicts the popular view that sexual variety improves sex for men'.[22] (Interestingly, cohabiting men consistently report having more sex, but married men report having better sex. The same is not true for women.)

In one study, wives were twice as likely as husbands to describe a relationship with a best friend as 'the person closest to them'. In another, 64 per cent of married women said they were more emotionally intimate with other women than with their husbands. Other research has shown that wives are less likely to talk over problems exclusively with their spouse. Husbands, by contrast, are far more likely to name their wives as their best friends or most trusted confidantes.[23] The conclusion is inescapable. As far as intimacy goes, men get what they need from marriage—either because women happen to give so much or because men happen to need very little.

Women's relative 'expertise' at intimacy has been widely noted. Yet we not only give more in the way of intimacy, we expect more. Social researchers Penny Mansfield and Jean Collard found that newlywed husbands and wives had starkly different expectations regarding 'intimacy' and 'togetherness'. As they put it, 'Most (though not all) men seek *a life in common* with their wives, a home life, a physical and psychological base; somewhere and someone to set out from and to. But for nearly all wives, their desired marriage was *a common life* with an empathetic partner, who would provide both material and emotional security.'[24] Men, this research suggests, see marriage as a set of two parallel lines: side by side, but separate. Women, by contrast, both expect and require frequent points of intersection.

If true, this finding implies a number of provocative possibilities—foremost among them that men may be more readily satisfied by marriage for the simple reason that they experience less emotional hunger. However elaborate a meal they are served, they may be satisfied with what, from a female perspective, looks like a handful of emotional crumbs. Women, by contrast, need something more sustaining. Or, to change the metaphor slightly, it's as if, emotionally, women need red meat—yet all men have to offer is celery and cottage cheese.

Perhaps the problem is not so much that women are unlikely to get everything they need from their male partners, but rather the expectation that they ought to. That they feel uncomfortable or resentful or even guilty about seeking that additional emotional sustenance elsewhere, whether from children or from female friends and relatives. A woman's husband, we for some reason believe, is supposed to meet her every emotional need. But…why? Especially if those needs are so much greater and more complex than his?

Contemporary men and women would both agree that they marry

'for love' and, as we have seen, this in itself represents something of an historical anomaly—a kind of social experiment whose outcome, at least at this point in time, appears dubious. As Germaine Greer has observed, 'modern marriage is fragile because the demands placed upon it exceed the tensile strength of the original sexual bond'.[25] This appears to be particularly true for women, who inevitably end up performing the lion's share of love's labour—in return for barely subsistence wages.

The idea of a marriage contracted 'for love' contains an explicit rejection of the earlier view of marriage as a primarily economic institution, not to mention of the much, much earlier view of monogamy as the most efficient means to an urgent biological end. 'Love' is supposed to be blind to little details like economic and/or evolutionary imperatives. In reality, of course, it has managed to keep a weather eye upon them at all times. The fact is, no matter what romantic ideal we may have collectively embraced, women have still required the material resources controlled by men, and men have in turn required the reproductive resources controlled by women.

Women who marry have also expected—and received—a host of social dividends. In many societies throughout the world, marriage remains the primary symbolic means by which young women attain adult status in the community. Where females are regarded as a form of property, marriage entails being 'given' by the father, and 'taken' by the husband. Our own marriage ceremonies still largely reflect this ancient form of patriarchal barter. As recently as sixteen years ago, when I was first married, it was still considered disrespectful to refuse one's father the privilege of this symbolic right of bestowal (or perhaps disposal!). Even in today's revised *Australian Prayer Book*, the celebrant still inquires 'Who gives this woman to be married?' as if she were a donation, or a parcel.

In a traditional setting, however, the transition from dutiful daughter to dutiful wife constitutes a definite step up in the status hierarchy. Hence the importance of the wedding as a universally acknowledged female rite of passage. Relative to husbands, wives may be weak. But relative to daughters, they are powerful adults, capable of establishing their own domestic dominions. To this extent, being 'given' in marriage has bestowed on women enormous social capital. And it continues to do so, even in our own putatively post-feminist world.

I have no doubt at all that women continue to pursue wifehood as a means of obtaining social legitimacy, particularly within their families of origin. I know I did. In retrospect, I can see that my own first marriage was a thinly veiled (as it were) way of announcing to my family, and especially to my mother, that I was a grown-up now. I would be very surprised if this were an isolated experience, even today. Using marriage as a fulcrum to achieve social leverage may be pathetic, but it still works. In my own case, marriage really did 'close the book' on my parents' sense of responsibility for me—a feat that none of the other maturational milestones I'd passed had satisfactorily accomplished. There was a tacit acknowledgment of this on all sides, even mine, though I'd have been loath to admit it consciously, let alone publicly. After all, the facts spoke for themselves. When I graduated from university, the family were proud. When I landed my first paying job, they were relieved. When I moved to my own place, they were exultant. But it wasn't until I became engaged that they rewarded me with celebrations and saucepans, crystal and cutlery and cold hard cash. Graduate, taxpayer, householder were one thing. Wife, quite clearly, was another.

Nevertheless, marriage has ceased to be the only or even the primary means by which females unambiguously attain adult status in the community. There are other paths to female adulthood now, other markers of our social legitimacy. Entrance into paid employment, usually after a period of specialised study, is the most obvious one. So, too, is setting up one's own home, particularly when it entails the purchase of real estate—milestones once inexorably tied to marriage for most women. Age is another factor in the changing status of marriage as a rite of passage. Even a generation ago, teenage marriage was commonplace. Today it has been relegated to a form of social deviance. In the US, the average age at which a woman becomes a wife is now nearly 26.7, and in the UK it's 27—a staggeringly late start on 'adulthood' by anybody's reckoning. This dramatic demographic shift is more a consequence of social change rather than a cause of it; nevertheless, it is a by-product that has begun to function in its own right as a catalyst for further change.

For many women, the social significance of 'tying the knot' is now dwarfed by another and far more enduring tie that binds: the experience of motherhood. Again, this is a consequence of prior social shifts. We have grown wary of investing too heavily in marriage because the risk of divorce is so very high—but of course the risk of divorce is so very high in part because we have grown wary of investing too heavily in marriage. One way or the other, we have been encouraged (or perhaps enabled) to see that the bridal advertisements were wrong. A diamond is not forever. With any luck a child will be. Husbands, sadly, may come and go. But motherhood endures. Unlike wifehood, a status all too easily reversed and remade, motherhood is a portal through which, once having passed, no return is ever truly possible. For this reason alone, first motherhood has become a far more appropriate occasion for the bestowal of adult female status than first marriage. Marriage may or may not 'take' the first time around, or even the second. Motherhood hasn't the luxury of such choice. It's now or never. I suspect that, among women themselves, motherhood has replaced marriage almost entirely as the point of cleavage in the great divide separating 'true' adulthood from functional or social adolescence. In terms of how men regard women, however, it is likely that marriage still occupies a position of eminence.

Throughout the ages, women have sought men in marriage as the sole means of achieving their own reproductive and economic agendas. More recently, women have also looked to marriage—although arguably to a lesser extent than have men—as a means for satisfying their emotional and erotic needs. Finally, we have seen that marriage functions as a form of social capital for women, a rite of passage into responsible adulthood. In each of these four respects—reproductive, economic, emotional and social—marriage continues to serve women's needs. Yet in none of them is marriage any longer *essential* to those needs.

Thanks to a powerfully synergistic combination of technological innovation and feminist-led social change, it is possible for a woman to (in a sense) have her baby and eat it too. Without marriage. Without monogamy. Without, in a significant portion of cases, any man at all. It's not necessarily easy or advisable to do so. But it is possible, and possibilities are in this instance the point. Emotionally, one could argue, marriage was never that great a deal for women. The ideal of marrying for love has in many respects been a male prerogative. Women have probably always relied more on female friends and kin for their emotional nourishment than our obsession with the heterosexual couple has allowed us to admit. Nowadays, we are simply more up front about it.

There are any number of conclusions that can be drawn from all this. But the first and most obvious one seems to me that we have reached the state where women need marriage less than men do. Once upon a time, marriage made women an offer they couldn't refuse. It does no longer. Today, it is men who have become the primary beneficiaries of the marital relationship.

I suspect this is a truth that would be universally acknowledged by women who have experienced marriage (and systematically withheld from those who haven't). Although it's not the sort of 'news' you read about in the paper or watch on television, this simple yet seismic shift in our relative dependencies as wives and husbands provides the answer to so many of the questions we struggle with. Including why marriage can feel so bad for women—even when, to all appearances, it looks so good. Why women now initiate three in four divorces, and remarry at less than half the rate of their ex-partners. Why, when women consider the alternative, single parenthood seems like a pretty good deal. Why, according to a *New York Times* poll, only one in twenty women considers 'being a wife' to be one of the most enjoyable things about being female (well behind both career and motherhood).[26] Why women turn for nurture to their children and female friends, rather than to their husbands. Why they perform so much less domestic labour than their mothers and grandmothers did, yet resent it so much more. Why wifehood is linked so strongly with depression, and being a husband linked so strongly with mental health. Why women feel, in short, that they are getting so much less out of this deal called marriage than they are putting in.

What it doesn't explain is why women keep making the effort anyway—why, having cut the most critical of their dependency ties to males, they continue to behave as wives in ways that bespeak powerlessness, vulnerability and even subservience. Before turning to that question, however, it is necessary to examine the behaviour of wives up-close and uncomfortably personal. What we will find is that most women continue to function in marriage as if the institution in general, and their husbands in particular, were still doing them a huge favour.

chapter 7

mars and venus scrub the toilet

'I don't know who does the bathroom.
She must do it, 'cause I don't.'
informant to Michael Bittman and Jocelyn Pixley, 1997

W ho does what around the house—otherwise known as the division of unpaid domestic labour—is almost as hot a topic among social scientists as it is in most marriages. Not at all coincidentally, many leading researchers happen to be married women.

Forty years ago, the topic didn't even exist. In those days, academic researchers didn't give a second glance to the grossly disproportionate way couples carved up the housework. Everybody knew that Her marriage was a site of on-going, unpaid domestic slog, and that His was a marriage of convenience. Or they would have known if they'd bothered to think about it. Like almost everyone else, researchers took the division of unpaid labour by gender as a given, a feature of the established order as inevitable and unremarkable as dust itself.

It wasn't until the mid-1960s that sociologists started to get the point that 'the established order' was the only thing worth studying in the first place. As late as 1974, *The Sociology of Housework*, the work of now-eminent British academic and feminist Ann Oakley drew sniggers from the academic community. Like much early work in the field, Oakley's groundbreaking research was more or less directly inspired by early feminist critiques, and it posed alarmingly simple questions: how much unpaid work does he do, and how much does she do? The answer—that in the 1960s women were performing a grossly disproportionate share of household work—surprised no one. The only truly 'startling' thing about these early studies was that they were conducted at all. At long last, sociologists had begun to take 'women's work'—i.e., unpaid work—seriously, counting it as 'real' labour and not as something women just sort of do, like their hair, or breathing in and out.

Before long, findings on the unequal distribution of household labour were being replicated across a huge spectrum of social and cultural settings. Gradually, the questions grew more subtle and qualitative, and researchers began to probe the variables that might affect the phenomenon. Does socio-economic status play a part in who does what? they wondered. How about participation in the paid workforce? Educational levels? Presence and ages of children? All were obvious suspects. Yet, funnily enough, none of them turned out to be culpable. Not even people's *ideas* about marriage and family life seemed to make a difference. Couples' perceptions about equality and gender roles in the abstract had almost no impact on how they lived their lives in specific.

In all this voluminous research, there was really only one variable that explained much at all. In fact, it explained everything. If you want to know who does what around the house in any particular marriage, it was conclusively demonstrated, you need look no further than gender.

Having established after decades of high-level academic inquiry what their grandmothers could have told them over a cup of tea and a biscuit, researchers have finally turned their attention from variability in the division of unpaid labour to the far more puzzling phenomenon of its persistence. In other words, they want to know why things *have failed* to change around the house when there have been so many dramatic gender shifts everywhere else.

But it's not only the persistence of traditional patterns at home that troubles researchers today. More and more, it's how we rationalise the persistence. As one sardonic academic has noted, 'researchers seem more troubled by the division of household labour than the women they interview'.[1] Particularly bewildering are recent findings suggesting that both spouses may be keenly aware of the inequities, yet not troubled by them. Even more perplexing, wives as well as husbands often perceive these gross asymmetries as 'fair'. Or so, at least, they tell researchers.

But I'm running ahead of myself here. Before we get to the interesting stuff we don't yet know about how men and women divide up the world of work at home, let's examine the interesting stuff we do know. There's a lot of it. The first thing the research has established is the enormous impact on domestic labour of marriage itself. 'When men enter marriage their participation in housework falls,' notes Anthony McMahon, author of *Taking Care of Men*.[2] Not surprisingly, their leisure time increases, becoming greater than at any other life-stage except retirement. For women, by contrast, marriage is hard work. 'A resident man creates extra chores, more washing, higher standards for cooking [and] more organisation to suit his schedule,' observes sociologist Joan Chandler.[3]

How much more? Well, estimates vary. According to Heidi Hartmann, a husband creates eight hours a week of extra physical labour for his wife.[4] Beth Shelton's 1992 study found that married women spend over five hours more per week on household labour than single women, whereas married men spend two fewer hours on household labour than single men.[5] According to Australian Bureau of Statistics figures, widows who are sixty and older do 25 per cent less housework than their married age peers—an awfully good reason to be merry. Widowers, by contrast, will find themselves doing 354 per cent more laundry, 226 per cent more cleaning and 208 per cent more cooking.[6] Males who move in the opposite direction—that is, straight from bachelor pad to nuptial bliss—reduce the time spent on those tasks by 75 per cent, 40 per cent and 50 per cent, respectively.[7]

Quite simply, the presence or absence of a wife is the main influence on the amount of domestic work performed by males. 'The remarkable thing about housework,' observes Steven Nock, 'is that the norms pertaining to it seem to inhere in the institution of marriage. Cleaning, laundry, or other daily household maintenance tasks do not appear to carry gender implications so long as there is no other person around who might do them. But once a man is married, there *is* another person.'[8]

When a woman is married, however, presumably there is not. Otherwise, why would a female who goes from living in a shared household to a marriage perform 50 per cent more laundry, 73 per cent more cleaning and 49 per cent more cooking? 'Conspicuous' is the word adopted by Michael Bittman and Jocelyn Pixley to describe the disparity between His housework and Her housework. One look at their 1997 figures and you realise how diplomatic this is. According to their study of Australian households, wives do on average 90 per cent of the laundry and 82 per cent of all indoor cleaning and tidying. Figures from the US are very similar, with employed wives still performing an estimated 70 per cent of all unpaid labour around the home—and this in addition to as yet untabulated burdens of women's mental and emotional responsibilities for family maintenance, including but certainly not limited to planning and organising all this physical slog.

This is not to suggest that the division of domestic labour has been entirely preserved from social change, snap frozen like some kind of glacier pre-feminist beast. In fact, recent US research has found that wives have cut their average housework hours almost in half since the 1960s, while husbands have almost doubled their contribution. That's the good news. The bad news is that even with these shifts, married women are still doing twice as much unpaid domestic labour as their male partners. And that is *before* factoring in time spent with children.[9]

When it comes to child care, wives typically contribute five times more than their husbands do. At the same time, for every hour a husband spends cooking, his wife will spend three.[10] After the birth of a couple's first child, almost all husbands and wives will conform even more closely to gender type. Yet even among Australian couples without children, women do six times as much cleaning as men.[11]

It would be easy to dismiss such findings if it were a matter of one measly little isolated study, or even one large-scale isolated study. But it's not. Figures like these recur endlessly—a bit like housework itself, really—in studies throughout the industrialised world.

According to the Humphrey Institute of Public Affairs, women constitute half the world's population, but do two-thirds of the world's work. In marriage, we do more like three-quarters of it. Research compiled for the 1993 National Child Development Study in the UK showed that women do 77 per cent of cooking, 75 per cent of cleaning, and 66 per cent of shopping. A survey published the same year found that only one British man in a hundred does an equal share to that of his wife.[12] Figures from the US are very similar, with employed wives still performing an estimated 70 per cent of all unpaid physical labour around the home—and this in addition to as-yet untabulated burdens of women's mental and emotional responsibilities for family maintenance, including but certainly not limited to planning and organising all this physical slog.[13]

For the moment, though, let's just stick to the topic of manual labour. Ironically, the domestic workload traditionally allocated to 'the weaker sex' tends to be more, not less, physically demanding than that of their mates. Indeed, as Germaine Greer has observed, 'the heaviness of work has never been a reason for women's not doing it'. On the contrary, 'as soon as a source of energy is found that makes work lighter, men take it over'.[14] Greer points out that in societies in which cultivation still happens by hand and hoe, gardening is women's work; when tractors come along, it's every man for himself.

I'm sure we could all think of similar examples closer to home. I think of the leaf blower a friend bought recently to deal with the seasonal fall-out from her Cape lilac tree. 'Since moving to our new house more than a year ago, I swept debris from this tree off our patio with a stiff-bristled broom at least three times a week,' she explains. 'My husband did it once. (And even then it was only because his mother was coming over and I forced him.) Finally, I decided there were some problems that technology really *could* solve, and this was one of them. I no sooner returned home with my new gadget—a nifty blow-or-suck job with detachable leaf bag—than Alan asked shyly if he could have a go. Within a few days, clearing the patio with this giant, motorised phallus had become His job.'

Unfortunately, the same effect has not often been observed with vacuums or washing machines. But it is true that the least technologised household tasks—the most physically demanding and unpleasant ones— are also the least likely to be performed by males. Perhaps this explains why, while there have been sightings of husbands who will dump clothes in the washing machine, the man who will retrieve them afterwards for *any* purpose—let alone to complete the full circle of drying, sorting, folding or ironing, and putting away—is a rara avis. Indeed, laundry presents an extreme case of gender-typing. British author Rebecca Abrams points out that even among dual-earner couples, 85 per cent of women do *all* the laundry and ironing.[15] In one large-scale Australian study, men neither laundered, ironed, folded nor put away clothes for 88 per cent of the days in which they recorded their activities. Its authors concluded that the husbands' avoidance of laundry was 'notorious'. (So, I'm certain, did their wives.) Among their more hilarious findings was that 'six husbands claimed the family possessed a twin tub washing machine or clothes dryer that their wives denied any knowledge of'. One of them even went so far as to claim that these phantom appliances were used 'mostly' by himself![16]

Less hilarious is the impact of such inequities of effort on the marriage relationship itself. It's a topic that almost no social scientist has been brave enough, or rash enough, to broach. For my money, there is something distinctly *maternal* about the act of caring for someone else's clothes. Dealing with dirty laundry, as the old adage suggests, is also highly intimate. The problem is that in this case the intimacy runs only one way. Perhaps it's not surprising that the husband who leaves his dirty socks on the floor has become something of a cultural caricature. Forty years ago, a wife's tolerance of such infantile behaviour was seen as a reflection of the depth of her gratitude to her male partner. Wifework wasn't exploitation. It was, quite literally, a labour of love.

This theme is captured beautifully in a short story that appeared in the *Australian Women's Weekly* in January 1958. 'The Perfectionist' is the cautionary tale of Jim and Judy: a young couple whose marital bliss is threatened when the wife momentarily fails to indulge her husband's slovenliness.

If only Judy knew how lucky she really was! After all, husband Jim was everything a woman could hope for: handsome, ardent, employed. But was Judy satisfied? No. She wanted all of that *and* she wanted him to stop throwing his dirty underwear around the bedroom. ('Judy looked up at her husband as she gathered up his clothes, which had been scattered about their bedroom, and realised that it would be easy to lose all patience with him—if she didn't love him so much.') Talk about a bitch! No wonder Jim's become so distant and depressed. Luckily, Judy has a good friend who sets her straight: a former workmate whom fate has doomed to remain single. This tragic figure reminds Judy of all the 'disagreeable things' she used to do for her former boss, Mr Harrow— 'things he could have done for himself, but didn't'. Hmm.

Is that the sound of gears grinding, or is Judy starting to think? 'She had done all that to make her job a success,' she reflects sorrowfully, 'and this morning she had rebelled at a few minor annoyances that might mean the success of her marriage.' Overcome with richly deserved self-loathing, Judy sets to work to right things. That night, she redeems herself with a pot roast and mixed vegetables ('because that combination was a favourite of his'), followed by a healthy dollop of steaming hot marital sex. Or any sex, really. As Jim swoops down for a pot-roast-scented kiss, 'Judy kicked his socks under the bed—the same two wrinkled blue socks that Jim had left in their usual place—on the floor.'[17]

It's easy to parody such stuff. There's a thriving segment of the greeting-card industry that uses domestic iconography from the fifties and sixties to do just that. I suppose it's our way of distancing ourselves from all that nonsense and naivete, from the made-up, mask-like faces of devoted wives like Judy and the looming virility of their cloddish but dependable Jims. It's so easy to feel superior and, well, *evolved* by comparison that we forget how recently these dinosaurs actually roamed the earth. In some ways, 'The Perfectionist' reads like a medieval morality tale—yet, as I was chastened to note, it appeared exactly one week before I was born. Judy and Jim represent precisely the marital milieu in which the baby boom was born and bred. Judy and Jim are the parents we grew up with, the parents whose marriage—for better or for worse—was modelled for us. Good grief. No wonder we're confused.

Judy and Jim are a scream, all right—but it's a whole lot less hilarious that marriages are held together today by essentially the same role structure. Which is why, both metaphorically and literally, so many of us are still picking up those goddamn blue socks off the floor. Sure, we resent it much more now. We may even resent it so much we're willing to end the marriage over it. Yet I suspect the real challenge lies in figuring out how to be married and female and *not* pick up the socks.

Stephanie Dowrick tells the story of a woman for whom the metaphorical socks—or, in this case, T-shirt—became grounds for divorce. 'In the end,' she told Dowrick, 'I thought my ten years of marriage had amounted to nothing more than his T-shirts. It wasn't washing them I minded. It was *turning them the right way out*! Why did he have to take them off and leave them inside out? Why couldn't he turn them out the right way himself?' Such a trivial thing. And yet, as I suspect this woman well knew, of enormous significance to the way we lead our lives. 'I don't like grown-ups behaving like babies,' she concluded. 'At the daily level of it, it is tedious, tedious.'[18] I have similar conversations with women on an almost daily basis. ('It's hard enough treating a child like a child,' says my friend Charmaine, 'let alone treating your husband that way.') Women hate acting like men's mothers. Yet not acting like their mothers doesn't seem like a viable option either, when it means wading to bed through a trail of soiled underclothes (or their moral equivalent).

Ingrid has been married to Simon for fifteen years, and she still seethes every time she matches a pair of socks for him. She seethes, but she does it. 'If I don't, who will?' she asks. Sarah says she feels she is 'making progress' with David, her forty-seven-year-old husband of three years. Although he still baulks at depositing his dirty clothes *in* the laundry basket, he now places them *on top* of it.

'Have you tried to talk to David about this?' I ask cautiously.

'Sure,' she replies.

'Have you been direct?' I persist. 'How have you framed the problem?'

She thinks about this. 'I think my exact words were: "What kind of bullshit is this, anyway? Just lift the fucking lid, for Chrissake." So I don't think directness was a problem.'

David's response to all this? 'Well, he laughed,' Sarah recalls. 'He got the point. But you know what? He still does it. It's perverse. Like he's trying to send me a message in code.' Which, of course, he is. Deborah, who's been listening to all this, feels very lucky. 'Gee, I guess Bob isn't as bad as I thought,' she reflects. 'He *always* puts his clothes in the dirty clothes basket.' And Deborah always washes, dries, folds and puts them away.

Laundry isn't the only area of housework that remains almost entirely women's business within marriage. There are plenty of other unpleasant unpaid tasks which almost invariably 'belong' to women. Scrubbing the toilet, for example. In one recent study, 91 per cent of wives who described the division of household labour in their marriages as 'fair' took sole responsibility for this task.[19] Appearances by the toilet fairy persist in nearly all marriages, regardless of spouses' protestations of 'equal sharing' of tasks. 'You can demand an orgasm,' one woman confided to a journalist. 'But you cannot demand that your man cleans the toilet.'[20]

So what's going on?

A generation ago, the answer was straightforward. The man was going out to work, for pay, and the wife was staying home to do it, for free. In those days, nobody—not even sociologists—had a problem with that. It may have been a drastic division of labour. But it was also a coherent and rational one, with boundaries high enough to trip over. Equally importantly, both parties to the agreement gave it their full consent—often, admittedly, because there was no alternative. Heaven knows, the so-called traditional division of labour by gender, in reality an artefact of quite recent technological and economic movements, was in no sense 'fair'. But it had at least the virtue of balance, of stability. Like all enduring family systems, the homemaker Mum–breadwinner Dad model was built on a foundation of intense mutual dependency. By the mid-twentieth century, having a full-time wife at home—someone who would in a sense live life for the two of them—made it possible for a man to be 'married' to his job. And only a man who was 'married' to his job could afford to have a full-time wife at home.

At one level, acquiring a wife was for a man a form of conspicuous consumption, a marker of his elevated economic status. As recently as forty years ago, the 'no wife of mine is going to go out to work' mentality reigned supreme in our cultural consciousness, if not precisely in our economic reality. A wife who worked for pay may have been an economic asset. But, far more importantly, she was a social and psychological liability—a direct hit not only on a husband's status in the community, but on his very identity as a man.

'My wife works and I HATE IT' bellowed an anonymous husband in a March 1959 issue of the *Australian Women's Weekly*. By turns condescending ('It all began about two years ago when she decided she was bored staying home all day. She wanted to get a job, to stop being a "potato", to meet people, to "express herself". You know the sort of things.') and plaintive ('I haven't seen a real pudding for weeks'), this real life story of one man's bewilderment and betrayal when his wife goes out to work makes riveting reading for a child of the baby boom.

This unnamed upstart wife and mother of two is among Australian literature's first Supermums; what befalls 'her' family in the wake of her 'selfishness' is the stuff of every husband's nightmare. 'The bath wasn't cleaned very often. The fridge often needed defrosting. The kitchen cupboards had a tired look.' The problem isn't that 'she' is lazy. Oh no. He's got to give credit where credit is due. 'My wife tries at night to get things straight,' the husband admits, 'and she works most of the weekend, and is exhausted by the time Monday comes. But she is always behind.' Eventually, her frenzy of fruitless effort gets so bad it even interferes with his golf. 'When I needed a golf shirt it hadn't been ironed and I had to do it myself, and it wasn't the last time either.' Even worse—if such a thing is imaginable—is the impact on the couple's children, aged twelve and fourteen, who have been driven next door to watch television after school 'even though we have our own set'. Oh, and their 'manners are deteriorating' too.

All hell is breaking loose, yet 'she' doesn't seem to care. She doesn't see 'the ever present danger of losing or damaging that something that makes marriage worthwhile'. (Pressed play-clothes? A frost-free fridge?) 'It's a hard word to use,' the husband concludes with a metaphorical shake of his head, 'but she is being selfish. As she has no need to work, her duty is to herself, me, the children, the home. And she is evading this responsibility.'[21]

Well, where does one begin? Firstly, perhaps, with the observation that the thinking this polemic expresses—however prehistoric it may appear—informs our own sensibility as married people to a degree few of us, male or female, would be comfortable acknowledging. Artefacts like this one remind us almost violently how huge a transition our generation has been required to make. They may also remind us how imperfectly we have managed it. No wonder. We've got one foot in a world where a wrinkled golf shirt stands as an indictment of our worth as women, and the other in a world that tells us we are in every respect the equals of the possessors of those golf shirts. Men feel an equivalent ambivalence, of course. Guys may not *think* they've got a special right to real puddings and a drawerful of ironed shirts anymore. But they may still *feel* that way. It's a head–heart split that reflects the particular historical moment we happen to occupy.

We absorbed one story about relationships, as if by osmosis, from the families we grew up in. Yet somewhere along the line, as we grew away from those families and into a social reality furiously reinventing itself, we lost the plot. In the place of that tiresome old tale called *The Breadwinner and His Wife*, we improvised a story of our own, complete with an all-new cast of hastily drawn characters. The old story was about hierarchy and neediness and mutual distrust; about 'knowing one's place' in the partnership and staying there. The new story was about discovering one's place; about sharing and equality and mutual respect. It had become clear to almost everyone that the old story had grown as musty and irrelevant as bad history. The new story, by contrast, was vibrant and full of hope. Aren't most fantasies?

chapter 8

believing in pyjamas

'It's a small world...But not if you have to clean it.' Anonymous

Between these two stories of married life—the original version we learned with our hearts, and the revised edition we tried to substitute with our heads—lies the tension so often experienced in marriage today, particularly by women. For it is the female character who has been by far most drastically revised. The differences between these stories are, as they say in the family law courts, irreconcilable. And this fact, I am convinced, explains both why we have stalled so spectacularly on the issue of who does what—and why we deny it.

Yet it would be a mistake to imagine that all this upheaval occurred suddenly, over the course of a single decade or two. It didn't. And the fact that it didn't is part of the problem. Take the simple but obvious variable of the employment of married women outside the home. Reading the fine print of the demographic detail exposes the 'sudden' demise of the breadwinner–homemaker family as something of a mass-mediated myth. In the US, for example, the labour-force participation rate of married women rose exactly ten percentage points per decade for each ten-year period from 1940 to 1990.[1]

For a revolution, that's an awfully orderly progression. It's also a deceptive one—providing just enough continuity over just enough time to sustain the illusion that nothing much has changed. Taking the long and privileged view of the social critic or academic historian, one would quite properly regard the magnitude of a 10 per cent rate of change, compounded over fifty years, as immense. In the US today, for example, only one in five families fits the traditional mould of breadwinner husband and full-time homemaker wife.[2] Yet on the ground, as it were— which is, after all, where we live—things look different. Living a trend is a very different experience from analysing one.

Perhaps a more abrupt break with tradition would have forced couples to confront the domestic division of labour as an urgent priority. As it happened, the measured pace of change from traditional to dual-earner marriage seems to have lulled the entire culture into a false sense of stability. As the *Weekly* article makes plain, there was a clear anxiety felt by husbands and wives alike to keep the sphere of paid work separate from that of unpaid work. There was no expectation that a woman's paid employment would purchase her freedom from unpaid domestic drudgery. On the contrary, wives' paid work was regarded as a kind of privilege, by women and men alike. The price of that privilege was continuing to accept full responsibility for what we have now learned to call 'the second shift' at home. Those who baulked at this deal—or even those whose frantic efforts to fulfil it fell short—were branded as 'selfish': the most unwifely stigma of them all.

The statistical proof of this pudding is both dismal and overwhelming. In an extensive review of the literature, the difference between the domestic workload of husbands with employed wives and husbands with non-employed wives was found to be exactly ten minutes a day. Husbands overall were doing about 33 per cent of what their wives did around the house; husbands of employed wives about 37 per cent.[3] Surely there are *some* husbands in dual-earner families who share the work equally? The good news is that, yes, of course there are. The bad news is that they range from a low of less than 2 per cent to a high of 12 per cent, according to the most recent research. In one study of marital equality and well-being, the researcher was forced to abandon her efforts. 'There were too few equally sharing couples to study,' she explained, almost apologetically.[4] Another sociologist, Harriet Presser, found that, when wives go to work outside the home, a third of husbands do more housework and child care, a third don't change at all, and a third actually do *less*.[5]

I mention some of these statistics to a married male friend, who looks distinctly uncomfortable. 'Yeah, OK,' he says. 'But, let's face facts. Even in dual-earner marriages, most guys work longer hours than most women. It's just a matter of time accounting.' He looks almost hopeful. And it *is* a nice thought. Unfortunately, it's not an empirically supported one. 'Husbands do not increase their participation in household labour in any significant way when their work demands decrease,' observes Janice Steil.[6] For women, the reverse is true. And when a woman works more hours, her husband's domestic load still does not change. Husbands of full-time employed women do no more housework than husbands of women who work part-time.[7]

But surely wives who work outside the home for pay do less housework than their stay-at-home sisters? As a matter of fact, they do. It's just that the slack is not being taken up by their husbands. According to Steven Nock's figures, US women were doing 2.5 times as much housework as their husbands in 1976. Ten years later, that figure had dropped to 1.9.[8] Yet in absolute terms, men were not doing substantially more, but women were doing less. Estimates suggest that about two-thirds of the reported change in the Who Does What? ratio is due to a drop in women's participation.[9] In 1992, for example, Australian women were spending an average of two hours less per week on cooking than they had five years earlier. Did men cook two hours more per week? No, they did not. In fact, there were no significant changes in men's participation in cooking in that period—although women increased the time they spent on home maintenance and car care, traditionally husband's business, by twenty-one minutes per week.[10] The decrease in time spent cooking reflected a change in consumer behaviour, not in gender roles, as working wives bought more prepared foods and takeaway.

Women are also doing less laundry now—about forty-four minutes a week less over the five-year period to 1992. Part of the reason, say researchers, is that ironing is now more likely to be outsourced to a paid worker. Another factor, I suspect, is that employed women are less fussy about laundry. Non-essential procedures like starching, bleaching, fabric softening and pre-soaking are now as vestigial as a hand-cranked mangle. So too are the days when a woman's self-worth was reflected by the whiteness and brightness of the clothes flapping on her rotary clothes-line. After all, we have dryers now. In the area of laundry, as in the area of cooking, we are becoming what my mother would not hesitate to call 'slack'. Or, as Bittman and Pixley put it, if more parity is being achieved, it's because 'women are behaving more like men rather than because "new" men have discovered how fulfilling housework can be'.[11]

Although the figures show that women are doing less cooking, their anxiety about the larger responsibility of 'feeding the family' remains as acute as ever. 'Though their part in food preparation has been to a large extent usurped by industry,' Germaine Greer writes, 'women are still held responsible and hold themselves responsible for what the family eats. In the matter of nutrition, as in so much else, they are confronted with the typical female dilemma of lack of control combined with total responsibility.'[12] According to a 1998 survey conducted by the BBC *Good Food* magazine, 90 per cent of women said they prepared the evening meal for their husbands or partners.[13] Arguably, however, the time spent chopping and cooking is the least of a wife's worries. More arduous by far are the mental burdens of planning and shopping for meals—not to mention the energy devoted to 'selling' them to children and men. These decision-making tasks are a constant part of most married women's lives, whether employed or not, whose toll on our time and attention has never fully been reckoned.

Ask any woman whose husband is away on business what she's having for dinner and I can guarantee the answer will be something along the lines of a gleeful 'Who knows? Who cares!' 'Women do not consume meals in the same way as men,' observes researcher Anthony McMahon, himself the happy product of a single-parent family.[14] Left to our own devices, women will often forgo 'proper meals' altogether, grazing contentedly on snacks and children's leftovers. Notes sociologist Joan Chandler, 'Food practices are patriarchal in that husband preferences dominate the family diet, men consume high-status foods and the timing of the day's main meal must fit the husband's return from work. Hence women only produce "proper meals" for other people and especially for men.'[15]

'Research shows that fruit cut into bite-sized chunks will be more acceptable to family members,' explained a nutritionist on a recent radio program. Why was I not surprised to learn that by 'family members' she meant children and husbands? Needless to say, the question of how women prefer *their* fruit remained unasked. When a marriage breaks up, how often do women console themselves by eating exactly what they want, and when they want it? I know I have done this and found it strangely satisfying in more ways than one. When my first marriage ended, I consumed ritual meals of long-forgotten favourite dishes: avocado salads, creamed spinach, garlic prawns, chicken livers and bacon. These were all foods my husband disliked; consequently, they were never served—in bite-sized chunks or otherwise—by either of us. I had honestly never thought about this. Like most married couples, we had simply adopted his food preferences as *our* food preferences. We ate brussels sprouts (yeech!) because he liked brussels sprouts. We avoided highly spiced foods because highly spiced foods gave him indigestion. We always had Diet Coke in the fridge because that was 'his' drink. There was no consultation about any of this. In fact, as far as I could tell, there was no awareness of it, either. Once I started really thinking about it, I realised that I disliked many of my own standard dishes— especially those of the 'meat and three veg' variety preferred by my strapping Aussie partner. Once I began substituting salads and sand-wiches for a heavy, meat-based evening meal, I felt a great weight—about the size of a leg of lamb, as a matter of fact—lift from my shoulders.

It has been justly observed that 'much depends on dinner'. Whether we like it or not, a family's arrangements for the taking in of nourishment are profoundly significant indicators of its domestic politics. I think of the women I know who describe themselves as 'lucky' if their husbands cook dinner once or twice a week, or even take responsibility for bringing home the takeaway. One friend boasts that she and her husband share the cooking equally. On her nights she cooks a balanced meal from scratch, and on his nights he buys a family-sized pizza or a bucket of fried chicken. She laughs about this, but always adds with a shrug, 'Hey, it's still three nights less I've got to cook.' I think how wistful references to 'real puddings' and 'proper meals' still have the power to inspire guilt in wives—and nostalgia in husbands. The myth of marital mutuality disguises the immense responsibility women continue to bear for men's bodies, from the inside out.

Nonetheless, it would be inaccurate to suggest that husbands' share of the domestic workload—cooking included—has remained unchanged. Men have assumed more responsibility around the house in the past forty years—just not as much as we may like to think. Between 1974 and 1992 Australian men's unpaid work increased by an average of 3.6 hours per week, or about thirty minutes a day. In the US, where the labour force participation of married women, particularly of married women with young children, is considerably greater, that figure is higher by as much as 25 per cent. Slowly, painfully, we seem to be evolving in the right direction. Yet, for most of us, the reality right now is that women are still working at roughly twice the speed of their male partners for less than half the benefit.

For it is still the case that the unpaid labour a wife performs is taken for granted, almost as if dusting or vacuuming or laundering were the discharge of some natural and therefore unremarkable function. In this sense, women's work remains 'invisible'—as unnoticed as it is uncompensated. And this is the case both in our own homes and in the wider society. Men's contributions to domestic labour, by contrast, are in many households still greeted with awe and ceremony, as befits an occasion. At the very least, wives are expected to show gratitude for a husband's efforts. We thank them—often fulsomely, as we would a child who has folded his first napkin, or surprised us by packing away her toys. By doing so, of course, we reaffirm the very gender divide we think we are eliminating. And that's frustrating. Realising that one shouldn't feel grateful when a man starts doing his own wifework, as it were, doesn't change the fact that one *does* feel grateful. And what about supplying 'positive reinforcement'? It works with dogs and kids and laboratory rats. Why not with husbands? The problem, of course, is not the 'thank you' itself but its subtext—a relationship message that reinforces the perception that when a man does work around the house he is doing a favour, yet when a woman does the same work she is doing her duty. In a more civilised world we would all be thanking each other. But as it stands, the gratitude runs in a single and utterly predictable direction.

One detects this dynamic in innumerable ways, both subtle and blatant. My friend Sarah's husband, for example, developed the habit of reciting his domestic achievements. 'I took out the rubbish, and fed the pets and washed the dishes,' he'd report proudly. 'It was almost as if he expected I was going to pin a gold star to his chest,' Sarah relates. '"That's nice, dear," I'd reply as blandly as I could.' In time, it occurred to Sarah that a far more effective strategy would be to mirror this behaviour and allow him to experience the double standard at first hand. 'The first time I tried it, he looked genuinely puzzled,' she told me. 'I could sense he was thinking "Is she for real? I mean who *cares* which vegetables she's peeled/what she put in the kids' lunchboxes/whether she vacuumed under the sofa cushions?"' After all, for a woman to expect praise, or even acknowledgment, for such effort would be a bit like seeking approval for brushing one's teeth, or successfully opening one's bowels. Needless to say, it didn't take long for the point to be made.

Researchers have observed that domestic wifework remains invisible partly because males trivialise it. They do this in both conscious and unconscious ways. Almost all men admit to having lower standards for household cleanliness than their wives. What's more, most of them are proud of it. This is so prevalent a pattern, despite some spectacular exceptions, that one is almost tempted to posit a biological basis for it. Did evolution select for tidy women because infants whose mothers were more careful about hygiene had a better survival rate? It's possible. Then again, if both parents were fastidious wouldn't that survival rate be higher still? Are females simply more tidy by nature than males? Or is our cultural conditioning to 'clean up and pack away like good girls' so incredibly successful that it only feels that way? Like many aspects of gender identity, I suspect it's a bit of both. Females may start out with a very slight biological predisposition towards orderliness, perhaps simply as a function of our marginally better visual acuity, a minimal advantage which culture has exploited to the max. We'll probably never know for sure—and, quite frankly, it couldn't matter less one way or the other. If males suffer from some sort of minor handicap in this area, it seems to me we have even more responsibility, not less, to assist in their rehabilitation.

After all, it's not as if there is some 'instinct to vacuum' which women have and men lack. The point is, we have clearly designated not-vacuuming as a boy thing anyway. There is no magazine called *Man and Home*, as Germaine Greer has pointed out. 'A man who is slovenly or untidy is considered normal,' she writes. 'The woman who is either is a slut or a slommack or a sloven or a slag. A woman who is dirty is dirt. The external attribute becomes a moral quality, as it does not for a man.'[16] Although they express themselves more sedately, most sociologists agree. 'Some types of housework are culturally defined as *women's*,' notes Steven Nock. 'This is particularly true of tasks performed exclusively in the dwelling: cleaning, ironing, or cooking, for example. If a man accepts this premise, there will be some tension about doing those tasks. Moreover, if he thinks *others in his personal community* accept it, there will be even more tension over doing housework.'[17]

These strong gender associations, researchers say, help explain why the contribution of males remains relatively unaffected by changes in hours of paid employment—either his or hers. A number of studies have even found that, for men, hours of paid employment are negatively correlated with hours of unpaid work around the house—in other words, he actually does less the more free time he's got. Unemployed men often do the least of all occupational groups. Researchers tell us this is an ego thing that cuts directly to the core of masculine identity, and its horror of dependency. To avoid adding private insult to public injury, so-called dependent husbands may refuse to participate in 'home duties' at all.

Some research suggests that men cope with such uncomfortable inequities by denying that housework matters—or, in some extreme cases, that it even exists! Michael Bittman and Jocelyn Pixley found that male respondents to their time-use study frequently 'tried to draw the interviewer into a collusive dismissal of the significance of housework and child care'.[18] One husband maintained that the issue of who did what around the house 'was never an issue'. 'No,' he assured researchers, 'it just happens.'[19] Bittman and Pixley also found that male partners were sometimes unaware that cleaners or other paid domestic workers were completing some of the work. All they knew—and all they needed to know—was that it was getting done, and by someone else. Another man admitted he did no cooking, but explained this was because he wasn't interested in cooked food. He ate it, mind you. Not because he wanted to, he insisted, but because, like Everest, 'it was there'.[20] Another husband betrayed a similar attitude when his wife suggested they might alternate responsibility for making the bed each morning. 'I don't believe in bed-making,' he announced, almost piously. Well, you don't need to believe in bed-making if it's always done for you. For that matter, you don't need to believe in housework, period. There's a fine line between the trivialisation of housework and the denial that it exists at all.

Non-contributing husbands often try to sweep the issue of unpaid labour under the rug (so to speak). But even worse than pretending that 'it's not a problem' is reframing housework as a form of pathology, suggesting that those who engage in it are, in some obscure way, their own worst enemies. There's a problem, all right, such men imply, and it's *hers*. One research team found that, where differing household standards prevailed, male respondents implied that their own attitude was 'tolerant' and their wives' attitudes were 'obsessive'.[21] I find it fascinating that we accept without question that there is a right way and a wrong way to perform traditional men's work—say, to change the motor oil, or mow the lawn, or hang a cupboard. Yet to most men, the suggestion that there might be a right and a wrong way to vacuum or fold a nappy or hang out the laundry inspires eyeball-rolling, or even disbelief. To me, this is another way in which we betray the very deeply held assumptions that what men accomplish matters, and what women accomplish doesn't; that what men know is knowledge, and what women know is prejudice. As a result, a women who persists in framing housework as skilled work, and who cares about the results obtained, is routinely stigmatised as 'too fussy' or—the ultimate marital put-down—a 'control freak'.

Among themselves, wives complain lustily and with caustic wit about their husbands' domestic hopelessness. This one washes dishes with no detergent. That one sweeps crumbs from the kitchen floor into a neat pile—and leaves them there. A third pegs out washing so ineptly that even the underwear needs ironing. A fourth cooks frozen peas in a wine-glass filled with boiling water. To hear their wives tell it, husbands are as laughably incompetent as a character out of a fairy tale—the dumb miller's son who carries cream cheese on his head, or puts the cow on the roof to graze. And it's even more entertaining when you consider that these same men masquerade in the world as engineers or marketing consultants, teachers or stockbrokers, medical practitioners or computer programmers. ('Come on. You mean to tell me a guy who struggles to defrost a loaf of bread managed to get himself through law school? As if!') One study found that 50 per cent of women reported that their husbands 'required supervision' with domestic tasks. Another looked at women's efforts at 'teaching' domestic practices to their husbands. In one case, after six months of tuition, the husband was actually doing the laundry. His wife concluded, 'I think I will train him to do the dishes next.'[22] Somehow or other, we find it reassuring to remind each other that our men are not only intellectually disabled, but visually impaired as well. 'He just doesn't *see* the mess!' we conclude ruefully, and on this point everyone agrees. It's not hard to see why. Such a fortuitous arrangement of rods and cones would get us all off the hook.

For a wife to criticise her husband's domestic accomplishments, it is widely believed, is the height of bad manners. More pragmatically, women also worry that criticism would be counterproductive—a negative reinforcer for a positive behaviour. These days, women also worry that, by maintaining some sort of household standard, they may be unconsciously colluding in their own oppression. Researchers call this phenomenon 'gatekeeping', a collection of strategies by which females may guard their traditional turf by subtly undermining male effort. The recent 'discovery' of gatekeeping by social scientists has inspired more trepidation than ever about resolving the issue of domestic work standards. When one of my girlfriends announced that she'd given her husband a detailed laundry-sorting lesson, the other women exchanged looks. 'Are you sure that's such a good idea?' somebody ventured. 'I mean, shouldn't we be praising instead of undermining them?' For a moment, it almost sounded like we were talking about our preschoolers. Another woman confided that, ever since she pointed out there were smudge marks on the glasses her husband washed, he simply left them in the sink. For her.

A third told the story of how her husband put the kids to bed in their school-uniform tracksuit-pants the night she went out with the girls. 'At first I was really upset about it. But when you think about it, he did read them a story and spend time playing cards with them. And I wanted to put the emphasis on that rather than on the negative stuff.' There were nods all around. 'Yet I couldn't help thinking,' she added quietly, 'why should I have to choose between getting the relationship thing right and getting the job done properly? Why couldn't he have done *both*? That's what I do.' ('How would you respond if a babysitter put the kids to bed in their day clothes?' I asked. 'She'd be an ex-babysitter,' she answered without hesitation.) There is no getting around the fact that we expect less of men—often a great deal less—than we do of women. Perhaps it's not so surprising then that less is what we get.

Tallies of hours worked do not, of course, tell us much about results achieved—a major structural flaw of most domestic labour studies. Yet the evidence clearly suggests that women not only work harder around the house than men, they work smarter too. One major difference, researchers say, is that women routinely engage in simultaneity of effort. In other words, unlike the husband who evidently didn't 'believe' in pyjamas, wives are expected and expect themselves to do two things at once—if not indeed five or seven. As a result, an hour of a wife's unpaid labour and an hour of her husband's unpaid labour are usually surprisingly incommensurate. (Well, it seems to be a surprise to academics, anyway.)

Overall, the research is clear that 'husbands do not modify their understandings of marital responsibilities when their wives are employed outside the home. Rather, they continue to believe that housekeeping is their wives' responsibility.'[23] The word *believe* is important. Because other evidence shows that most men no longer *say* that women should look after them. In 1990, well over half (57 per cent) of randomly selected adults in a nationwide survey described the 'ideal marriage' as one in which both husband and wife have jobs and share in the responsibilities of child-rearing and caring for the home. Among respondents aged eighteen to twenty-nine, the figure was closer to three-quarters.[24] In an Australian study conducted in 1992, for example, 89 per cent of men (and 97 per cent of women) agreed with the statement 'If both husband and wife work, they should share equally in the housework and child care'. Even the more unconditional statement that 'Men should do an equal amount of work in the home' was endorsed by 86 per cent of men.[25]

At one level, we are convinced we have entered a brave new world of marital equality, where this aspect of wifework has become extinct. Yet at another, men evidently still believe they have a right to such services. Even stranger, their wives do too.

For many women, wifework is a bit like the weather. Everybody talks about it, but nobody seems to do anything about it. Women may gripe to their girlfriends, but few ever really call a spade a spade, and a mop a mop, and a toilet brush a toilet brush, and bewail the injustice of it all. On the contrary, somewhere between two-thirds and three-quarters of wives tell researchers that a 70/30 division of unpaid labour is actually 'fair'.[26] Compare this with the proportion of marriages described by researchers as genuinely 'equal'—around 10 per cent.

Michael Bittman and Jocelyn Pixley, who interviewed husbands and wives separately, tried to get beyond buzzwords like 'fair' and 'equal' to see what was really going on in households. They cite one case in which the man claims to do vacuuming, washing up and taking out the garbage. His female partner agrees, adding that the two of them perform these tasks 'equally'. Yet with a little probing it turns out that the husband does these things '"maybe once a month" (vacuuming) and "once or twice a week if I'm lucky" (washing up)'.[27] In another study, on the transition to first parenthood, a young wife proudly explained that she and her husband chose to bottlefeed their newborn son in order to allow them to share the burden of night-time feeds—you guessed it—equally. 'Saturday morning he sleeps in—till midday, if he wants to. And Sunday morning I do the same,' she reported. Further questioning revealed that the wife was still doing the 5 a.m. feed on her ostensibly 'free' morning. She also declared that, on weekends, her husband took responsibility 'for all night-time feeds until 2 a.m.'. Once again, the 'equality' evaporated under examination. It turned out that the baby fed at 11 p.m. and 3 a.m.![28]

Equality researchers Daphne Spain and Suzanne Bianchi propose that we resort to such obfuscation (OK, lies) as a way of reconciling the tension between expectation and reality, 'for better or worse'.[29] Janice Steil also found fairness perceptions to be remarkably resilient. For women, for example, neither their own nor their husbands' hours in paid work made a difference to how fair or unfair they perceived their unpaid workload to be.[30] Other research, however, has indicated a trade-off between perceptions of fairness and husband's income. The more money he makes, the more likely she is to see her situation as fair. (Money may not buy you love but, if you are a married man, it may purchase you a modicum of peace.) At the same time, wives who admit to researchers that the division of labour in their marriages is manifestly unfair are more often economically dependent than independent.[31]

Another strategy for maintaining the illusion of equity is to refuse to compare goose with gander. Studies conducted by Linda Thompson in the US and Ken Dempsey in Australia have found that women are much more likely to make intra-gender rather than inter-gender comparisons. In other words, they compare their situations within marriage to those of other women, not to men. Similarly, wives are more likely to judge their husbands based on how they perceive other husbands, rather than relative to themselves or other wives. A woman who counts herself 'lucky' because her husband 'helps' can generally justify this with reference to some 'unlucky' friend or acquaintance whose husband 'does nothing'. This is a bit like being overjoyed to have haemorrhoids because it's so much better than a brain tumour. To a greater or lesser extent, this is something we all do. In my first marriage, I would often find myself telling someone how 'lucky' I was to have a cleaner, as if employing someone else to wash my floors while I worked for pay was a form of

pampering—a self-indulgent luxury like taking a bubble-bath in the middle of the day. And anyway, why didn't I say that my *husband* was lucky to have a cleaner? Because husbands don't have cleaners, that's why. Wives have cleaners. And husbands have wives.

Another way women keep a lid on their sense of injustice, I believe, is to make their comparisons inter-generational—to measure their husbands' performance, or their own 'privilege', against those of their fathers and mothers. Again, this is an understandable and even a useful analytic perspective. We *need* to view our lives in some sort of historical context, if we are ever to make sense of them. On the other hand, history can also blinker our sense of justice, by substituting relative measures for absolute or objective ones. (Compared to slavery, racial discrimination looks like a veritable moral triumph.)

In my second marriage, I keenly felt the weight of inter-generational history. As the fourth in a working-class family of ten children, my husband had been raised by a mother who often toiled literally from sun to sun, stretching her husband's salary with her own astounding labour. A more modest and unassuming woman than my ex-mother-in-law is impossible to imagine. Yet her shadow hung over my marriage like a spectre of doom, daring me to complain about *anything* in my comfortable, middle-class milieu. My mother-in-law, bless her heart, made no comparisons at all between her own lot and mine. But her son never stopped doing so. 'Don't talk to me about "juggling" three kids and a part-time job,' he'd practically sneer.

Ken Dempsey found that 'fairness' was used by women as a kind of code for 'marital satisfaction'. If the marriage was working on an emotional level, women were unlikely to complain about equity. Any woman who's been married for longer than about a week and a half can see the point. After all, if the price of justice is a chronic cycle of hurt feelings, fruitless negotiation and pervasive discord, and the only things a couple is really 'sharing' are the guilt and resentment…well, it's no wonder injustice starts to look like a minor annoyance. Compared to beating your head against a brick wall—which is the way most women phrase it—even ironing business shirts can be fun. And, in the final analysis, what's more important anyway, your marriage or your pride? The sanctity and stability of your family, or some abstract ideal of equity that, in your heart of hearts, you may not even be sure you believe? These are hard questions—and no woman should be glibly judged for the way she answers them.

And yet, on the other side of the brick wall (as it were), there are a number of equally troubling issues. First among them is the seemingly fathomless capacity of women to 'settle' for whatever it is they think they can get, their collective horror of 'rocking the boat' or, to use one of my mother's favourite expressions, 'pushing their luck'. It's as if love and justice together in the one life were too much to ask—as unrealistic as expecting bedtime stories *and* pyjamas.

There's another concern too. And it's the one about the relationship *between* equality and intimacy. What exactly can it mean to say that an 'emotionally satisfying' marriage is better than an 'equal' one? Without equity, one wonders, what does or can intimacy really mean?

To me, it seems obvious that both men and women want very badly to believe their marriages are fair. We want to reduce what psychologists call the 'cognitive dissonance' between word and deed in order to create coherence in our heads and to ensure harmony in our homes. This is all entirely understandable. It is also delusional. With exceptions so negligible researchers often can't even locate them, marriage continues to exploit the willingness of wives to perform roughly three times the unpaid domestic labour of husbands—and to take responsibility for nearly all of it. Intellectually, we rejected the concept of wifework a long time ago. Emotionally and behaviourally, we remain stalled within the old patriarchal paradigm: the one that warns us that a good man is hard to find and even harder to hang on to—so if a woman is lucky enough to snag one, she needs to keep those puddings coming, for life.

and baby makes two and a half: the myth of shared parenting

'Take a few minutes to wash the children's hands and
faces (if they are small), comb their hair and, if necessary, change their clothes. They are little treasures
and he would like to see them playing the part.'
from a 1950s home economics textbook

Former Fortune 500 executive Daniel Petre claims he has no regrets
about tossing in his chances for 'ultimate career success' in order
to devote himself to his family. As a vice-president of Microsoft, Petre
routinely worked a sixty-five-hour week. Then, one day, it hit him. 'I
chose to have a family so I should be there.' After much agonising Petre
made the ultimate career sacrifice. *He cut down his working week to fifty
hours.* Well, naturally, he wrote a book about it. I mean, we're talking
about a revolution here…Aren't we?

Petre, author of *Father and Child*, does not apologise for holding down
a full-time-plus job: he runs Kerry Packer's ecorp, when he's not writing
books on making time for fathering. On the contrary, Petre boasts about
it. And why not? He's participating. Petre drops the kids at school *and*
manages to get home for dinner 'two nights out of three', a miracle
of organisation he accomplishes by scheduling kid time into his diary
and treating it 'with the same importance as a business meeting'.
Does he sound a trifle hard-hearted? Well, don't be fooled. Inside,

Petre's a pushover. 'We're all insecure, sensitive creatures [who] build facades to protect ourselves from the outside world,' he explains.[1] It's reassuring to know that even if Petre looks, sounds and acts like a self-congratulatory opportunist, he isn't one.

At the same time, though, one can't help but wonder about Mrs Petre. How, exactly, does *she* fit into all this? Does she too manage to work fifty hours a week for pay and still feel sanctimonious about her parenting? Has she also learned the secret of elevating her children to the status of a business meeting? And what about her record on 'getting home for dinner'? Does she, like Dan, win brownie points just by turning up? And, once she gets there, does a meal materialise for herself and the kids, just as it seems to do for him? Does Mrs Petre get written up in *Family Circle* magazine because she no longer believes her kids' needs must be sacrificed on the altar of her own career goals?

In all likelihood, if Mrs Petre works for pay at all, she is too busy hurtling through family life to write many books about it. Chances are, she is more like Susan Reiche, a public policy manager and mother of two featured in a 1999 *New York Times* article on women for whom 'the pinnacle of stress comes after work ends'.[2] For working mothers like Ms Reiche, we learn, on-the-job stress is as nothing compared with the 'second shift' at home—a veritable nightly marathon of unpaid tasks that in Reiche's case includes picking up two children from day care, shopping for dinner, cooking it, bathing the kids, helping with homework, doing a load of washing and putting the kids to bed. (Oh yes! She also 'says hello to her husband'. That little detail is important. Because without it, we might be forgiven for assuming there *was* no Mr Reiche.)

The problem, according to journalist Alice Lesch Kelly, is that 'all the roles [women] juggle—employee, mother, wife—come crashing together as they try to separate from work, spend time with their children and reconnect with their spouses'. Alice D. Domar, director of the Mind/Body Center for Women's Health at a Boston teaching hospital, agrees. For working mothers, coming home *is* the most stressful part of the day. This is the case even for 'women whose husbands pitch in'.[3]

The stresses suffered by working mothers are by now the stuff of journalistic cliche. Superwoman is dead. The second shift is unfair. The 'mommy track' gets you nowhere. Juggling multiple roles is stressful and exhausting for most women, the articles always seem to conclude, but then again it's a whole lot better than *not* juggling multiple roles. (Well, isn't it?) And then there's the wishlist. If only day care were more flexible. If only school hours were longer, or work hours were shorter. If only businesses adopted more 'family friendly' policies. If only extended families still existed. If only we did more 'outsourcing' or less 'gatekeeping'. If only kids understood the meaning of quality time. If only we could be in two places at once. If only parenting could somehow be *shared*.

I can't be the only observer who has noticed the lack of articles on stress suffered by working fathers (even those whose wives 'pitch in'). Maybe no one comments on it because for a sizeable majority there isn't any—unless you count the stress of dealing with the fallout from their wives' stress, or unless those fathers are divorced. Indeed, 'fatherhood', far from conflicting with 'employment', almost universally implies it— which is why the term 'working father' is unknown. In the interests of even-handedness, journalists and researchers often refer euphemistically to 'the phenomenon of the dual-career couple'. Nine times out of ten what they're really concerned with is how Mummy manages.

'Given the choice of dealing with all these stresses or making a job change,' writes Alice Lesch Kelly, 'many couples opt for change.' Yet it's not the *couple* that changes. It's the wife. 'After her second child was born, Mrs Parker, the former magazine editor, gave up her three-day-a-week job in Boston because the numbers didn't add up. "I don't regret my decision for a minute," Mrs Parker said.' I know just how Mrs Parker feels. But did Mr Parker? Did he consider giving up his job because 'the numbers didn't add up'? Mrs Parker, Kelly tells us, 'subtracted day care costs of $4.50 an hour for each child...and added the stress of commuting two hours a day' in order to reach her decision.[4] Again, perfectly understandable. But why wasn't the cost of day care—or even half the cost of day care—subtracted from Mr Parker's wage? I'll tell you why. Because the Parker children, like almost all children growing up in intact families, live with two parents, but belong to only one of them.

Before we plunge headlong into this most explosively emotive of topics, let me say that I believe there are huge and substantive differences between mothering on the one hand and wifework on the other. Yet conceptually, as well as in our day-to-day lives, we are prone to blur the boundaries of these two aspects of 'women's work'—at times to the point where it is almost impossible to determine where child care ends and husbandcare begins. Women's commitment to mothering is a social privilege—with attendant social liabilities—built upon the bedrock of biological necessity. We have a moral responsibility to mother our young, an urge we experience not as the result of some kind of 'false consciousness' or patriarchal conspiracy, but simply owing to the immense honour of being female. In other words, it is not our mothering which needs rehabilitating.

Our 'wifing' is another story, of course—especially when it involves a felt imperative to mother men. This *imagined* responsibility has nothing to do with women's biology, let alone our destiny as females. In the present environment, it is maladaptive for everyone involved—the women who stagger under its emotional and physical toll; the children who see Daddy, in some ways correctly, less as a man than an overgrown sibling; the men who are both prevented and prevent themselves from experiencing parenthood at full throttle. The fact is, the dream of shared parenting remains just that, and the reimagination of fatherhood is just another in a series of 'stalled revolutions' on the exit ramp of twentieth-century life.

The only real revolution is that we now envisage parenthood and partnership as separate entities—divergent paths into unknown territory, rather than a convergence towards a foreseeable future. The paradigm shift is evident in our sudden interest in 'the impact of children on marriage'—now a growth industry in the social sciences. It's a question that, until recently, would have been akin to pondering the impact of food on digestion. Children were what marriage was *for*, for heaven's sake.

Today, all that has changed. We no longer marry to have children (or, if we do, we don't admit it publicly), or have children simply because we are married. The invention—or perhaps discovery—of 'the couple' as a primary social unit is another of the unanticipated side effects of contraceptive technology. For married women, the conceptual untethering of the roles of mother and wife has created a painful gulf between maternity and sexuality. Women, in addition to their responsibilities for children, now shoulder the weight of 'the relationship'—a beast with needs separate from those of offspring, and often in direct conflict with them. Indeed, it has become commonplace to castigate mothers for 'failing to put the relationship first'. Yet what *is* the relationship, anyway—beyond a euphemism for 'the needs of the husband'?

The task of reconciling marriage with fatherhood, by contrast, is an item on nobody's agenda. It's much like the problem of working fathers (i.e., there is no problem). The notion that a man would be criticised for failing to put his wife before his children is almost unthinkable. Men don't feel torn between the demands of fatherhood and those of husbandhood for the simple reason that those demands are not terribly onerous—either singly or in tandem. It is debatable whether there really *are* any 'demands of husbandhood' per se. A married man may still be expected to be the family's major breadwinner—admittedly, a huge service rendered. Then again, upon divorce, a man does not normally stop working, change jobs or even reduce his hours. Is he employed because being a husband 'demands' it, or because being an adult male 'demands' it? Or is there, as some commentators have suggested, very little difference between the two?

When a husband becomes a father, his brief enlarges; but it does not really diversify. He is now expected to be an even better breadwinner.

We pay lip service to the quality of a father's relationships with his children. But the reality is that we continue to measure a father's performance in crude dollar terms. Beyond breadwinning, all he really has to do to feel good about himself—and to be felt good about by the community at large—is to turn up. Think about it. A man who spends time with his kids every second weekend and pays child support regularly is called a good father. A woman who does the same is called abusive, or worse. Of course there are plenty of divorced fathers who would do anything to spend more time—much more time—with their children. But that's another point entirely.

You don't need me to tell you this. You've seen for yourself the huge fuss we make over the Dad who shows up for kindy roster ('Children, we have a very special helper today!'), who gives up his Saturday golf game to take the kids swimming or to the movies. Even a father who does nothing more extraordinary than pick up the phone to arrange a play date inspires admiration, if not awe. The Dad of one of my six-year-old's friends rang to accept a party invitation yesterday, and it was all I could do to stop myself congratulating him. Maybe I should have just gone ahead and done it. We've had twenty-three kids' birthday parties in this family in the last ten years—which works out to a total of perhaps 500 guests—and I can recall only one other instance of a married Dad doing the RSVP-ing. (And in that case the child's mother was recovering from a stroke.) Divorced fathers quite often do such things, of course—an interesting reflection in itself, I think. But where there is a mother present in the household, the day-to-day responsibilities for child care are, as they say, her baby. Sure, our parenting is 'shared' now. Except that in all but a handful of cases, Mum remains the default parent and Dad the back-up. That's not how we *say* our families work. But behind the rhetoric of the 'revolution in fathering' lies a reality as radical as a pair of argyle socks.

Let's begin at the beginning, with a look at the literature on the transition to parenthood—a body of research as consistent as it is depressing.

In a nutshell, the birth of a first child will destabilise even the sturdiest of marriages. But it will have a wildly disproportionate impact on wives. Becoming a mother, the research shows, almost inevitably transforms a woman's identity from the inside out. It also changes men. A little. At the very least, the transition to first parenthood will reconfigure the gender balance within marriage. At the worst, it may knock it off the scales. Where small gaps existed between the unpaid contributions of husbands and wives, great, yawning chasms will appear. Within a year, His marriage and Her marriage—once parallel tracks following the same general trajectory—will diverge dramatically.

For a sizeable minority, that divergence will stretch the marriage to its breaking point. In the US, one-quarter of all divorces take place before a child is old enough to remember living with both biological parents. Approximately 40 per cent have taken place by the end of the child's kindergarten year. Among couples who survive what has been called the Great Divide of parenthood, almost a quarter report that their marriages are in some distress by the time their first child is eighteen months old.[5] 'A baby,' writes Nora Ephron, 'is a like a hand grenade thrown into a marriage.'[6] Few couples who have experienced the joys and traumas of first parenthood would disagree—although even fewer, I'm sure, would wish to throw it back again.

'The birth of a child entirely revamps the internal landscape of marriage,' writes leading family psychologist Judith Wallerstein. 'Becoming a father or mother is a major step in the life course, a step that requires inner psychological growth as well as changes in every part of the marital relationship and the extended family.'[7] While I agree— and I believe it's a point that should be made more often, and much, much more loudly—there's a secret even deeper, darker and more depressing than this one. The birth of a first child will affect a woman's internal landscape like an earthquake, followed by a flood, followed by a volcanic eruption. For a man, it will be more along the lines of a heavy thunderstorm.

Marital dissatisfaction skyrockets with new parenthood. But so too, oddly enough, does spouses' commitment to one another. In a longitudinal study of nearly 100 couples, Carolyn and Philip Cowan found that fully 97 per cent of husbands and wives reported more conflict after the baby arrived than before.[8] Paradoxically, however, parenting actually increases marital stability. Other research has found that the divorce rate among families with a preschool child is half of that of childless couples.[9] When partners become parents, it seems, they like each other less and less but stay together more and more. As one researcher rather bluntly noted, 'love decreased and ambivalence increased for both partners' following the birth of a first child. The effect is particularly evident among wives.[10]

As the Cowans and other marital researchers have stressed, parenthood exaggerates and hardens gender differences within marriage, pushing husbands to become more 'husbandly' and wives more 'wifely'— and then leaving them there to get on with it. After the birth of her first child, the research suggests, a wife will do even more housework, cooking and shopping than ever before, and she will also work fewer hours outside the home and for less pay. And all of this will be in addition to assuming major, and in many cases overwhelming, responsibility for child care. The new father, by contrast, will perform even fewer household tasks, and work longer hours for pay outside the home. Sure, he'll spend time playing with the new baby. He may even bath it or feed it or change its nappy. But his parental responsibilities, relative to those of his wife, will remain largely abstract, centring on his role as financial provider. As far as the child's day-to-day care and well-being are concerned, the husband will begin his fathering career as a second-string parent—and, in most cases, he'll end it that way too.

These are just predictions, mind you. But they are also predictions whose efficacy has been demonstrated in study after study, and in family after family. Is there a chance that things might work out differently in your marriage? Of course there is. But it's a very slim chance. Once children enter a marriage, resisting the forcefield of gender stereotyping is about as feasible as ignoring a second-stage contraction. And the comparison is an apt one, because it is invariably the wife who labours hardest and longest. Co-parenting is not impossible, but it is surprisingly arduous—in part because it means making almost everything up as you go along, at a time when both partners' creative energies are at a low ebb. It's no wonder so many couples decide, whether consciously or not, to capitulate. For wives, caving in to tradition is an obvious case of taking the path of least resistance. For both partners, it may be an implicit acknowledgment that having some rules, even bad ones, may be better than no rules at all.

It is impossible to underestimate the extent of our collective denial of these unpleasant realities, and the tendency of women to seek refuge behind a self-protective 'mask of motherhood' has been well documented. Yet the evidence also suggests that, as our hard-won marital mutuality regresses to some awful 1950s archetype, we are at some level aware of what's happening. One recent study found that 60 per cent of new mothers admitted being haunted by the ghosts of gender roles past, a phenomenon noted, perhaps predictably, by only 33 per cent of their husbands.[11]

For most husbands, parenthood will produce no negative effects on well-being whatsoever. For wives, by contrast, becoming a parent is almost inevitably associated with a steep decline in well-being, across a huge range of physical and mental health indicators. Researchers Rosalind Barnett and Grace Baruch found that, by and large, women's traditional roles are far more stressful than paid work—a finding seconded more recently by Arlie Hochschild in her influential study of dual-income earner couples, *The Time Bind*. Typically, motherhood has been portrayed as the most arduous of these traditional roles. In the words of Janice Steil, the work of mothering consists of a 'unique combination of relentless demands, great responsibility, and minimal control'. No wonder it is so 'rarely associated with improvements in well-being for women and is often associated with distress'.[12]

Is it really parenting per se that drives women to ill-health, depression, loss of identity, lowered self-esteem? Obviously not. Because 'parenting' is also what fathers do—isn't it?—and fathers may barely even register the birth of a first child as a significant transition. In a sense we are right to point the finger at 'motherhood'—which is what women do—as distinct from the generic 'parenting'. What we have resisted reckoning is the extent to which the overwhelming burden of parenthood that women bear is in fact a subclause in the larger job description of wifework itself. Motherhood, in other words, at least as we have socially constructed it, is yet another service women render to males, another way women free men up to pursue even more autonomy and advantage in marriage and in life.

We have managed in theory to separate marriage from parenthood. In reality, for the vast majority of us, they remain tenaciously intertwined. According to recent US figures, for example, only 13 per cent of ever-married women aged thirty-four to forty-five are childless today. Although that represents an almost 50 per cent increase over the past twenty years, analysts maintain most of that difference is owing to delayed fertility—women having babies later in life—than higher rates of childlessness within marriage.[13]

In Australia, the trend seems to be similar. (The picture is complicated by the fact that, since the mid-1970s, the Australian Bureau of Statistics has collected detailed fertility data by age, not marital status.) On the one hand, rates of childlessness for women born since 1943 have increased consistently. Among women born in 1951, who were forty-five years old at the time of the 1996 Census, for example, 11 per cent were childless. As we read in the headlines, this represents an increase of 18 per cent in a mere twenty years.[14] Viewed in a slightly wider historical perspective, however, this seemingly massive increase in childlessness reverses itself altogether. It has been estimated that women first married in the 1950s had more babies than any generation of women born since the 1890s.[15] The baby boom, we seem to have forgotten, was so named because of its *atypical* fertility pattern. All indications are that childlessness figures will rise significantly over the next thirty years—but the shift is more properly seen as a corrective swing of the pendulum than a 'revolution'.

Although today's marriages are probably as likely to yield children as ever before, they are definitely producing fewer offspring. What's more, men and women are now significantly older when they marry, and older again when they have their first child. In the US, the average male marries at around age twenty-nine and the average woman at twenty-seven. In England and Wales, first marriages take place even later, with the typical groom now thirty-four and the bride twenty-eight. In part, this shift reflects the growing trend towards pre-marital cohabitation.[16] In the UK, 75 per cent of women now spend time as 'de factos' before entering into legal marriage.[17] American women are much more conservative about cohabitation, though. Currently, only about one in three women aged twenty-five to thirty-nine lived with their male partners before marriage.[18]

Parenthood typically follows within two to four years of marriage. In Australia, for example, the median age for married fathers is now an astonishing thirty-three, and for married mothers thirty and a half. The interval between tying the knot and cutting the cord has scarcely changed at all over the past two decades; the baseline has simply shifted upwards.

Family size is another variable that has changed significantly. We are having *fewer* children, both within and out of wedlock. In the US, the average number of births per woman is now 2.03, and has been below the replacement rate of 2.1 since 1971.[19] In Australia, the total fertility rate is even lower—1.76, according to 1998 figures—and in England and Wales lower still, at 1.70 in 1999.[20] There are clear trends indicating that the proportion of one-child families is rising, while that of families of three or more is falling.[21]

Theoretically, parenthood has now become an option for married couples. In reality, the only real options are 'when?' or 'how many?'—not 'whether'. As any childless-by-choice married couple will tell you, a marriage without children is still widely regarded as a social aberration. The phenomenon of the 'optional parent' is another of those social revolutions that seems to exist largely in our mass-mediated imagination, an illusion perpetuated by a hunger for trend-spotting and a willingness to accept raw statistics at face value.

'First comes love, then comes marriage, then comes Susie with the baby carriage.' We used to sing that jingle in the schoolyard. Today, my kids are still singing it. And no wonder. Although much else has changed in the past thirty years, the high probability that husbands and wives will become fathers and mothers has not. Back then, the progression from partnership to parenthood was seen as natural and unproblematic, and so was was the division of parenting labour along the faultlines of traditional gender roles. Today, the transition to family life is still a natural step, yet we are far more likely to experience it as a free-fall into chaos. We are especially shocked when we revert to gender type—enacting the Mummy and Daddy roles we were sure we'd written out of the script for good.

equality go bye-byes: parenthood and partnership

'Clearly services applied to children are not appropriated by them, but by the person who would have to perform the work if his wife did not provide the totality, i.e., the husband.' Christine Delphy

Researchers estimate that, in the US, women still do about 80 per cent of the child care—*as much as in the 1960s*. And most of the time men do spend with their children takes the form of what sociologists call 'interactive activities' rather than 'custodial activities'.[1] In other words, Dads play—and Mums pay. According to research published in 1997, the arrival of a first child more than doubles a wife's domestic load, working out to an average *increase* of thirty-five hours a week.[2] One large-scale study conducted in 1991 found the increase in domestic labour to be as high as 91 per cent for new mothers—while the fathers' (lower to begin with, of course) did not increase by a single minute.[3] To put it bluntly, Mummy becomes the work horse and Daddy the show pony.

'Parenting is increasingly shared,' maintains Lancaster University psychologist Charlie Lewis, co-author of the 2001 study 'What Good Are Dads?' Adds David Bartlett, of UK-based advocacy group Fathers Direct, 'Nobody can take refuge in discredited stereotypes suggesting fathers are insignificant'.[4] 'Increasingly shared' parenting may be, and 'insignificant' fathers are certainly not—yet even the staunchest fathers' rights types can't fight the figures. At best, parenting between the genders remains a 75/25 enterprise, with the average Mum expending at least twice the energy of the average Dad. The fact that fathers have increased their levels of active parenting—and they have increased them, to be sure—is progress. But it is a long way from equality.

It's not that Dads don't do anything. It's more that they don't do anything too taxing or too unpleasant. In Australia, men perform on average only 16 per cent of the labour involved in looking after their own children—yet they claim 40 per cent of time spent in play or recreation.[5] Virtually all studies of the division of parenting tasks have shown that blokes invariably get the good bits: the 'tasks' of playing with, reading to and conversing with their kids. It's a phenomenon one researcher has aptly described as 'skimming off the cream'. Is it any surprise that a number of studies have found that fathers enjoy their kids more than mothers do?

All work and little play not only makes Mum a dull girl—it makes her a cranky one too. As one informant confided guiltily, 'I'm really glad he's spending more time with the children. They really enjoy it. But it's beginning to make me look more like the meany. Daddy plays with them and tells them stories and other nice things while I do the disciplining, make them wash up, tidy their toys and never have time to play because I'm cooking supper.'[6] I suspect there isn't a married mother alive who doesn't sometimes, or maybe even constantly, feel the same way. In the language of social research, 'fathers engage in fewer punitive episodes, conflictual interactions [and] negative emotional expressions'.[7] The 'Wait Until Your Father Gets Home' generation—if it ever existed in the first place—is a thing of the past. In today's families, it's Mummy who calls the disciplinary shots, reserving for Daddy the role of resident Mr Softy, the charming goof-off whose cameo appearances provide comic relief in the often grim business of contemporary family life. Sure, Mum gets tired of being the heavy, and sometimes she worries whether it's true that she's simply a 'control freak'. But what can you do? The buck's got to stop somewhere. And anyway, she shouldn't complain—he's so good with the children!

How it happens that a wife ends up being the only grown-up in a family with one too many children is a mystery—especially among couples who know for absolute certain that it's not going to happen to them. Perhaps most mysterious of all, though, is why we pretend otherwise. Why we insist upon projecting an image of harmony, equality and symmetry when the reality is so clearly fraught with conflict, injustice and disproportion. It's not just couples themselves who misrepresent the realities of family life. Researchers have been known to do it too—like the investigators who counted child care as 'shared' if the husband looked after his children without the wife present 'at least once a week'.[8] Or the ones who were so determined to find evidence of shared parenting that they analysed the total amount of time fathers spent in the same room with their children![9] Subtler forms of misrepresentation, part of the everyday reality of most families, are even more insidious. Like the woman who boasts to her mates about how 'lucky' she is to have a husband who'll 'babysit' while she works shifts—yet never mentions what it's like coming home to a scene of domestic devastation and wakeful, unwashed children. Or the man who ostentatiously changes a nappy, while his wife hovers to whip away the soiled wipes, find the pins and—ultimately—scrape it, wash it, hang it on the line to dry, and fold it up again for next time. One couple I know 'take turns' cooking dinner for their blended brood of five—except the only thing he ever prepares is pasta and sauce. Tomato sauce.

The common perception among women that men are less responsible caregivers has a sound basis in empirical fact. For the most part, men's fathering remains largely a matter of 'just following orders'; like good children, or low-ranking public servants, they do as they're told. One US study found that 70 per cent of a random sample of fathers were not responsible for *any* child-care tasks, and an additional 22 per cent were responsible for only one such task. (The researchers defined 'responsibility' as 'remembering, planning and scheduling'.) That left only 8 per cent who took responsibility for two or more child-care tasks.[10] The man cited above who feeds his children pasta and tomato ketchup defended himself by explaining 'there's usually nothing else in the cupboard worth cooking'. When his wife suggested he might stop off at the supermarket and buy something 'worth cooking', he looked hurt. 'I can't do *everything*,' he protested. And she wondered if she'd gone too far...

It is precisely this mental work—the 'remembering, planning and scheduling' thing—that is the most arduous of all parenting tasks. It also happens to be the work that married fathers steadfastly avoid doing. Married mothers not only carry out the lioness's share of parenting work, whether they work for pay or not. They shoulder the additional burden of administering the endless minutiae of family life—a task which consumes untold gigabytes of a woman's intellectual hard-drive. Husbands may go shopping, but wives still write the list, Dad may take baby to playgroup, but Mum will enrol her, pack her nappy bag, organise her lunch, and settle her to sleep when she comes back home again.

When baby gets a little older, Dad may consent happily to supervise when she has a friend to play on the weekend—as long as he can do it from the couch in front of the footy, or from behind his laptop. But the odds that he will take responsibility for cultivating her social life are somewhere between poor and nil. And the same goes for taking her shopping for new sneakers, or noticing that she needs them, seeing to it that her room is navigable, keeping tabs on her homework assignments or dental appointments, paying the piano teacher (or even remembering the piano teacher's name). In the words of one recent study, fathers have made little '(if any) progress relative to mothers in the "management" of child care, which involves being generally responsible for planning and scheduling child care and a child's daily activities'.[11] Spending time with kids is one thing. Actually *thinking* about them—not just responding to needs, as directed, but autonomously anticipating and planning for them—is quite another. In intact families, it's a Mum thing.

Within individual marriages, especially those in which partners pride themselves on their commitment to 'equal sharing', facing up to these realities can be acutely painful. Typically, discussions about the balance of parenting within marriage are minefields bristling with shallowly buried hurts and resentments. Husbands feel their contributions as parents are undervalued; they feel 'attacked' or 'controlled'. Wives, for their part, often feel ripped off and betrayed; abandoned by their mates as parents and stripped of their options as people. The fact that a man has the luxury to *choose* his level of involvement in parenting, and women don't, rankles. It's no wonder that, when it comes to discussions about shared parenting, so many couples make a decision at some tacit level not to 'go there' at all. They collude instead in the socially correct fiction that their parenting is 'basically equal' or 'pretty well shared'.

There is a price to be paid for this denial—and there is no doubt that, over the short term, it is women who will pay it: in extra work, extra stress and a toxic build-up of unspoken anger and resentment typically leading to depression and/or anxiety. Among professional working mothers, according to research conducted by University of California psychiatrist Elizabeth Ozer, a woman's belief in her capacity to enlist the help of her spouse for child care was the strongest predictor of her well-being or distress.[12] Over the longer term, men will also pay dearly. At the very least, such fathers will miss out on genuine intimacy with both their children and their wives, perhaps even to the point of becoming the 'odd man out' in their own homes. In the worst cases, they may find themselves expelled from family life altogether, as resentments that have been allowed to simmer reach boiling point, and destroy the very basis of the marriage. A recent survey of 5,000 British working women found that a stagging 93 per cent of women felt stressed by the task of balancing career and family, with symptoms ranging from headaches and exhaustion to backache and insomnia. Three-quarters believed they had or would suffer emotionally as a result.[13]

The gender politics of parenting may be highly controversial within individual families, but on the empirical level it is almost entirely uncontentious. 'Fathers are especially unlikely to have overall responsibility for managing children's environments or for structuring their schedules and setting limits,' blandly summarises one recent family studies textbook, citing a string of references long enough to hang nappies on. 'Fathers' direct interaction and accessibility increases only modestly when mothers work outside the home,' it goes on, 'while virtually no change occurs in fathers' overall responsibilities for managing children's lives.'[14] In other words, it is not simply women's perception that marriage leaves them holding the baby. It is also the reality, in most cases—a reality which has been repeatedly observed and quantified. Britain's much-touted parental-leave initiative, introduced in December 1999, created a level playing field for entitlements to paternal and maternity leave. Yet even the government that formulated the scheme predicted that the take-up rate for fathers would be a minuscule 2 per cent, compared with an estimated 35 per cent for mothers.[15] Much reporting on 'the new fathering' emphasises Dad-friendly details, often at the expense of the bigger parenting picture. A study conducted in 2000 by Jonathan Gershuny of the UK-based Institute of Economic and Social Research, for example, found that daily fathering time of young children had increased 800 per cent since 1961. Yet mothering time, which of course started out at a much higher baseline, had increased 'only' 400 per cent in that period. Overall, the division of childcare ratio was still seriously lopsided at 3:2.[16] Yet by international standards, that's about as good as it gets. Gershuny's study, based on the time diaries of more than 60,000 parents worldwide, found that British Dads reported spending more than twice the parenting time as their counterparts in other countries.

The day of what UK journalist Pete May calls the 'refusenik dad' is over. Indeed, in Tony Blair's New Labour Britain, fathers are feeling downright smug. Says the sanctimonious May of his fellow Dads, 'Unlike mothers, we don't feel trapped by childcare.' He doesn't appear to wonder why. Instead, the self-proclaimed 'Lad Dad' boasts that 'carrying a baby turns you into a babe magnet. Overnight.'[17] In *Taking Care of Men*, Anthony McMahon argues that the so-called New Father represents a shift in image, rather than in substance. We have turned up the heat on the emotional climate of fatherhood, no question. We have made it positively sexy to be a Dad, in fact. But being a parent and doing the parenting are two very different propositions. Paternal 'engrossment'—as the psychology literature terms it—is a wonderful new string to the New Dad's emotional bow. If only we could say the same about his behavioural repertoire, we'd really have something to applaud.

Nevertheless, it would be misleading to suggest there have been no changes at all in the husband's participation in child care. This is the one area of male unpaid labour which has shown clear and unidirectional change. In Australia, the increased time men spend parenting is a trend that has been evident since 1974. This is especially the case for men aged thirty to thirty-four, a group in which child care participation increased nearly two full hours per week in the single five-year period 1987 to 1992. Given that the average married father is thirty-three when his first child is born, this strongly suggests that men are becoming significantly more involved with infant care. Also encouraging is that roughly one-quarter of the rise in fathers' participation in child care has been in the area of physical care. Less encouraging is that three-quarters of it remains concentrated in the 'interaction' or 'play' area, or what researchers simply call 'accessibility', which pretty much boils down to just being a warm body.[18]

These statistics are enough to give even the most cynical woman reason for hope. Yet it turns out that mothers have increased their participation in child care too—to an almost precisely proportional degree. This development initially surprised observers, but most now attribute the increase in time spent on child care by both parents to a steep raising of consciousness about childhood development, coupled with an equally precipitous rise in our expectations of what 'good parenting' entails. One unexpected consequence of all this is that the working mothers of today may actually be spending more time with her children than the stay-at-home Mum of a generation ago. (So much for the Selfish Bitch theory about mothers in the workforce.)

These findings may refute the argument that today's kids are being 'neglected' by dual-career parents with busy lifestyles. But the ratio of father care to mother care remains as absurdly unbalanced as ever before. Bottom line? Australian women continue to perform 84 per cent of the physical care of children. Those women in full-time employment get a break, of course. They do only 76 per cent.[19] The picture is similar in the US, where, according to a recent literature review, 'the movement towards coequal parenting seems fairly localised within samples of highly educated fathers, especially European American fathers with considerable formal education'.[20] What the revolution in fathering all adds up to is little more than a playground skirmish.

A 1998 Canadian study of 225 dual-earner families found that only 14 per cent of married mothers reported that their partners were 'emotionally supportive and sensitive to the needs of the family'.[21] A longitudinal study of parental involvement with children aged up to five years found that mothers provided more than 80 per cent of the care of infants, regardless of parents' employment status. The only childcare 'task' shared equally by mothers and fathers was play—a finding consistent with the results of numerous other studies.[22]

One can find surveys that purport to show strikingly different patterns to this one. But on closer examination, the 'hard data' often conceal a soft centre, artificially sweetened by the biases of a sponsoring advocacy group. One such study, carried out by the Families and Work Institute, found that working fathers now spend an average of 2.3 workday hours caring for, and 'doing things' with, their kids. The dubious boast that 'working fathers now spend more time doing things with their children than they spend on themselves' was trumpeted as some sort of watershed for shared parenting. Reporting on the study, *New York Times* journalist Tamar Lewin warned that the data were based on self-reported time-estimates, a methodology regarded by social scientists as notoriously unreliable. Findings such as these, Lewin cautioned, may be reflective of little more than a shift in respondents' views of socially desirable responses. This is not to suggest that such attitudinal changes towards shared parenting are insignificant, or negligible. But the frame is *not* the picture; and there is no necessary correlation between the talk and the walk.[23]

Taking responsibility for children is not simply a series of administrative or managerial tasks. If it were, the project of 'equal parenting' wouldn't be nearly as daunting. It might be solvable, like any other managerial task, through better time-management or more effective delegation. As it happens, raising children—though it is undoubtedly very hard work—is a task peculiarly unlike any other. Like housework, with which it is often unthinkingly lumped, child care is unpaid labour. But unlike housework, it is labour for which the rewards are both profoundly meaningful and highly specific, in the sense of being impossible to replicate through other means. No one achieves transcendence through vacuuming. We don't arrive at a new definition of self by making beds or scouring pots. We are not forced to rethink our priorities every time we cook supper. Yet raising a child will entail all of that and much more. Having said that, it is also true that in some respects we have tended to overplay such rewards at the expense of confronting their costs. In the process, I am convinced, we have trivialised the enterprise of parenting. In our public discourse, we have tended to reduce the epic poetry that is parenthood to mere doggerel.

Child care, unlike housework, is for most parents a genuine labour of love. The work of raising children is not only infinitely enriched by this love, it is infinitely complicated by it. The fact is, there are no lines of cleavage between the emotional labour of parenting on the one hand,

and its physical and intellectual demands on the other. Indeed, in evolutionary terms, the love we feel for our children may be the most successful adaptation of all: compelling us not only to meet their needs and to keep on meeting them, no matter what, but also to *want* to do so, indeed to yearn to do so. What's more, there seems to be a genuinely reciprocal relationship between the physical care we perform for children and the emotional attachments we feel for them. All other things being equal, the parent who does more *for* the child will generally experience a deeper bond *with* the child. It's a bit like a self-correcting equation, or a self-tightening noose, depending on your point of view!

Studies of parental behaviour bear this out, invariably concluding that nurturant behaviour is far more highly correlated with time spent on physical care than it is with gender. It's not 'maternal instinct' that makes females more involved, more responsible parents. It's the reverse. It's our involvement and sense of responsibility that makes us truly 'maternal' in the first place, and keeps us 'maternal' over time. Whether we happen to be male or female. (It is worth noting that we reserve the term 'paternal' to describe a biological relationship rather than an affective one.) The evidence does suggest that females start out their parenting lives with a certain biological edge; given the mechanics and biochemistry of human pregnancy, birth and lactation, any other arrangement would be highly impractical. In any number of observable ways, women really are more tuned to their infants. In the first few hours and days after birth, for example, they are better able to identify them by smell and by the sound of their cries. But these so-called mothering instincts are both short-lived and exceedingly limited in scope. Like the Moro or startle reflex in infants, which once served an important survival function, they have become largely vestigial. In every important sense, the skills of child care are for human beings just that—a set of learned behaviours. We are born with the urge to procreate, and the propensity to love and protect our offspring. But beyond that, we are all of us on our own. There is no instinct that tells any of us how to parent—let alone how to be a good parent—any more than there is an instinct that tells us how to unfold a stroller or choose a school or when to start toilet training.

Nature gives biological mothers a kick-start in the nurturing game, especially if they breastfeed. Culture does the rest, encouraging and validating and extending that slight advantage out of all proportion to biology. Things don't *have* to be this way. It's just that changing the course of the prevailing current will consume significantly more energy than not changing it. The extent to which we are able to find that energy is, I suspect, as much a function of raised affluence as it is of raised consciousness. There's got to be substantial surplus in the system to make such a change in direction even thinkable, let alone practicable.

But there's another obstacle to change as well—one summed up very nicely by the old joke about therapy. 'How many therapists does it take to change a light bulb?' 'Only one, but it's got to really *want* to change.' In the case of parenting, much more so than in the case of housework, many marriages don't achieve equality for the simple reason that neither party is entirely certain it wants it. This ambivalence is particularly striking among women, who have more to gain by the establishment of coequal parenting but also more to lose. A much-cited study conducted in the US more than fifteen years ago found that only a minority of women actually desired increased involvement from their husbands in child care.[24] More recent research continues to indicate that women's 'support for father involvement' cannot be assumed, either within marriage or without.[25] In a study of more than 600 dual-earner mothers, Brigham Young University researchers Sarah Allen and Alan Hawkins classified 21 per cent as 'gatekeepers', whose 'reluctance to relinquish responsibility over family matters by setting rigid standards', need for 'external validation of mothering identity' and 'differentiated concepts of family roles' effectively prevented their husbands' active collaboration as fathers.[26] A smaller-scale study by Washington State University sociologists June Ellestad and Jan Stets found that women with a 'prominent mother identity' responded to hypothetical father–child interactions with feelings of jealousy and possessiveness. Understandably, the authors speculate about how 'such mothers' emotion may unintentionally serve to maintain social structural arrangements with respect to parenting'.[27]

Family therapist Anna Dienhart, author of *Reshaping Fatherhood*, found extensive evidence of mothers' anxiety to retain their status as 'parent of first contact'—as well as an 'elusive sense of loss' when they took steps to establish greater equality of parenting. 'Women's acculturation seems to nag at them to hold on to deeply felt, perhaps unconscious, expectations about motherhood,' she concludes.[28] There is no doubt that motherhood is far more central to most women's sense of identity than fatherhood is to most men's. Again, this may be a matter of individual dispute, and it may hurt the feelings of some men to put it this way, but for now, that's the way it is. Whether that's the way it will always be is another and far more open question. Yet for me Anna Dienhart's certainty that gatekeeping behaviour is due to women's acculturation 'nagging' at them is more in the nature of a political statement than a scientific observation—as political as the opposite contention, that gatekeeping is the inevitable consequence of in-built 'maternal instincts'.[29]

The problem with the whole concept of gatekeeping is that it frames women's emotional responses as aberrant, problematic and—beneath the psychological gloss—just plain selfish. At its crudest, it is merely another example of what Paula Caplan calls 'mother blame'.[30] ('He wants to help, but she *just won't let him!*') For my money, gatekeeping puts the emphasis on the wrong syllable: identifying the strength of women's identity as parents as 'the problem' rather than the relative weakness of men's.

At another level, I also see so-called gatekeeping behaviour as a form of psychological teaming: reflecting an 'us versus him' mentality that may be a consequence, rather than a cause, of the failure of intimacy between husbands and wives. The less available Dad is—emotionally as well as physically—the closer Mum and the kids become, eventually perhaps closing ranks entirely. Women who, before children, felt their marriage was a matter of 'he has his life, and I have his life too' may well seize upon motherhood as an opportunity to carve out some territory of their own. They may wish to flaunt their competence as caregivers, consciously or unconsciously belittling that of their husbands, just as their husbands may have flaunted their physical prowess, say, or their capacity to earn income. ('I'm the one with the real job,' the high-salaried husband reminds his part-time employed wife. 'Yours is just a hobby.' 'I'm the one who's the real parent,' she retorts. 'You're just the babysitter.') Or, to put it even more bluntly, maybe women will be more willing to share parenting when men are more willing to share everything else.

And yet, the fact remains that most women are already willing to share parenting. For, whatever else we can say about gatekeeping, it is important to remember that it is a minority experience. You could say the real problem is that women are overly generous—all too willing to settle for the parental equivalent of the burnt chop, while we give the choicer cuts away to Dad, who accepts them (as he does so much else in life) with an unexamined sense of entitlement.

It's not that Dads can't do things differently, or that some Dads don't always. Such behaviour exists. The real question is whether it exists broadly enough to constitute what social scientists call a 'norm'. Abundant research tells us conclusively that it is not. Even more persuasive is the evidence of our own experience. You and I don't need a PhD in sociology to know if something is outside the norm. When our expectations of social behaviour are violated, we take notice. When they are fulfilled, we don't. This is why when we see, as I did yesterday, a bloke out shopping with a baby strapped to his back and a toddler in the pram, it is an occasion to be remarked. And when we see a woman doing the same—well, nine times out of ten we *don't* see her, or we don't at least take particular notice. This is not to say we should aim to make the bloke equally invisible. In my own case, I tooted my horn at him and raised my fist in a sisterly (?) salute. In the best of all possible worlds, I'd do the same to another woman.

People tell me all the time that they know couples in which the guy is the 'wife': where he stays home, or works fewer hours for pay, and looks after the kids and the housework. I know families like this too. And I also know that the reason we talk about them in the first place is not because they are typical but because they are not. That may sound too obvious to bother stating, but I do state it because it is a point that crops up so often in the parenting debate.

Not long ago, I wrote a magazine column on the division of household labour. Among other responses was a letter from a male reader offended by what he called my 'generalisations' about gender roles. It turned out that this man was a 'house husband' who took major responsibility for child care while his wife worked full-time. 'I work part-time *and* I manage the household, including two school-age children,' he declared in a published letter to the editor. I know from intimate experience that this achievement is a substantial one, but it struck me that the very fact of this letter's existence was the most eloquent corroboration of my 'generalisations' I could ever hope for. Can you imagine a magazine editor in the universe publishing such a letter from a woman? Can you imagine a woman writing one in the first place? It would be like a man boasting in print he could walk *and* chew gum.

None of which suggests even for a moment that fathers feel less love for their children than mothers do, or that men are somehow constitutionally irresponsible when it comes to parenting. On the contrary. I am convinced that fatherlove is a hugely powerful force in many men's lives, and one that has been tragically underplayed in our social constructions of masculinity. At the same time, there seems little evidence for the proposition that fatherlove and motherlove are easily interchangeable. Analogous, yes. Complementary, definitely. But equivalent? No. At our present stage of evolutionary development, our emotional repertoire remains in almost every way shaped by gender. Why should parenting be any different? This is an unpopular position in feminist circles, now that it has become fashionable to shun any view of gender that smacks of 'essentialism'. Yet to pretend for the sake of political expediency that we have somehow evaded membership in the biological community is gallant but absurd. Exploring our biological inheritance—beginning with the acknowledgment that we have been shaped by the same evolutionary forces as has every other created thing—does not, to my mind, imply accepting some pre-determined destiny. If there's anything evolutionary theory has taught us, it is that destiny is meaningless. The only thing 'essential' or 'determined' about any species—our own very much included—is a tireless capacity to adapt to change.

Ultimately, we need to grapple with the issue of why males and females parent as they do, which is to say differently. There is scarcely a species on earth that has not evolved a division of this most arduous of labours. Birds do it. (Indeed, they do it extraordinarily equitably.) Bees do it. (They invented day care, as a matter of fact.) As we have seen, co-parenting evolved in our own species not because human beings decided it was fairer that way, but because the survival of our young depended on it. And anyway, biologically speaking, co-parenting does not imply 'equality' but co-operation. In the case of our own species, the role of fathers came to centre on protection and provisioning. Dad made sure you ate (and were not in turn eaten)—a considerable contribution in the scheme of things—and Mum did pretty much everything else.

Despite substantial cross-cultural variations, this basic theme continues to characterise parenting in human groups today. And in all but a small minority of those groups it continues to prove not only highly adaptive, but almost entirely unproblematic. The minority in question is the tiny but disproportionately visible slice of humanity living in middle-class conditions within the industrialised world. Inhabitants of this rarified habitat—you and I and our mates and our offspring—have been afforded the extraordinary privilege of looking beyond the imperative to survive. For us, and for the first time in human history, issues related to the *quality* of existence have been allowed to take centre stage—not just for a few, but for the many. Today, we struggle, not to survive, but to prosper; not simply to find food and a mate, but also happiness and (dare I say it?) justice. Partly as a consequence of the transformation of our physical environment through technology, we have transfigured our moral universe as well. And parenting is very much part of that universe.

Exactly how we will adapt to accommodate that changed environment remains uncertain. But the necessity to adapt is undeniable. So too, fortunately, is the evidence of our capacity to do so. 'Doing what comes naturally' is, thank heavens, a highly mutable enterprise. As Dorothy Dinnerstein reminds us in *The Rocking of the Cradle and the Ruling of the World*, it was once 'natural' to go about on all fours.[31] Without doubt, most of the persistent asymmetries we observe in human co-parenting are also 'natural' or—to use more technical language— 'genetically encoded' or 'biologically based'. But this observation does not end the argument about achieving equity. On the contrary, it bids it begin.

chapter 11

the wifely art of emotional caregiving

'A young woman becoming a wife should think of
her new state not as one that is to make her happy
but as one in which she is to make her husband
happy. Her own happiness will be a by-product.'
Father D. F. Miller, *Catholic Weekly*, 1953

In the 1960s, pioneer marital researchers Robert Blood and D. M. Wolfe called it the 'mental hygiene function'. In the 1970s, sociologist Jessie Bernard—who 'told it like it was' in *The Future of Marriage*—dubbed it 'the stroking function'. In the 1980s, Arlie Hochschild suggested the term 'emotion work'. Today, call it what we will, the reality of 'doing the intimacy' in marriage remains pretty much what it always has been: wifework. 'In the vast majority of couples today,' writes psychologist Pepper Schwartz, 'the relationship exists on the women's skills. Perhaps the biggest job women carry is to be the expressive member of the couple.'[1]

The art of emotional caregiving is arguably the most demanding and depleting aspect of wifework a woman will undertake. It is also the most invisible, the least likely to be acknowledged, and the most difficult to outsource. Ironing ladies are a dime a dozen, but intimacy ladies—at least in this culture—are not. Nevertheless, the average wife typically directs so much energy towards the care and maintenance of her husband's emotional equilibrium that researchers Jean Duncombe and Dennis Marsden have dubbed it 'The Third Shift'.[2]

There is no doubt that a lopsided division of emotional labour establishes itself early on in a marriage. One study of newly married couples found that, after only three months, the wives' main complaint was that although they were 'understanding, tender and reassuring to their husbands', their men did not reciprocate. Another study of married women found the greatest source of unhappiness was men's failure to 'do the emotional intimacy'.[3] The division of emotional labour within marriage is naturally much harder to quantify than other forms of unpaid labour. But the evidence is clear that the imbalance between husbands and wives is at least as drastic as it is in the more visible areas of housework and parenting.

We are now able to discern that domestic labour and child care are things that women do, rather than expressions of what women *are*. We remain very far from the same insight about the emotional caregiving wives lavish on their male partners. There is virtually no public debate about this aspect of wifework at all, and only fledgling academic interest. It's no wonder the issue has been described by researchers as 'the last frontier of gender equality'.[4] It is treacherous terrain indeed.

The provision of nurturance and care to others—but especially to children and men—is widely acknowledged to be a central feature of our social construction of femininity. It is women's work par excellence. To be sure, men also care for and nurture their wives and children. It's simply that, compared to women, the energy and effort they typically expend on emotional caregiving is negligible. This is not my opinion or experience or observation, but the consensus view of those social scientists who have begun to study the matter systematically, in depth and over broad populations.

The duties and responsibilities of this 'biggest job' are diffuse. Yet researchers agree that they involve the efforts of spouses to understand and empathise with one another, and to incorporate imaginatively the other's feelings into one's own. The issue is clouded still further by the fact that, to many non-academics, this sort of thing goes by a simpler name: love. If you think about it, you'll realise that this sort of 'love' is highly gender-specific. Within the context of the family, it is something women give, and men (and children) receive. It is wifelove (and, in a different form, it is motherlove, too). But it is not husbandlove. And we all know it's not. At some deep level, the asymmetry of emotional care-giving—of love itself—is accepted unanimously and unconsciously by almost all of us. 'Both men and women view these activities as women's spontaneously offered expressions of love,' notes Janice Steil. 'Men, for whom such work is seen as less natural, are free to provide less but are disproportionately appreciated for what they do.'[5]

Emotional caregiving is a form of wifework that most women perform so spontaneously, so effortlessly (or so it seems) and so successfully that it is rarely seen as a form of work at all, but rather the expression of an innate quality, a way of simply 'being' in the world. Yet it is clear that the skills of empathy and listening, the eagerness—or at least the the willingness—to be emotionally 'on call' as needed, are primarily learned. Academics have long been aware that 'women's intuition', for example, might more aptly be termed 'underlings' intuition'. As feminist critic Jean Baker Miller has observed, 'Subordinates…know much more about the dominants than vice versa. They have to.'[6] Historically, women have *needed* to be more aware of men's feeling states than men have needed to be aware of women's. It was all part of the biologically driven process of catching a man, and continuing to hold him captive. Women's superiority in emotion-reading may also have once served an important survival function, as an acquired compensation for their relative inferiority in the brute strength department. There was a time—rather a long time, in fact—when a woman's skill at 'soothing the savage breast' of her male partner may have spelled the difference between life and death for herself and for her offspring. For women in abusive relationships, it remains a widely used strategy.

When I was growing up in the 1960s, girls were still routinely advised to try to 'draw out' their dating partners by 'finding out what his interests are'. The implication was clear: it was 'unfeminine' to talk about one's own interests—or even, perhaps, to have any. For a girl, the key to successful dating, the courtship ritual paving the way to marriage, was to 'be a good listener'. It is hardly surprising that this good advice—because, let's face it, it probably worked—has been carried over into so many contemporary marriages, however ostensibly 'equal' they may be in other respects. As wives, women tend to remain the Good Listeners, the conversational firelighters and tenders of the relationship flame.

This emotional selflessness can mean that, even after ten or twenty years of marriage, a woman is still acting like she's on that same first date: still accommodating herself to 'his interests'—just as she so often accommodates herself to his taste in food, or music—still 'drawing him out' at the end of each day. In most cases, of course, there is a show of pseudomutuality between partners. 'Oh, yes, he asks about the children,' an informant in one study explained. 'But it's just to check out the state of the nation, no child development chats or anything like that. He loves the children, but he doesn't seem to need to know much, you know what I mean?'[7] Other women find that their husbands have a similarly low tolerance for detail when it comes to their wives' work or their friendships. The questions may be dutifully asked, but the quality of attention makes it clear that it is a duty. As Pepper Schwartz observes, 'A husband may say, "Tell me what happened…" but if his eyes glaze over and halfway through the story he displays impatience with the amount of narrative detail, he reinforces his wife's alienation and self-editing.'[8]

My girlfriends and I used to have a name for the glazed eye experience: the Venetian Blind look. (You can practically see the slats closing over!) I don't suppose there's a woman alive who hasn't encountered it from time to time—and learned to adjust both the style and content of her self-disclosures to prevent it happening more often. I am equally certain that there are women who go into Venetian mode when their husbands start talking; it is, after all, just another prerogative of the powerful, and not every set of power relationships within every marriage is dictated by gender. Yet I suspect that the numbers of female offenders are few relative to those of males. And the social opprobrium of such behaviour perpetrated by a female would be greater by several magnitudes.

It has even been suggested that women's reluctance to 'cut men off', as it were, has profound psycho-sexual underpinnings. Carolyn Heilbrun argues that the emotional deference with which women continue to favour males reflects a trans-gender conspiracy to protect the male ego from intimidation, both sexually and otherwise. Heilbrun believes this protection of the male is 'the key to success for both partners in a marriage, not only literally, but figuratively'.[9] Other observers believe it's more a case of women's self-imposed martyrdom—pursued in the mistaken belief that 'only a wife's self sacrifice assures reliable family bonds; her desire promises chaos and abandonment'.[10] At the least, it is clear that husbands and wives have a very different sense of entitlement to nurture. What's more, there is often a tacit acceptance on both sides that this is simply 'the way it is' for heterosexual couples.

In my second marriage, this tacit acceptance was made suddenly blatant in an argument we had about what I described as his emotional avoidance (and he described as being tired!). 'But you never even listen to my concerns, you're not interested in what I think or what I'm feeling,' I accused. Imagine my dismay when my husband didn't even attempt to deny this. 'Come on. You have your girlfriends for that,' he countered instead. I must admit, it was a response I never expected. Stated so baldly and without shame, it seemed such an admission of defeat. It was also absolutely true. Like most other married women, I loved my husband, but I felt closer to—I suppose, more intimate with— my girlfriends. The difference between us was that I saw this as problematic, and he didn't.

In our time, the importance of something called 'communication' within marriage has been drilled into all of us. One large-scale study showed that most divorced people cited 'communication problems' as the number-one reason for their marital breakdowns.[11] The problem is that the word 'communication' has been rendered almost meaningless with overuse—a catch-all category for everything from infidelity to in-law problems. Yet whatever else it may mean, 'communication' is unquestionably the wife's bailiwick. It is she who greases the relationship's wheels, changes its oil and brings it in for servicing.

For some researchers, the problem is that we have 'feminised' love itself: we have chosen to define love with reference to women's emotional strengths and capacities, not men's. As a result, men may not get credit for the style of intimacy they're best at. Although no one seems certain what that style consists of, most agree that men's caregiving contributions tend to be less expressive and more instrumental than women's. One researcher suggested—seemingly with a straight face—it could take the form of paying the insurance, for example. This is all well and good, yet the fact remains that if we wish to expand our definition of emotional caregiving to include concrete acts of care towards others, we will hardly succeed in redressing the gender imbalance. Awarding intimacy points for paying the insurance makes no sense unless we do the same for scrubbing the toilet, doing the ironing and paying for child care. Let's say we agreed on a definition of emotional caregiving in which actions registered at least as loudly as words. The contribution of the average wife relative to that of the average husband would be more lopsided than ever. Given the huge disparities of effort and reward experienced by males and females within marriage, giving men *more* credit for what they do as husbands seems a strange sort of solution. Indeed, I would have thought this was the problem.

The depiction of emotional caregiving as a wife's *job* (implying perhaps that it might be a husband's hobby?) is commonplace in the literature on marital intimacy. Social scientist Carol Tavris, author of *The Mismeasure of Woman*, goes so far as to characterise marriage itself in these terms. 'Marriage is the wife's territory,' she writes, 'her domain of expertise. It is her *job* to know how everyone is feeling in order to head off problems at the pass.'[12] There's a very good reason women are motivated to become the intimacy experts in marriage, says Tavris. It's because they will be blamed if something goes wrong. Other observers argue—or imply—that the real impediments to achieving equality of intimacy go all the way back to biology, to a 'mothering instinct' that gets switched on indiscriminately whether the baby in question happens to be forty weeks, or forty years, old. More persuasive, and far subtler, are psychological theories that look to the early mother–child bond to locate what one researcher has called women's 'special virtuosity in relationships'.

Has it ever seemed to you that the men in your life suffer from a form of mild to severe emotional disability? Well, it seemed that way to psychoanalyst Nancy Chodorow too. In research published in the 1970s, Chodorow set out to investigate how the formation of gender identity in early childhood might advantage females and stunt males, at least in terms of their caring skills. She argued that males raised by females—which is to say, virtually all males—develop a deep-seated anxiety about gender identity that females raised by females do not. One result of this anxiety is a lifelong ambivalence about the giving and receiving of intimacy, and an intense fear of emotional vulnerability.

Chodorow argues that boys raised by women are forced to deduce what it is to be masculine from the premise of maternity. Put simply, in order to become a little man, a little boy must reject mother and all that she represents: love, vulnerability, tenderness. Masculinity is constructed negatively, to be whatever femininity/maternity is not. In the case of female children, exactly the opposite occurs. The little girl's dependence on female love and power, in the person of her mother, is exactly the same as her little brother's. Only in her case, it will prove psychologically adaptive. For the little girl, who will herself become a mother one day, the intensely experienced identification with her mother provides a solid foundation for her identity as a female. Far from being a developmental 'problem', it is a huge psychological asset.

For boys, the emotional identification with Mother starts out equally strong, but within a few short years will become socially problematic. The thing of it is, boys will *not* become mothers. They will become men. Thus, their identification with Mother—and the dependency that goes along with it—must be at some stage redirected towards some masculine other. But who? Most boys don't really 'know' any men. Like all children, little boys' lives are full of female caregivers, relatives, teachers and babysitters. Sure, they know Daddy—but not wholly, fully, from the inside out, the way they know Mummy. Understandably (or so the theory goes), little boys are scared. They don't want to leave the safe female cocoon for the harsher, stranger, more rough-and-tumble world of men. They don't want to, but they must. Even worse, the 'push' often comes from the mother herself: an act of emotional abandonment whose scars will last the average male more or less a lifetime. Mothers who don't push their sons from the nest, it is assumed, will inflict even worse damage.

To paraphrase Oscar Wilde, boys cannot become mothers; that's their tragedy. Girls can; that's theirs. In the case of males, the tragedy is perhaps particularly poignant. The rejection of mother and all things female not only disables males as caregivers, it results in a compulsion to control women as a way of disguising a crippling emotional dependence on them.

Nancy Chodorow believes that the only way to break this dreary cycle of 'reproducing gender' throughout all eternity is for men to assume equal parenting responsibilities for young children. This would allow boys and girls alike plenty of opportunity to observe nurturant role models of both genders. Yet, as critics of her theory have pointed out, Chodorow never got around to explaining how men so intrinsically disadvantaged as caregivers could ever be persuaded to become equal parents in the first place. What's more, there is some evidence that shared parenting—particularly in families in which gender roles are otherwise traditional—may do little to challenge the status quo anyway. Even more seriously, Chodorow's attempts to describe how basic gender differences arise have been construed by some feminists as an endorsement or justification of those differences. Finally, she has been criticised for failing to consider the role of social and economic institutions in reproducing gender stereotypes. (The fact that she happens to be psychologist, and not a sociologist, is presumably not a good enough alibi!)

Nevertheless, for my money, Chodorow's theory remains a powerful explanatory tool for anyone interested in the link between gender identity and what we have learned to call 'emotional intelligence'. I suspect it will become less powerful over time, assuming that the incremental increases in the amount of time men spend in fathering young children start to add up. Another factor will be the increase in households headed by women, although it remains to be seen whether single-mother families will do more to entrench gender-role stereotypes (as Chodorow's theory seems to suggest) or undermine them. Certainly, there is reason for optimism on this score, given recent research showing that fathers, not mothers, are more instrumental in the formation of rigid gender identities. Mums, whether partnered or not, tend to treat their children equally; if anybody's going to lay a snakes-and-snails-and-puppy-dog-tails thing on a son, it's Dad. But all that lies in the future. As far as the present generation of adult males is concerned—the ones whom many readers of this book are married to—Chodorow's analysis has much to teach us.

Psychiatrist Julian Hafner, author of *The End of Marriage*, agrees, arguing that the central psychological dilemma faced by most men in our society is to avoid feeling dependent on a woman. Yet most men in our society *are* dependent on a woman. Emotionally, marriage means swapping one maternal figure, i.e., mother, for yet another, i.e., wife. 'As adults,' writes Hafner, 'any feelings of being dependent on a woman threaten to evoke Oedipal stirrings…To protect himself from the confusion, anxiety and guilt attached to this dilemma, he must preserve emotional distance between the woman and himself.'[13] This not only explains the source of men's fabled 'commitment phobia', but also why ambivalence towards intimacy persists even within a committed relationship. Within marriage, at least, most men appear to have little trouble *receiving* emotional caregiving from females, and in exactly the same unexamined spirit of entitlement with which they received such care from their mothers. Reciprocating such care is another story. To do *that* is to risk acting like a mother or—even worse—a girl.

I thought about this a few weeks ago, as I watched my ten-year-old daughter and her girlfriends perform as cheerleaders for the Perth Orioles, a professional women's netball team. To be honest, I hadn't been that keen on chaperoning the event. Sport is not my thing at the best of times. As for cheerleading, it was all tied up in my mind with prom queens and pep rallies and grunting jocks encased like bugs in a carapace of moulded plastic padding. Even as a freshman in high school I was repelled by the whole concept, more on aesthetic grounds than owing to any ideological concerns, to be honest. But the night I watched my daughter and a hundred other girls cheer, scream and stamp their feet for a bunch of other girls…now that was something else again. I found, to my amazement, that cheerleading could be incredibly moving. To see girls expend that kind of supportive energy on *girls*—publicly and in huge numbers—was a revelation. I couldn't wait to tell my daughter how proud of her I was, a reaction that both pleased and bemused her. Bless her heart, she had no idea how radical an event she had just participated in. For me, it was difficult to imagine anything more subversive. And then, a week or so later, I did.

What would it be like, I found myself wondering, if the Perth Orioles had had a *male* cheering squad? A serious one, with pompoms and complicated choreography and clever clapping rhymes? A squad that swooned in disappointment over a girl's missed goal, that yelled itself hoarse with excitement when she redeemed herself with a spectacular interception? What would it be like for girls to be able to count on boys cheering from the sidelines, secure in the knowledge that their every step was worth watching, their every achievement worth celebrating?

Well, I'm not sure what it would be like. Except that it would be drastically unlike the world we live and get married in right now. In the average marriage—no matter how 'democratically' constituted in other ways—a wife still functions as a kind of one-woman emotional cheering squad to her husband's centre-court performance. A marriage in which that role structure was reversed almost defies imagining. Try it. Picture to yourself a marriage in which the husband performs continuous and unreciprocated emotional labour on behalf of his wife—bolstering *her* self-esteem, applauding *her* successes, salving *her* hurts and disappointments, acknowledging *her* hard work, protecting *her* physical well-being, sacrificing his leisure so that *she* can rest and recharge, tailoring his sexuality to *her* preferences and desires. What kind of a man would do all that for a woman? What kind of a man would do for a woman, in other words, what almost all women do throughout their married lives for men? The kind, I'm afraid, who lives only in women's wildest fantasies.

Theories of gender identity development seem to suggest that males are constitutionally incapable of providing unambivalent nurture to women to the same degree that women do to men. It's an assessment with which many wives would agree. 'It's just not in a man's nature,' they say. 'When it comes to dealing with feelings, guys just don't get it.' All of which probably explains why the Emotionally Incompetent Male has proved a more enduring stock character of post-feminist life than his unmarried alter ego, the Sensitive New Age Guy. (Q: What's a guy's idea of foreplay? A: You awake?) John Gray, author of the internationally bestselling Mars and Venus books, has made a virtual industry out of explaining His quaint habits and customs: His propensity to try to 'fix' problems before actually listening to them; His unerring ability to divorce sex from intimacy; His infamous tendency to 'retreat to His cave' during times of stress. Like the hapless husbands who inhabit Mere Male-type columns in the women's weeklies—a journalistic fossil with as much post-feminist credibility as a girly calendar—He wanders in a curious kind of gender-specific oblivion, forever losing his keys, misplacing the kids, or just plain missing the point. He's exasperating, clueless, out of touch. But what can you do? The guy can't help himself.

It seems to me that it's one thing to entertain the notion that males may be at an emotional disadvantage relative to females. Yet to accept— even to celebrate—self-absorption and cloddishness as a necessary feature of the masculine condition is quite another.

Maybe it's not even necessary to drag developmental theory in, kicking and screaming, in order to explain men's lack of awareness of the needs of others. Feminist critics like Anthony McMahon, Christine Delphy, Diana Leonard, Susie Orbach and Barbara Eichenstein, for example, see men's emotional incompetence as just another in a long series of entrenched male privileges. Like an aristocratic Victorian lady unable to lace up her own corset, a man may never learn to provide emotional caregiving to others for the very simple reason that he has never had to. According to this view, men can afford their extravagant lack of awareness only because 'those needs are continually met by others who have (indeed who are obliged to have) such an awareness'.[14] No points for guessing who those 'others' are.

chapter 12

giving, receiving...
getting depressed

'When women are ready to believe that a man's saying,
"My wife doesn't understand me" means "I behave
unreasonably towards my wife", feminism will
have got to first base.' Germaine Greer

For many couples, the sense of male entitlement to emotional care
is often so entrenched neither partner in a relationship is aware of
it. Even fewer consider the ways in which men's entitlement to receive
nurture—or women's imperative to supply it—structures a wide range
of behaviours within marriage, from conversational style to sexual
relating to patterns of leisure and recreation. In almost every area in
which husbands and wives relate, the 'pipe and slippers' mentality is
appallingly alive and well in marriage today.

In a study of dual-earner families during 'crunch times'—in the hour
before leaving for work and school in the morning, and the hour upon
returning home again in the evening—researcher Susan Donath found
that in the mornings, husbands slept later, watched more television, spent
28 per cent more time eating breakfast yet 34 per cent less time cooking
it, and exerted 67 per cent less effort in caring for children. At the other
end of the day, the picture was just as skewed. For one thing, three-
quarters of all wives were already home by the time their husbands
arrived. Wives' first activities upon arrival were equally divided between
household work and leisure/eating. For their male partners, by contrast,

71 per cent engaged in a leisure activity first, while only 28 per cent performed a household task first. Overall, in the first hour following splashdown, husbands spent forty minutes in leisure activities—or 25 per cent more time than their wives did. This included roughly twice as much TV-watching, about two-thirds more eating and drinking, and a third more sleeping. Only 8 per cent of males did not participate in at least one leisure activity in that first hour at home, compared with 17.3 per cent of their wives.[1]

Not surprisingly, given what we have already observed about the division of labour in marriage, research into the division of leisure confirms that wifework leaves most women little time for fun and games. One large-scale Australian study of dual-earner families with children under ten showed that husbands enjoyed sixteen hours more uncommitted time *per week* than their wives did. In families with older children, the gap decreased to seven hours.[2] In a study of labour and leisure patterns in 'high-demand households'—families with young children where both partners worked for pay—leading US sociologist Arlie Hochschild came up with a very similar leisure gap: fifteen hours.[3] A study published in 2000 in *British Social Trends* did not distinguish between married and unmarried respondents. However, on the basis of BBC audience-research figures, the annual General Household survey and weekly time diaries of more than 2000 people, it found that the average British woman enjoyed 50 minutes less leisure time per day than the average man.[4]

According to Rebecca Abrams, author of *The Playful Self*, the 'pressure to put others' needs before one's own is one of the key reasons why so many women have such difficulty when it comes to finding either the inclination or the opportunity to play'.[5] Psychotherapist Susie Orbach goes so far as to argue that women have difficulty even *recognising* their own needs, let alone seeing to it that they are satisfied. It's the old burnt-chop syndrome all over again. In extreme cases—which happen to be extremely common—the husband's idea of leisure is a two-hour game of tennis followed by a beer with the boys, and the wife's idea is five minutes alone in the bathroom.

The research strongly suggests that men have no problem at all claiming their inalienable right to leisure. Bob and Linda, a couple featured in Arlie Hochschild's *The Time Bind*, are typical in this respect. Both partners worked full-time, and both felt the need for time off, just to relax and have fun. The difference, writes Hochschild, was that 'Bill simply climbed in his truck and took his free time'. He didn't ask permission, hang back, or apologise. He just did it. Linda felt irritated by this—because it left her holding the baby at home—and retaliated by grabbing her own version of 'free time': at work. That's right. Linda's so-called leisure-time pursuit was working for pay.[6]

Was Linda hopelessly neurotic, or simply a very dull girl? It's hard to say. Her plight may be pathetic, it's certainly not unusual. On the contrary, Linda's solution to the problem of shoe-horning some leisure into the gap between paid employment, child care and wifework is a very common one. After all, leisure is a relative concept, when you stop to think about it. And compared to running after toddlers while washing the skirting boards even the dreariest office work can seem like good sport. In my experience, many working mothers with young children regard their worklife as a form of leisure. I know I did. There were times when I hung out to go to the office—even to attend a departmental *meeting*, for crying out loud—the way normal people (i.e., male and/or childless) hang out for a long weekend, or a day on the beach. I felt guilty about this, and implied to people that I was only working because I had to. Well, I did have to. But the truth was, financial necessity was only a convenient alibi. I would gladly have worked for free.

Leisure became a huge issue in my second marriage. I now know that it almost always does when there are preschool children in the picture. In our case, the usual scenario was further exaggerated by the small age gaps between our children. For a brief but memorable time—except that I really remember very little, doubtless out of sheer self-defence—we had three under the age of four. This meant that there was a period of almost five years in which I was continuously either pregnant or lactating. I was also profoundly sleep-deprived and had no family within a 20,000-kilometre radius of my neighbourhood. To say that I needed 'a break' now and then would have been a profound understatement. Of course, the same could be said of my husband, who worked long hours in a hectic professional practice. Not surprisingly, when the opportunity arose for some leisure time, he was quick to grab it. His version of 'jumping into the truck' was playing a round of golf on a Saturday. He would leave around lunchtime, tee off at 1 p.m. and be home sometime around five, looking tired but happy. My version of 'jumping into the truck' was going grocery shopping without the kids—from which I'd return tired but…well, tired.

'Resentful' is too weak a word to describe my feelings about this inequity. 'Enraged', 'aghast', 'furious', 'consumed with malice' come a lot closer. Here I was, a nearly forty-year-old academic in the last decade of the twentieth century—a whole generation beyond *The Feminine Mystique* (or so I thought)—and I was still being treated like a subordinate, a sort of trainee grown-up, a *housewife*, within my own home. It seemed almost surreal, and so incredibly unfair. But, unfair or not, our Saturday morning arguments always ended up exactly the same way. 'I work hard all week,' he'd remind me through clenched teeth—for the hundredth time—'and I am entitled to play a round of golf on the weekends if I feel like it.' And then he'd leave. And that, we both knew, was his trump card: that he could leave—that he *would* leave—and I couldn't. I wouldn't. When women walk out on their families for five hours on a Saturday, it's called abandonment. When men do it, it's called entitlement.

I'm the first to admit that mine was a fairly advanced (or should I say regressed?) case. Most of the time, the inequities in the distribution of leisure by gender are subtler, or at least more artfully concealed. Often, for example, a husband's 'long day at the office' incorporates a multitude of opportunities for leisure and socialising. One common scenario sees him scoring major brownie points for working from eight to six—during which time he manages to read the paper, take several coffee breaks, eat lunch at a cafe and catch up on the latest office gossip. Her 'part-time' hours of paid work from ten to four sound like a comparative doddle—and they would be, too, if she didn't have sole responsibility for almost everything else that keeps the household running: getting the kids off to school, picking them up again, planning and shopping for dinner (which she does during her lunchbreak), cooking it, supervising home-work, organising baths, folding the laundry, etc. etc. The opportunities for 'concealed leisure' in such a schedule are few indeed.

The fantasy that equates time at home with so-called free time is a strictly masculine delusion. Yet the myth that men 'deserve' their leisure because they work longer hours for pay is something we all continue to buy into. 'All studies show that leisure is a masculine privilege,' writes Germaine Greer.[7] What they don't show is the extent to which wives collude in protecting that privilege—often by denying it exists. Greer is a fund of quirky information about the leisure gap that lurks beneath even the most egalitarian households. She notes that the major record companies have more or less given up on trying to sell music to adult women. Even among those who can afford CDs, market research has shown, most don't have the time to listen to them. Speaking as someone who hasn't sat down to listen to music for probably ten years, that sounds plausible to me. And then there's the shopping mall in Birmingham, UK, where shopkeepers have clubbed together to organise a 'husband creche', where men can be dropped off to enjoy snacks and telly while their wives to do the weekly shopping. Greer may be a better polemicist than social scientist. But her conclusions agree entirely with those of the most rigorous academic studies into the division of leisure within marriage.

The relationship between leisure and freedom has been noted by many observers—including my ten-year-old daughter who, like most students, regards any assigned reading as 'work' and any freely chosen reading as 'fun'. The principle is fairly obvious. Among other things, it explains why preparing a four-course gourmet dinner party can be fun while frying sausages and mashing potatoes can stress you out of your skull. As one wife explained when asked by researchers to define 'leisure': 'Leisure is the time that I get to choose what I want to do for myself.'[8]

An interesting study conducted in 1994 found that the more leisure time fathers spent with their children, the greater their parental satisfaction. For mothers, there was no such effect. The researcher speculated that the reason was that mothers had no choice but to spend time with their children. For mothers, parenting was an obligation (albeit an often pleasurable one). For their male partners, who had the luxury of picking and choosing their paternal moments, parenting was a form of 'leisure'.[9] As one mother explained to researchers in another study, 'My mind says that I should say "yes" that I spend leisure time having fun with my children, doing things with my children, but to me, I guess that's not really leisure...I wasn't doing something for myself. I was doing it for my children'.[10]

Researchers in the growing field of leisure studies have found that, in general, the more roles undertaken by an individual, the less personal leisure he or she will enjoy. As the popular press never tires of reminding us, married women with children juggle more roles than any other group in our society. We hear about the mother role, the paid-worker role, and the housekeeper role, but very rarely if ever about the wifework role, which implicates all of the above yet encompasses an exhausting additional agenda which is documentably husband-specific. As one researcher rather politely put it in a wide-ranging review of the current literature on women and leisure, 'A contradiction seems to exist between addressing the relationships and roles that are central to a woman's life and needing time for oneself.'[11] Canadian researchers Patricia Hunter and David Whitson deduced bleakly that, for 'anyone in a caregiving role, leisure as free time may be irrelevant'.[12]

Their study suggested that married women more often find themselves in the role of leisure facilitators than leisure consumers. Their 'fun', in other words, typically consists of arranging or attending recreational activities for the benefit of other family members. In extreme cases, wives' leisure may be little more than a by-product of overseeing or witnessing the leisure of others. At the most obvious level, this may consist of keeping an eye on children in the playground or in the surf (with or without their fathers), or watching husbands play cricket or football. Wifework also entails the kind of leisure facilitation that makes possible the typical Sunday afternoon picnic, or the family holiday. Such family 'leisure' occasions entail a remarkable degree of hidden labour—from the planning, shopping and food preparation to the packing, washing and putting-away again. No wonder Mummy's idea of a good time is to be left in peace for five minutes! Daddy, meanwhile, scores Good Time Charlie points playing cricket with the kids and rather ostentatiously donning an apron to fire up the barbie. For him, doing the cooking is fun—a performance, almost. University of Akron sociologist Rebecca Erickson points out that a wife, by contrast, never simply cooks meals; she 'orchestrates' them.[13] For her, the backstage work of stage-managing everybody else's good time can be a real drag, even when it is acknowledged and appreciated. And most of the time, it isn't.

To what extent this is all a matter of self-imposed martyrdom—or even pathology—remains open to conjecture. On the one hand, we live in a society which has constructed gender such that women are expected to find their primary gratifications through the gratification of others. Yet, on the other, we are quick to point the finger at women who have 'made themselves' subject to the ruling desires of men and children. 'Get a life!' we advise them, as if we, ourselves, had the problem all sewn up. 'You're allowed to nowadays, you know.' Women who take this advice to heart may find it's not as easy as it looks—especially without wads of disposable income to spend on takeaways, extra child care, and household support. The problem is not getting a life; the problem is sharing a life. And sharing a life is something no woman can simply decide to do on her own, or accomplish through sheer force of will.

Rebecca Erickson's 1993 study of 205 women in dual-earner marriages provided plenty of evidence for what she calls 'marriage burnout': 'a state of emotional exhaustion that is associated with working intensely and intimately with others over a long period of time'.[14] In extreme cases, a woman's failure to cut free from the yoke of servicing others will be diagnosed with the clinical label of co-dependency, and she will be encouraged to 'seek treatment'. 'Society is more comfortable with women who feel inadequate, self-doubting, guilty, sick and "diseased",' Harriet Goldhor Lerner noted, 'than with women who are angry or confronting.' What's more, she adds, 'women are too'.[15] By now it should be clear that blaming women for perpetuating gender stereotypes like these is every bit as obtuse as adopting an 'all men are bastards' approach.

At the same time, the desire to blame somebody or something is very understandable. The relief that finding a scapegoat provides—even if that scapegoat is oneself—can prove almost irresistibly seductive. Guilt feels bad. Living with ambiguity feels even worse—especially when it means accepting that our free will is inevitably compromised, even at our most intimate moments, by a social and biological history utterly separate from, and indifferent to, our most deeply cherished notions of 'gender equality'. As the novelist A. S. Byatt observes in *The Virgin in the Garden*, 'It is not possible to create the opposite of what one has always known, simply because the opposite is believed to be desired.'[16] At the very least, it is not possible to do this over the course of a single generation or even two or three.

Wifework and playfulness are very nearly mutually exclusive, though the reasons why have little to do with either the natural martyrdom of females or the innate obtuseness of males. Perhaps more vividly than in any other area of married life, this division of seriousness reflects how closely we are still following somebody else's script for our relationships.

It emphasises how far our marriages seem to have taken us from the people we've always said we wanted to be. Women allow themselves to be silly with their girlfriends, perhaps; but find it difficult to be other than the Grown-up with their spouses and children. 'Well, somebody's got to be,' as women often say to one another, knowingly. Yet taking on the mantle of the 'serious adult' in the family surely comes at a cost.

Although its implications for women's psychological and physical health can only be imagined, there is plenty of evidence to suggest that playfulness in outlook and conduct is highly correlated with creativity, happiness and a youthful outlook. A study conducted by clinical psychologist David Weeks, for example, found that extremely playful people are twenty times less likely to visit their doctor than non-playful people.[17] Based on that finding, one could deduce that women engaged in wifework would be more likely to visit their doctor than almost any other group. One would be absolutely correct.

To me, it is sensible to look at leisure—including the provisions we make for it, and our sense of entitlement to it—as a concrete manifestation of the emotional division of labour within marriage. Doing this makes clear the obvious relationship between who does what in relation to emotion work and who feels what in relation to marital satisfaction and overall well-being.

This failure of men to 'do intimacy' in marriage contrasts painfully with women's success in the same endeavour. The price wives pay for their success as emotional caregivers has yet to be reckoned, but it would be surprising if it were not implicated in measures of marital satisfaction that lag significantly behind those of their male partners and in rates of depression several times as high.

Rebecca Erickson found a direct link between husbands' performance of emotion work and wives' levels of marital satisfaction. In fact, this was the single most powerful predictor of wives' well-being. Men who were 'there' for their wives emotionally, Erickson found, were forgiven almost anything else that may have needed forgiving—including painful inequities in the performance of domestic labour and child care. (Significantly, however, when men did perform housework, it was perceived by wives as 'emotionally supportive behaviour'; when wives performed housework, it was perceived by husbands as...wives performing housework.)[18]

Understanding how emotion work is negotiated can help us understand a great deal about gender differences in the way marriage is *experienced*. It will not be news for you to learn that the major beneficiaries of emotion work in marriage—husbands—experience marriage much more positively. The response on the part of the major providers of emotional care—wives—ranges from 'less than effusive' to 'clinically depressed'. Oxford University Professor Michael Argyle spent eleven years studying human happiness, and found marriage to be a much more salient factor for men's sense of personal well-being than for women's. 'Marriage provides companionship, particularly during leisure time, and a great deal of emotional help and support, especially for men,' noted Argyle. 'Husbands are not very good at providing that or being very good listeners. But they seem to need it more than women.'[19] One Australian study conducted in 1993 found that men rated marriage as the greatest source of happiness in their lives. Among women, it barely rated a mention.[20]

Research over many decades, and across a wide spectrum of disciplines, has found marital satisfaction more important to personal well-being than occupational success, religion, housing or finances combined. As one researcher has noted, 'it appears that having a "very happy" marriage is almost essential to being personally "very happy"'.[21] Our cynicism about the institution notwithstanding, we continue to regard the possibility of achieving happiness outside of it as, at best, remote—as most single people in our society over the age of thirty will readily (and wearily) attest. No matter how privately awful we may have experienced marriage to be, we publicly pity whomever we perceive as having 'missed out'. We regard adults who remain single in much the same way as we do couples who remain childless: with suspicion.

Both men and women are reluctant to admit bluntly to 'unhappiness', even where it plainly exists. 'The ideal of marital happiness is so strong,' comments social psychologist Blaine J. Fowers, 'that spouses deceive themselves about the degree to which their marriage meets the criterion.'[22] Studies show that both parties engage in what social scientists call 'positive illusions'—and the rest of us call wishful thinking—about their chances of divorce, for example. They are also prone to 'endorsing unreasonably positive statements about their spouses', exaggerating virtues and concealing private hostility with public protestations of loyalty and affection. We have seen that women are at least as prone as men are to 'protect' their marriages in this way. Even among our closest friends, we may complain blithely, or bitterly, about our husbands' flaws—but invariably conclude that 'compared to other women, I've got it great' or 'compared to other men, he's fantastic'.

Most researchers now accept that this protective strategy is so strong and so well documented that crude self-report data is virtually useless. If people were as happy as they say they are in their marriages, there would be nothing to study!

If both husbands and wives pretend they are happier in marriage than they really are, the evidence is clear that women pretend more. This is yet another facet of the emotional asymmetry that continues to characterise contemporary marriage. Wives not only experience greater dissatisfaction, frustration and resentment in their marital roles than their husbands do, they find more gratifications outside of marriage than within it. For men, it is clear, marriage still functions as a kind of refuge, a 'haven' as Christopher Lasch has called it 'in a heartless world'. For women, it is often marriage itself which constitutes the 'heartless world'. How shameful that a 'women's refuge' is a place to which women flee *from* their marriages.

Researchers have struggled for decades to explain why being a husband feels so much better than being a wife. Even the least cynical and most conservative is sure it has something to do with power—

something feminists have been saying for more than three decades. Interestingly, marital satisfaction is high for both partners where husbands and wives agree unambivalently that the bloke is boss—where it is overtly preached as well as covertly practised.[23] Research conducted among 150 Israeli couples in 1997 showed that equal role-sharing and decision-making were highly predictive of women's marital satisfaction. Unfortunately, they were equally correlated with marital *dis*satisfaction for husbands.[24]

One of the privileges of the powerful in any relationship is to enjoy superior access to resources. In marriage those resources are not only material, but also emotional. Husbands have access to vast resources of 'emotional capital' in the person of their wives. Women in search of emotional sustenance, by contrast, tend to look outside the marriage, to children, friends, or family. Wives are twice as likely as men to describe a best friend as 'the person closest to them'.[25] According to one recent study, between six and seven out of ten married women said they were more emotionally intimate with women, compared with only one in ten who found greater intimacy with men. Other research has found that wives are less likely to talk over problems exclusively with their spouse than husbands are, while husbands are much more likely to name their spouse as 'best friend' or 'most trusted confidante'.[26] In the Australian study, *Living Decently: Material Well-Being in Australia*, men cited marriage as their greatest source of happiness. Women nominated friends, health and family support—in that order.[27] Pepper Schwartz believes that it is 'typical' in traditional marriages for women 'to make the children her real emotional community—in place of her partner. In a sense, he just seeds the family and visits it.'[28] On those visits, a husband's expectations of nurture from his wife remain high. Many researchers believe, in fact, that men actually feel 'entitled to excessive emotional dependence on women'.[29]

Yet being on the receiving end of so much emotional largesse may have a downside for men as well, argues English psychiatrist Julian

Hafner. Hafner maintains that the failure of males to take responsibility for their own emotional health is one reason they don't live as long as women do. (In most western societies, the 'longevity gap' is about seven years—and it has remained constant for decades.) Along with men's neglect of their own physical health, Hafner cites the emotional dependency of males on females as 'one of the most sinister and destructive aspects of the current relationship between men and women'.[30] Other researchers, however, stress the 'importance' of wifely nurture, seeing it as the main reason for the 'protective effect' of marriage on men's health and happiness. The possibility that men's emotional dependence on women may be ultimately infantilising—an inhibitor of personal growth—is rarely canvassed.

As we have seen, that protective effect for married women is much weaker overall, and in certain key respects it is missing altogether. The reasons for this hole in the marital ozone layer should at this point not be hard to understand. Marriage is harder work for women. It takes more out of them, and it gives less back. This inconvenient fact is widely ignored by recent apologists for marriage, including Linda Waite and Maggie Gallagher, authors of *The Case for Marriage*. The neotraditionalist mantra that marriage makes life better for everybody not only rests on a highly selective look at the relevant data. It glosses over the fact that marriage makes life much, much better for men, and only somewhat better for women—and with significant and telling exceptions. One of those exceptions is mental health.

Marriage not only fails to protect the mental health of women, there is evidence that it is a direct risk factor for depression. Notes Howard Markman, head of the Center for Marital and Family Studies at the University of Denver, 'Many problems brought to individual psychotherapy are really relationship problems. First and foremost is depression in women.'[31] When one considers that, as Orly Benjamin puts it, 'the silencing of women's concerns has traditionally dominated the sphere of intimacy' the link between marriage and depression is not hard to understand.[32] University of Washington psychologist Neil Jacobson estimates that married women are twice as likely to be depressed as their husbands are.[33] Depression expert Dr Ellen McGrath describes the link between marriage and women's depression as 'psychology's dirty little secret'.[34] The link is particularly evident where wives' educational attainments are low and financial dependence is high. One recent study found that unemployed wives with a high-school education were at a fourfold risk of depression compared with college-educated wives. Indeed, not working for pay more than doubled the risk of depression for all women, whatever their educational level.[35]

Then again, living with an emotionally independent partner (or, at least, one who is not emotionally dependent on *you*) may provide protection against depression for men, but not for women. One recent study of 317 elderly couples found that husbands had fewest depressive symptoms when they perceived their wives to be emotionally independent. Wives, by contrast, had lowest levels of depression when they felt their husbands 'needed them' emotionally. In the same study, high 'couple closeness' scores were associated with fewer depressive symptoms in women, yet *more* such symptoms in their husbands![36] The suggestion seems to be that men are not particularly motivated to seek an intimacy that is mutual: a one-way flow of nurture is fine with them. For their wives, however, the issue of mutuality is crucial.

Unfortunately, they are far more likely to strive for mutuality than to find it. Janice Steil believes that the level of mutuality a couple achieves will be ultimately determined by the husband, 'the partner who prefers more distance and less interaction'.[37] If Steil is correct, the result is an almost inevitable structural impediment to wives' emotional and psychological well-being in marriage.

Other research has found a strong link between depression and 'emotional reliance' among women. This is hardly unexpected. A wife who is 'emotionally reliant' on her husband will almost certainly experience distress, given men's well documented inability (or disinclination) to provide emotional caregiving. A study of 1393 Canadian adults found that education and occupational prestige reduced perceptions of emotional reliance. Marriage increased these perceptions, especially for men; but in their case, the increase was not associated with increases in depression. Again, the reason may not be so mysterious. A man who becomes emotionally reliant on his wife stands an excellent chance of having his needs met beautifully. The emotional reliance of males on females is not only not problematic, it appears to be positively adaptive. Exactly the opposite is the case when females are emotionally reliant on males.[38]

Women's rates of depression are much more closely keyed to the state of the relationship than their husbands' are. Research reported recently in *Mental Health Weekly* found a strong link between women's depressive symptoms and their husbands' 'hostility ratings'. Wives' 'hostility ratings' had no effect at all on men's depression.[39] Although other studies suggest that negative interactions with spouses are strong predictors of depression for both genders, it has been clearly established that women's depression is more strongly linked with marital quality than men's depression.[40] Then again, women generally are more vulnerable to depression stemming from events with the extended family, while men are more likely to become distressed by financial and work events.

It's not that men do not suffer equally when a relationship turns rocky. But their distress is likely to take other forms—especially alcohol abuse and other 'acting out' behaviours.[41] One psychologist who studied how men express emotional distress found the following to be typical: 'frantic work', heavy drinking, trouble concentrating at work, restlessness and hyperactivity, physical ailments and stress symptoms. 'Many of the men had low scores on standard depression scales,' Carol Tavris notes in *The Mismeasure of Woman*, 'yet their lives were in a shambles.' Tavris believes the clinical definition of 'depression' is based almost entirely on female modes of coping with grief and distress: crying, staying in bed, talking about one's misery, developing eating disorders. As a result, Tavris notes, 'it is easy to infer that men suffer less than women when relationships are in trouble, or even that men are incapable of love'.[42] Obviously, nothing could be further from the truth.

Nevertheless, as University of Washington psychologist John Gottman points out, in unhappy unions—as in happy ones—it is the wife who takes on the burden of 'fixing' the relationship. Gottman sees this as one more piece of evidence that 'marriage disproportionately benefits men'. Bowling Green University sociologist Gary Lee attributes the so-called 'happiness gap' between husbands and wives in part to women's role strain—a euphemism for wifework—and in part to women's higher expectations of marriage. 'Women are still socialised to believed that marriage is the most important life transition they will make,' Lee maintains. 'It is not the same for men. So when the marriage isn't perfect, it may be a bigger disappointment for women than men.'[43]

The relationship between the emotional division of labour in marriage, marital satisfaction and depression is a complex one. The question of whether males and females have different emotional 'needs'—or simply different chances for getting needs met—remains contentious. Possibly, women seem so hungry for connection not because their intimacy needs are greater, but simply because their intimacy needs are less likely to be fulfilled. One day we may have better answers. For now, all we can be sure of is that emotional caregiving in marriage remains something that women largely give, and men largely receive.

not tonight, darling: wifework and sex work

'Women, despite doing more activities they did not
wish to do than men—domestic, child care tasks
and sex—generally indicated that they saw the
relationship as equal.' Sally and Rudi Dallos

'I don't know anything about sex, dahling,' drawls Zsa Zsa Gabor. 'I've been married my whole life.' Behind the ditzy deadpan is a reality every married couple can identify with. Ironically, the more 'stable' the relationship the more problematic sex can become. Familiarity may not breed contempt, exactly; but it rarely ignites a great deal of passion either. Recent research has confirmed what you, your partner and your Aunt Harriet always knew: sexual passion fades fast. In three years—tops—the average sexual flame has more or less consumed itself. Professor Cindy Hazan of Cornell University interviewed 5000 men and women across thirty-seven cultures and found that just about all of us seem biologically predisposed to be 'in love' for precisely eighteen to thirty months. Her study also indicated that men fall in love more quickly than women and that most relationships are terminated by women. Hazan and many others cite extensive evidence that the role of 'chemistry' in human sexual attraction is more than just a metaphor. It's phenyl-ethylamine, dopamine and oxytocin too—the brain chemicals that scientists now believe are 'triggered' through social conditioning.[1]

Sociologists are more apt to talk of going off the boil in terms of 'habituation': a concept which pretty much translates into people getting bored—something they do rapidly once married. Most research shows that the 'coital rate' drops by about 50 per cent within the first year of marriage—a result so predictable that it has been termed 'the honeymoon effect'.[2] In the words of one recent US study of the incidence and frequency of marital sex, based on the 1988 National Survey of Families and Households, 'sex satiation and habituation occur very quickly after the honeymoon'. Researchers describe the initial fall-off in erotic interest as 'precipitous…with a steady decline thereafter'.[3]

Indeed, there is some indication that sex within marriage is so moribund that the reluctance to study it is almost as pronounced as the reluctance to engage in it. As late as 1983, one researcher observed that marital sex 'remains more the topic of jokes than of serious social scientific investigation'.[4] Another observed that out of 533 articles on the topic of 'human sexuality' indexed in a major academic database between 1987 and 1993, only one dealt with sex between partners married to one another! One thing researchers do seem almost obsessed with, however, is the frequency of marital sex. Most recent studies seem to confirm that, for married people aged between thirty and fifty-five, most couples have sex about seven times a month, or somewhere between once or twice a week.[5] If anything, the evidence suggests that these figures are probably exaggerations. Unmarried, cohabiting couples are documentably hornier. On average, they 'do it' about twelve times a month, or almost twice as frequently as their married counterparts. Keep in mind, though, that the average cohabiting couple is younger, and the relationship newer and, as it were, greener.

What is it about marriage that makes it a kind of metaphorical cold shower for everyone involved? The answer is much more complicated, I suspect, than simple 'habituation'. One of the relevant factors seems to be that passion is, as Pepper Schwartz notes, 'to some extent maintained by tension and anxiety'.[6] Yet the decision to marry, for most people, represents a resolution of uncertainty. The making of the commitment typically allays the anxieties both partners feel during the courtship phase—only to replace them in short order with *new* tensions and anxieties, to be sure. Although marriage signals an important new beginning for a relationship, it also functions as a definitive punctuation mark. Whatever other excitements marriage may herald, the thrill of the chase is not among them.

As we have already seen, parenthood will also have a depressing, in some cases even a terminal, effect on marital libido. And for most couples parenthood follows almost as closely on the heels of marriage these days as it has ever done: somewhere between two and three years, on average. Not at all coincidentally, I'm sure, the arrival of a first child occurs just at the point at which a couple's most intense sexual longing for one another is seriously on the wane. The baby will pretty much put paid to what's left—whether for months, years or even decades. US researchers Carolyn and Philip Cowan, in their landmark ten-year study of the impact of parenthood on couples, found that both husbands and wives universally reported a negative change in their sexual relationship after the birth of a first baby. Couples were equally divided between those who felt sexual quality had declined most, and those who were most worried about frequency.[7]

Most researchers agree that the reasons for this are partly physical—sleep deprivation is a biggie, followed closely by pain from healing episiotomies, caesarean scars, cracked nipples from breastfeeding, etc.—and partly psychological. 'I have this little voice that begins to nag at me, saying, "Parents don't have sex,"' confided one new parent rather sheepishly.[8] In other cases, it's a matter of finding the time and the energy for sex. When the Cowans asked one couple about any changes in their sexual relationship after having a baby, they both laughed and asked, 'What sexual relationship?'[9] It's an exceedingly common scenario. Parents who believe that 'things will get back to normal' once the baby sleeps through, or turns one, or starts walking, or even starts school, are often shocked to discover that things never get back to normal, if by 'normal' they mean the relationship as it existed BC: Before Children.

Yet there are plenty of other variables (besides the ones running around in nappies) that help explain the decline in marital sexual activity. Critic Dalma Heyn points out that the role of 'wife' is seen as the antithesis of sexiness. She tells the story of how her first book, *The Erotic Silence of the American Wife*, was rejected by the bookbuyer for K-Mart because of the word 'erotic'. 'Although I was stunned and angry,' she recalls, 'I was also oddly pleased by this perfect illustration of the book's thesis: the literal silencing of *erotic* for wives, the cultural inclination to talk about women's pleasure.'[10] Couples who don't consciously believe any such thing—certainly the majority of young married people today— nevertheless seem affected by it. Quite possibly, it was a message conveyed wordlessly but powerfully in our families of origin, one among many that we later attempted to 'unlearn' with only partial success.

In my first marriage, I was very much struck by the change in my partner's attitude towards my clothes and behaviour—neither of them what you'd call outrageous—once we became engaged. Sexy outfits that were once a turn-on suddenly became 'cheap' or 'inappropriate'. I remember once he checked to make sure I was wearing underwear! I didn't know whether to take it as a compliment or an insult. But I eventually decided it was an expression of his 'commitment' to me—that I'd reached some sort of new status. (I had, of course.) Years later, when we broke up, I took enormous pleasure in flouting what had become my wifely dress code. Like buying and eating the food he hated but I loved, it felt like an important way of getting back in touch with the person— me—I'd lost in the role. It was only much, much later that I read the words of psychologist Carol Gilligan: 'I have rarely met a woman in a conventional marriage who is not leading a double life in her relationship, who does not speak in this false voice in relationships.'[11] In my own first marriage, I was not only speaking in a false voice. I was wearing a costume to match.

Yet it is clear there is no corresponding erotic dampener associated with the role of husband by either women or men. In fact, and somewhat contrary to popular belief, sex is one of the many areas of life that marriage seems to enhance for men. According to research conducted by University of Chicago sociologist Linda Waite, married men more often report that sex with their wives is extremely pleasurable than either single guys or men living in de facto relationships. Husbands may not get as much sex as they like, but there is no doubt they like the sex they get. Whether their wives feel the same way is a more contentious question. An unabashed apologist for marriage, Waite found that physical satisfaction with sex is no worse for married women than for non-married, but it is certainly not better. She argues, 'Since married couples expect to carry on their sex lives for many years, and since most married couples are monogamous, husbands and wives have strong incentives to learn what pleases their partner in bed and to become good at it.'[12] If only life were like that!

In the average marriage, the question of who does what in bed turns out to be every bit as fraught a gender issue as who does what around the house. In fact, the intricacies of what researchers have begun to call 'the politics of intimacy' within marriage are enough to pour cold water on even the hottest couples.

A growing number of scholarly observers has begun to argue that, for many married women, sex is simply another form of wifework—another way in which women routinely service the physical and emotional needs of their male partners at the expense of their own. Historian Sheila Jeffreys argues that in contemporary marriage women do not experience sex primarily as a form of recreation, or an act of intimacy, but as a form of work: 'a "skill", like housework, that women need to acquire'.[13] Researchers Jean Duncombe and Dennis Marsden agree. In doing 'sex work', they argue, individuals strive to manage their emotions according to an accepted set of 'feeling rules' that govern how sex ought to be experienced.[14] Their research suggests that, in most marriages, those 'feeling rules' have largely to do with the simulation of desire and the suppression of 'distaste'—and in a huge majority of cases it is women who work to abide by them. There have been sightings of husbands who engage in sex work, too, of course. But for the most part, sex work is women's business—perhaps the subtlest and trickiest, and certainly the least discussed, aspect of wifework of all.

It's important to understand that referring to sex as a form of 'work' does not imply that wives do not often, or even usually, enjoy it or that by having sex they are simply submitting to the will of another. Christine Delphy and Diana Leonard point out that pleasure and work are hardly mutually exclusive; nor, of course, are work and free will. 'After all, most people could be said to enter paid employment willingly within our society, and some get considerable pleasure out of it.' Unpaid work, whether around the house or garden or in the bedroom, is no different, they argue.[15]

Observers who use the word 'work' to describe the strategies used to manage a couple's sexual relationship might in an earlier era have simply referred to a wife's 'duty' to have sex with her husband or, conversely, to his 'conjugal rights' to have sex with his wife. Indeed, it is difficult to get one's head around the notion that 'wife rape' was legal in the UK until 1991. Prior to this, note husband and wife researchers Sally and Rudi Dallos, the marriage contract was seen as binding on women to provide sexual gratification to their partners. Refusal to do so was a breach of that contract, pure and simple. Under such circumstances, a husband's resort to physical force was regarded as a legitimate measure.[16] By contrast, British wives who have sought divorce on the grounds of their husbands' loss of interest in sex have been laughed out of court on the grounds that such behaviour is 'not unreasonable'.[17]

No one seriously entertains the notion of 'wifely duty' anymore. Or do they? Many observers—a category which emphatically includes wives—would argue that while our language and our frames of reference have changed, our expectations about marital sexuality remain, to use Susie Orbach's vivid metaphor, 'strangely stuck in the most appalling groove'.[18] The traditional view saw a wife's sexual withdrawal as a breach of contract. Today, we say there is something wrong with her, or she is 'abnormal'. Nevertheless, what researchers call 'sexual reluctance' appears to be almost as rife among today's wives as it was for our grandmothers, lying there 'thinking of England', or its moral equivalent. The resulting guilt for women is probably even worse.

Sexual reluctance ranges from 'being somewhat uninterested' and 'complying but not enjoying it' to 'complaining afterwards' and 'making no effort to be "attractive to the partner"'.[19] Despite the politically incorrect overtones, sexual reluctance—whether in marriage or outside of it—is not an affliction that appears to affect many men. Well, why should it? As many commentators have observed, it is a long-standing marital tradition that sex occurs according to the husband's erotic schedule, and in response to his perceived sexual needs. Although men and women have always had difficulty in decoding one another's sexual signals, notes Pepper Schwartz, the dilemma has traditionally been resolved 'by men doing what they want and women adapting'.[20] Schwartz argues that our notions of eroticism are so tied up with hierarchy and differences in power and status that the idea of 'peer sexuality' is highly problematic. Translating the idea into reality is even more difficult.

Few observers have gone as far as Andrea Dworkin, the radical lesbian separatist who infamously insisted that heterosexual intercourse is by its very nature oppressive to women and has no place in an egalitarian relationship. Yet there is no denying that in our ruling erotic narratives—from Mills & Boon up—it's the *differences* between lovers that kindle their appetites, whether those differences are to do with power, status, education, age, sexual experience or even height. But it's not just difference that matters. If it were, we would be reading trashy novels about tall, greying female CEOs who spot a 'certain something' about their under-educated but plucky accounting clerks. No, the kind of difference that we find sexy has the man securely positioned 'on top', the dominant or alpha animal. 'The woman can say yes or no,' writes Schwartz, 'be strong in her tastes and willingness to give her body or her mind, but she is ultimately responsive rather than aggressive.'[21] Perhaps even more troubling, this dynamic is a turn-on not only for men, but also for their female partners.

In a study of what men and women 'really' want out of sex, UK-based researchers found that although women valued tenderness and sensitivity, they still 'wanted a man to be a man', not a 'wimp'. Specifically, wives told researchers that they wanted their husbands to be 'dominating, but in a gentle sort of way'! Husbands, for their part, placed almost as tall an order. They wanted their wives to take more initiative in sex, but dreaded the prospect of female partners 'taking over'.[22] Is it any wonder US sociologist Lillian Rubin, author of *Erotic Wars*, deduced in exasperation that the ideal sexual partner for the average male is 'a sexually experienced virgin'?[23] It's no wonder, either, that surveys repeatedly show how married people commonly resort to solitary masturbation.

When you stop to think about it, sexual frustration of one kind or another is almost inevitable in a long-term relationship. Tellingly, many of us never do stop to think about it before we get married. Once committed, and particularly once past the thirty-month 'itch' stage, sexual problems often hit both members of the couple as a nasty bolt from the blue. And there is no doubt that men and women both are capable of using sex within marriage to achieve their own aims. One wife interviewed by Duncombe and Marsden openly admitted she found sex with her husband 'distasteful' and had even moved bedrooms to escape his advances. Yet 'she still allowed him sex when she wanted a new dress or a day out'.[24] This study was conducted in the 1990s, not the 1950s. I know another woman—who happens to earn enough money to change dresses hourly, if she feels like it—who rewards her husband with a blow job for remembering to take the garbage out. 'I don't make value judgments,' she comments wryly. 'But I can tell you: it works.' A male informant complained to researchers that his wife sometimes refused point blank when 'I just want her to let me put it in and do it'. 'It would be no skin off her nose,' he sniffed. 'Sex is *part* of marriage,' this husband insisted, 'and I can't see that anything's changed enough to alter that.'[25] We can make fun of such attitudes if we like. But the fact remains that what this man says is true. Sex *is* part of marriage, and women still feel pressure to put out, or shut up.

There is considerable evidence that the pressure on married women to 'perform' sexually may be greater today than ever. The 'new' sexual contract to which we are all now supposed to subscribe sees male and female erotic desires and entitlements as equal. In reality, however, that contract rarely extends beyond the life of the courtship. Duncombe and Marsden comment that 'it seems to be only relatively briefly (before marriage!) that the "new" man is prepared to do sex work for his partner'.[26] Almost all of us now believe that women, whether married or not, have at long last gained 'permission' to be sexual creatures. Yet for many married women, this gain translates into yet another obligation: a sort of imperative to be sexually assertive and orgasmic whether one really feels like it or not. Sally and Rudi Dallos cite the case of 'Wanda', an informant who routinely initiated sex with her husband for exactly the same reason her grandmother may have passively submitted to sex with hers: because she thought she owed it to him. 'I'd initiated it,' Wanda explained, 'but the reason was that I would not get any back-lash…so it was not the right reason…if I initiated I'd have this sinking feeling that it was not what I wanted but I better had.' Afterwards, Wanda reported feeling not so much satisfaction as sheer relief. 'Once I had done it…it was phew…that's all right for a few weeks.'[27]

Another study participant explained her sense of obligation to her husband—even down to having, or faking, an orgasm 'for his sake'—this way: 'women are responsible for what the man enjoys and it is important for the woman to enjoy it because that means the man enjoys it more. If the woman's not enjoying it, that's not fair for the man because that means he can't enjoy it.'[28] The idea of enforced enjoyment ('I'll have fun for your sake, darling') has decidedly Huxleyan overtones. It amounts to a kind of 'be spontaneous' paradox, in which the wife feels obliged to drum up a sexual eagerness she may rarely (if ever) feel. If the current research is to be believed, the familiar problem of 'faking orgasm' has been transmuted into something more subtle and twisted. This involves not just acting a part in someone else's sexual drama but doing what Duncombe and Marsden call 'deep acting': a form of self-delusion in which one convinces herself—albeit usually only temporarily—that she is actually feeling whatever it is she is 'supposed' to. A common pattern involves women 'deep acting' at the start of a relationship, as a way of dispelling doubts about sexual compatibility. Later, however, they may 'rewrite the narrative to acknowledge that they always knew "at some level" that something was wrong'.[29]

In other cases, such knowledge is right on the surface. 'Maryann', an informant in one large-scale study of marital sexuality, had no illusions about her participation in oral sex with her husband. It was, to use her exact words, 'a chore'. 'He takes a long time to come, and my jaw is always aching, which makes the whole thing more like work than anything else,' Maryann confided to researchers. 'It's real important to him, so I do it,' she added, 'but it's not something I really enjoy. I think the alienating part of this is that I don't think he notices that I'm not comfortable.'[30] So much for the sexual revolution 'empowering' women in marriage—dutifully fellating one's husband, RSI of the jaw notwithstanding.

Having said all that, I would like to add that there are of course as many men in marriage performing sex work on behalf of their wives as vice versa. I would like to, but I can't. Although I'm told cunnilingus can be an equal pain in the jaw, the evidence is abundant that the balance of power in marital sexuality remains disproportionately weighted towards the gratification of male desires. It's not that husbands never need to 'work' at having sex with their wives; probably all do at some time or other. For wives, however, the obligation appears to be a much heavier one, and the pay-off a good deal less...satisfactory. Researchers have observed that it is 'surprisingly common for women to "confess" that they had always at some level found their sexual relationships [with their husbands] unfulfilling'.[31]

A generation or two ago, it was considered outré to acknowledge that female sexual desire existed at all, let alone to suggest that it was of equal magnitude or importance to that of males. Yet even a cursory look at the history of western sexuality confirms how recent, and culturally aberrant, such a view is. In other times and places, the intense power of female sexuality has been feared, or revered—often simultaneously. We are now used to congratulating ourselves on our sexual savvy, and in some respects, we are entirely justified. It was, after all, an alarmingly short time ago that Masters and Johnson 'rediscovered' the clitoris—stating definitively to a dumbfounded American readership that they could find no evidence whatsoever for something called a 'vaginal orgasm'. I was in high school then and I'd never even *heard* of a clitoris. (Nor, I venture to say, had my mother.) Remember the joke in Woody Allen's *Annie Hall* about the woman who had an orgasm but was told by her therapist it was 'the wrong kind'? Anybody under the age of forty wouldn't get that joke today—and in many ways that's a relief, I think. Today's men (and women) are so much more knowledgeable about female sexuality. How successfully, or willingly even, we translate that knowledge into action is very much open to question.

A generation ago, husbands might not even have tried to arouse their wives. Even the so-called 'sexologists' of a few decades ago—the ones who took it upon themselves to teach couples how to do it—were astonishingly male-centred in their approach. In the 1970s, Alex Comfort's hugely best-selling *The Joy of Sex*, for example, became the Bible for a whole generation of 'adventurous' married couples. Yet Comfort's focus on male sexuality was relentless. He was forever admonishing readers to consider 'what the male turn-on equipment requires'. It was as if the female 'turn-on equipment' somehow didn't count, or maybe didn't even exist. English psychologist and sex therapist Paul Brown recalls with appropriate horror some of the 'good advice' he and his colleagues were giving clients in the 1960s—like prescribing copious amounts of lubricant to combat vaginal 'dryness'. Eventually, Brown reports, 'we understood that to ask a woman to use cream to aid penetration when there was no excitement, and hence no lubrication…was much the same as asking a man to tie a splint to his penis if there was no erection'.[32] It would be interesting to know exactly how widespread Brown's insight has become today, among the 'lay community'—if you'll forgive the expression—in most marriages. I suspect it would still sound pretty radical.

The literature on marital sexuality is laden with complaints about the perceived perfunctory nature of men's attempts to 'stimulate' their wives. One woman complained of her husband, for example, that 'It was like he knew there had to be foreplay so—a couple of squeezes up here, then a quick rummage about down there and straight in'.[33] The perception that women don't care a great deal about sex anyway (so why go to too much trouble?) appears to be common in many marriages. It's an attitude not wholly lacking in foundation. There is some evidence to suggest it may be entirely justified in more cases than either gender would care to admit.

However politically incorrect it may be to acknowledge it, the study of 'sexual reluctance' in marriage clearly indicates that a lack of interest in sex is much more likely to be a girl thing. And I suspect that even those who have never had the dubious privilege of reading the literature will fail to be surprised by that. Women who spent most of their single lives running after sex often find that they spend a good deal of their married life trying hard to avoid it. Of course, the evidence shows that it is couples—men and women both—who have less and less sex as the marriage matures. Obviously, it would have to. But one can't help wondering how much of this is attributable to wives' reluctance in spite of the continuing high level of interest by husbands. Doubtless, we will never know for sure. Depending on which discipline you happen to consult, the notion that men are more highly sexed than women will either be derided or justified. Psychologists, in particular feminist psychologists, are nowadays very much in the former camp, as are cultural critics who see the myth of insatiable male sexuality as simply another 'discourse' that entrenches gender stereotypes.

One psychologist, for example, refers with deliberate cynicism to something she calls MSDD, or Male Sexual Drive Discourse: the belief that men 'will always feel like "it" whatever the circumstances; that women, not men, are likely to refuse'.[34] Or, to put it in the language of folk wisdom, 'marriage is the price a man pays for sex; sex is the price a woman pays for marriage'.[35] Females, the argument goes, are more likely to engage in a 'have/hold' discourse—a relational, rather than a biological, take on sex that sees emotional intimacy as pre-eminent. The suggestion, of course, is that neither of these 'discourses' actually bears much relationship to reality—or, more subtly, that they represent only a small and selected slice of reality.

The perspective of sociobiology, by contrast, views the same behaviours through a different prism. Male sexual marauding has been explained as an evolutionary imperative to sow as many seeds as possible, whenever possible, with whomever possible. Female sexual behaviour—which is seen as more discriminating and more 'naturally monogamous'—is similarly regarded as a case of production for use. Women are more relational and nurturing because they have been built that way, because mothering requires it, and mothering is what being female is ultimately about. Such views have been widely, and often justifiably, criticised for constructing female sexuality as somehow biologically passive, and therefore inferior, to that of males. Correcting biases is one thing. Throwing the baby out with the bathwater (pun gravely intended) is quite another. Natalie Angier's *Woman*, for instance, is a typical example of a concerned feminist at great pains to refute such politically offensive sociobiological wisdom. For Angier, who calls evolutionary psychology 'a cranky and despotic Cyclops, its single eye glaring through an overwhelmingly masculinist lens', it appears to be an article of faith that males and females have been created sexually not just equal but indistinguishable—and any evidence that tends to refute it is either ignored, misread or derided. (Women don't 'really' find older men attractive, she argues. Why? Because we all know baldness is not sexy.[36])

For me, the notion that males and females are equally sexually *strategic*, each pursuing with equal vigour, cunning and ferocity his or her particular reproductive game, has been an important corrective of bias on both sides of the gender equation. What's more, it allows us to see male and female sexuality as highly differentiated at the same time as we acknowledge them to be equally central to the joint business of perpetuating the species. It is entirely glib, not to mention documentably untrue, to say that females are 'monogamous' and males are not. Indeed, evolutionary psychologists are now positing that it is females, not males, who develop the itch that leads to the break-up of potentially long-term relationships. According to Dr Helen Fisher of Rutgers University's Center for Evolutionary Studies, human females may have a biological predisposition to stay with a male mate only as long as it takes for a child born of their union to survive on its own. Fisher bases her theory on the interesting cross-cultural finding that the incidence of divorce reaches a peak during the fourth year of marriage and that, as we have already observed, up to three-quarters of divorces are initiated by women.[37]

Is it really necessary, I wonder, to keep insisting that there are 'in fact' no differences at all between male and female sexuality? That men only *seem* like they come from another planet, sexually speaking? That women only *think* they need less sex, and more intimacy? In 1985, in her pre-*Woman* incarnation as a feature writer for *Time* magazine, Natalie Angier herself wrote a lively little piece titled 'Finding Trouble in Paradise: Do Women Really Prefer Cuddling Over "The Act"?' which concluded that yes, as a matter of fact, they do. The article is a report on a 'massive survey' conducted by the most widely syndicated columnist in the US which found that 'almost three-quarters of the women in America would happily give up sexual intercourse for a little tenderness'. The real shocker was that four in ten of these wannabe celibates were under the age of forty. 'Women have had access to the Pill for nearly 30 years,' wrote Angier, 'and many now unabashedly woo reluctant dates with phone calls and American Express gold cards. But they are still not sure what to make of sex.'[38] Well, that was putting it mildly, under the circumstances. The women who responded to this poll—a self-selected sample, to be sure—seemed to know exactly what to make of sex: namely, a whole lot less than their male partners.

Sally and Rudi Dallos are convinced that women's well-documented sexual reluctance has less to do with biology than it does with politics. Specifically, the Dalloses argue that women in highly unequal relationships—which, by their reckoning, includes almost all marriages—use sex as a kind of bargaining chip in an ill-fated and largely unconscious attempt to even up the score.

'Either as a deliberate tactic or otherwise,' they maintain, '"going off sex" appears to be clearly related to inequality of power' in the relationship. In the couples they studied, the dynamic was especially evident in cases where wives were financially dependent on their husbands. They also noted a striking correlation between sexual reluctance and 'an unequal distribution of domestic and child-rearing tasks, often associated with women attempting to persuade men into sharing these tasks more equitably but failing to succeed'.[39] The Dalloses see these 'associations' as causally linked; that is, they believe the awkward lack of fit between His interest in sex and Hers is the *result* of other inequalities, not a further expression of them. Their data show that where wives are financially independent—at least theoretically—a couple's sex life seems to be less skewed. They measured this empirically, in case you were wondering, by asking couples about who initiates what, and how often, and who holds the power of veto, and how frequently they exercise it.

They did not, however, look at the impact of women's earnings on other areas of inequality—an omission which hardly inspires confidence in their hypothesis.

On the other hand, it would be rather strange if sexuality were exempt from the assumptions that underlie marriage in every other respect. In all likelihood, more equal relationships would be more equal in this respect as well: with women doing less 'acting', more genuine initiating and presumably saying 'no' less frequently. To me, all this stands to reason. And yet I can't help wondering, as I ponder the research, whether it doesn't tend to perpetuate the same 'masculinist' bias it's supposedly meant to efface. Almost every study I've read, including every feminist study, takes male sexuality as the baseline of erotic behaviour within marriage. Why, even the term 'sexual reluctance' itself reflects this unconscious bias—definitively locating the problem as belonging to women. I have certainly never read a study that set out to solve the issue of male 'sexual pushiness' in marriage, or heard of a sex therapist who strives to dampen down a man's libido to harmonise more naturally with his wife's. Maybe, just maybe, the libido of all those women out there is not 'depressed' at all—but simply struggling to keep pace with what may turn out to be the more naturally, well, *wired* sexuality of their husbands.

Feminists like Natalie Angier take enormous pride in showing the world that, for example, the sexual adventurousness of female chim-panzees is every bit as staggering as anything their boyfriends can dish out. But, speaking personally for a moment, I resent being lectured to by *anybody*—female or male, fascist or feminist—about what I ought to be feeling in order to qualify as a card-carrying 'natural woman'. My own theory, which I admit to be utterly unsubstantiated by any data beyond my immediate acquaintance, is that it is perfectly natural and entirely appropriate that a woman's interest in sex should abate after the birth of her children. From an evolutionary standpoint, it seems to me it would be quite bizarre if this were *not* the case. Women are fecund for a very brief time, compared to men, who can theoretically continue to inseminate to the grave. It's just possible that the reason men consistently appear to be more interested in sex over the life of a relationship, is that they are.

A friend of mine mentioned to her live-in partner recently that, prior to meeting him she had been celibate for three years. He laughed. She asked why. 'It turned out he simply assumed I'd been joking—which also explained why he'd forgotten that I'd told him all this ages ago,' she told me. 'When I assured him I was serious, he looked so horrified it was my turn to laugh. "Now wait a minute," I told him. "You know how bad my marriage was. You know I had two preschoolers. Come on. Who had time to have sex? Who had time to think about having sex?" Well, he was quiet for a moment, and I figured I'd finally got through to him. And then he said, with total conviction, "I would."'

To paraphrase Will Rogers, all I know is what my girlfriends tell me. And what they tell me is that this experience is not that aberrant. And maybe even that it's perfectly normal. Perhaps women's sexuality—at least some women's sexuality—is more like a tap than a raging current, a force that can be turned on and turned off. Perhaps not exactly at will, but with greater ease than the so-called masculinist discourse of 'human' sexuality would have us believe.

To be perfectly honest, having come of age at the height of the sexual revolution, I believed for decades that the fact that I'd never had a casual sexual encounter was a kind of character flaw, almost shameful evidence that my soul was insufficiently advanced. With age, I've become less and less inclined towards self-flagellation and more and more cynical about the necessity to conform to anybody's expectations, however 'nonconformist'. For me, sex has never had meaning outside of a committed, loving relationship. And, even within a committed, loving relationship, I experience sex as pleasurable and even at times profound—but, once past the thirty-month itch stage, very rarely if ever as an urgent necessity. I have a hunch there are a lot of women in a lot of marriages who feel the same way. I'm sure there are men who do also. But I'd stake my life that they are pitifully outnumbered.

In an important sense, the 'real' answer to the riddle of human sexuality is irrelevant. Whether a reflection of our deepest nature, or a shadow cast by culture, the unequal division of sex work within marriage is an empirical fact. Perhaps your own marriage is exempt. But for the majority of couples today, sexuality remains yet another aspect of post-feminist married life still characterised by asymmetry and imbalance. Does this mean sex within marriage is normally a battlefield, fraught with ill-feeling, resentment and disgust? Of course not. Sex may be a form of 'work' for wives, but it is work women often enjoy immensely. As to the question of whether, on the whole, they enjoy it as much as their husbands do—to be honest, the answer is probably no, not really. After all, as the statistics on marital satisfaction make abundantly clear, married women enjoy almost everything about marriage less than married men do. Why should sex be any different?

chapter 14

excuses, excuses:
why wifework persists

'I wouldn't let him do it, he's a man, he'd wreck it.'
informant to researcher Ken Dempsey

Internationally acclaimed family psychologist Judith Wallerstein tells the story of inviting a group of female colleagues to participate in a study of 'long lasting marriages that are genuinely satisfying for both husband and wife'. The words were no sooner out of her mouth, Wallerstein recalls, than 'the room exploded with laughter'.[1] She remembers feeling disturbed and puzzled by this response. Yet it's hard to believe that a marital researcher of such long standing could have been surprised by it.

The charge that contemporary marriage is a raw deal for women may sound dissident. But recent research shows that, in their own quiet way, a surprising proportion of contemporary men and women already believe it. According to Australian sociologist Ken Dempsey, who has spent his professional career studying marital equality, many men and most women see marriage as offering a better deal to men.[2] Young women, evidently, are the most cynical of all about what you might call their marriage prospects. Research published by the Australian Institute of Family Studies found that only 11 per cent of twenty-something women agreed with the statement 'married people are happier than single people'.[3]

A 1999 report commissioned by the Economic and Social Research

Council at the University of Kent has predicted that by the year 2010 'millions of women will choose to live alone, unfettered by the demands of a husband and children, instead enjoying a fulfilling social life and realising their ambitions both professionally and personally'. According to the report's author, Richard Scase, a visiting professor at the university, there is 'growing segregation between the lives of single men and women'. 'The hard truth,' says Scase, 'seems to be that living alone is good for women, but bad for men.'[4]

Of course, some married people really are happier than their single counterparts—and most of them are male. Yet it would be misleading and just plain inaccurate to suggest that marriage is not a highly constraining institution for males. The very real limitations to a man's freedom marriage imposes, especially his sexual and economic freedom, are beyond dispute. They are what the cultural iconography of the 'commitment-phobic' male is all about—or the complaints of his older brother about the 'ball and chain' or 'trouble and strife'. There is not the slightest doubt that marriage can be exceedingly hard work for men too. But, on the whole, the nature of that work is different, both in degree and kind. The work of husbands, in other words, while arguably complementing the work of wives, in no way parallels it.

By tradition, the work of husbands in marriage has been identified almost exclusively with 'breadwinning'. A husband is someone who 'provides for' his wife and children; whose 'sun to sun' dedication to paid employment provides the economic substrate without which family life would be unliveable. It's important, however, to adopt an historical perspective about what is 'traditional'. Conditioned by the relentlessly present-centred bias of our media, our view of history has become perilously foreshortened. We think of that far country, 'the past', as consisting of the generation or two before our own. In fact, in almost every time and place except our own, the productive labour of two—not one—adults has been necessary to sustain family life. In a pre-industrial society, bread is not 'won' at all. Its elements are planted and grown, harvested and processed, and then mixed and kneaded and baked—none of which could be accomplished without the co-operative, joint labour of two pairs of adult hands (and often several little pairs as well).

There is no society in the world, nor is there any evidence to suggest that there has ever been one, in which male and female labour has not been highly differentiated. Wives have always done one set of jobs, and husbands another. But to suggest—as people, including 'experts', often do—that women's work has been traditionally limited to the reproductive sphere and men's to the economic is wrong. Looked at from a broad historical perspective, females have typically assumed *primary* responsibility for feeding their families, generally through agriculture rather than hunting. Men's contributions may have been more highly valued—meat having greater prestige value than vegetables—but it was the herbivorous food supplied by females that formed the staple diet.

Industrialisation changed all that, to the point that the home ceased to function as a site of what economists call 'primary production', except of offspring. It was not 'human nature' but rather the demands of waged work that created the sharp split between economic and reproductive responsibilities that we have come, erroneously, to call 'traditional'. The imperative to go out to work—not to the barnyard, or a neighbouring field, but all the way to a factory or shopfloor—redefined first motherhood, and then wifehood itself, as economically unproductive activity. You can raise kids on a farm alongside the grain and potatoes, but you can't raise them on an assembly-line. *Somebody* had to stay home, and an avalanche of biological and social factors ensured that this somebody would be the wife. Heaven knows, the industrial revolution did not create the concept of male dominance, nor the associated notion that servicing male needs is a primary duty of females. But it did skew the balance of power in marriage in new and more drastic ways: increasing the already considerable biological dependence of females, and concentrating economic resources in male hands.

In many ways, these developments have proved disastrous for

everybody. For women, the resulting disempowerment—there is no female equivalent of the term 'emasculation'—would eventually culminate in the short-lived mid-twentieth-century ideal of the Happy Homemaker. For men, the result was a cardboard cut-out construction of masculinity that reduced the husband's role to a middle-class John who paid out for sex, children, and assorted other domestic products and services: a character often treated as a 'walking wallet' because that's exactly how he acted. Ironically, it is that eye blink of human history— that anomalous moment balanced between the Industrial Age behind and the Information Age ahead—which we call 'tradition'! Yet, in another sense, we have every right to do so. For these were our traditions. The traditions of our century, our culture, our own childhoods.

The situation we face today—with males and females contributing jointly to the economic support of their families—feels more radical than it is. In fact, in important ways, this kind of family structure is as 'traditional' as it's possible to get. It is our own families of origin that are aberrant. Having said that, there are important respects in which the structures underlying our marriages today are not entirely different from those we grew up with. 'Breadwinning', for instance. Despite all the changes of the last fifty years, in the majority of middle-class families today, including dual-earner families, the husband remains the more highly paid partner. Despite their high participation rate in the US labour force, only 25 per cent of married women in America earn more than their husbands. Overall, working wives contribute 30 per cent of family income in the US. Where wives work full-time, an ever-more-common scenario, the average ratio of male:female earnings is about 60:40. Research by the UK Office for National Statistics in 1999 showed that the average full-time male worker was earning £23,412 annually, compared with a female average of £16,481—a difference of 30 per cent.[5]

This difference may seem slight, but if the social construction of gender can teach us anything, it's that little things mean a lot. Any advantage by either party, however minimal, will tend to be exploited and overelaborated to the max. We have already observed the operation of this principle with regard to biological advantage. Well, as in biology, so in the social sphere. In our society, males remain not just slightly but quite significantly more likely to earn a higher salary than females. Despite our laws governing 'equal pay for equal work', the pink-collar ghetto is alive and well, and 'women's work' continues to be systematically undervalued in occupations ranging from hairdresser and child carer (vis-a-vis, say, mechanic or plumber) to teaching, the 'caring professions' and the wide range of people-skill occupations in areas like human resource management, marketing and tourism and hospitality. Even in professions where women have made impressive inroads, such as medicine and law, females continue to dominate the ranks of the 'unspecialised' and command proportionally 'unspecial' salaries.

Without getting into the multitudinous reasons why one female dollar still buys only about seventy-five cents in 'real' currency, the fact of the matter is that economic inequality remains at the core of today's marriages. The gap has narrowed enormously over a short period of time. But narrowing is one thing, and closing is another. Today, the specialist physician (male) will be married to a GP instead of a nurse. (A friend's husband is a psychiatrist, and if I cited the number of his colleagues who are married to psychologists you would think I was making it up to prove a point.) CEOs are these days more likely to wed their vice-presidents than their PAs, and publishers to marry executive editors than executive secretaries. In relative economic terms, in other words, husbands are still very much the household gods of marriage. Hypergamy, the 'Iron Law of Marriageability' that sees women marrying up the socio-economic scale—and men inevitably marrying beneath them—has not been abolished, only adjusted.

The question of how much money matters within the broader politics of marriage is more complicated than it looks. One recent Australian study found that the average salary of employed wives was only slightly more than half that of their husbands. The author speculated that this disparity—especially in combination with the presence of dependent children—'may have encouraged many of them to be grateful for the material contribution of husbands and to view an unjust division of labour as fair'.[6] The link between women's access to paid work and spiralling divorce rates is well established. Women who would formerly have had no choice between staying in a bad marriage on the one hand and penury on the other have been liberated indeed by their economic power, relative though their gains may be. This is a fact frequently forgotten by people who marvel at the apparent 'success' of arranged marriages—as if wives in societies that practise such marriages actually had a choice in the matter. My own mother, who has been married to my father for some forty years ('We met in the nursery of the maternity ward,' my Dad jokes), admits candidly that economic realities played an important role in getting them through the tough times. 'There were so many times I would have left,' she told me recently, 'if only I'd had a financial alternative.' She didn't, she stayed, and today they seem more in love than ever.

Today, thankfully, that kind of financial dependence is uncommon. Yet the skewing of financial resources is not. For the 50 to 60 per cent of couples who choose *not* to divorce, how, if at all, does this impact on the relationship, and specifically on the distribution of power and privilege? By way of answer, I'll tell you a true story from my first marriage. Shortly after we had both finished our doctoral degrees, we moved from New York to Perth, Western Australia, where my husband had been offered a job. I didn't have any difficulty finding employment as a casual tutor, but full-time work in my field proved dismayingly elusive. After several months of renting, we talked about the possibility of buying a house. I was very much in favour; he was less keen. Ultimately, as in so many other areas of common life, I found myself capitulating. A few days later, still fuming, I decided to confront him. 'Now wait a minute. Why is it that, whenever we have a difference of opinion about how to spend money, your say is always final?'

'Easy,' he replied. 'Because I earn most of it.'

It was baldly put, but it was also hard to refute. I thought for a moment. 'OK, I can accept that,' I told him. 'But if the day ever comes when I earn more than you do, I'm the one who's going to be calling the shots, you know.'

'Fair enough,' he replied.

Well, the day did come, of course, and a lot quicker than either of us anticipated—only a year or so later. The turning point had not even been remarked upon—it was only a matter of a couple of thousand dollars anyway—until the next time we found ourselves grappling over the issue of home ownership. 'Well, I'm the one who's earning more money now,' I reminded him triumphantly, 'So I guess what I say goes.'

'Don't be ridiculous,' he replied. 'Surely we're not *that* crass.'

In disbelief, I reminded him of our discussion of a year ago.

He laughed. 'Don't take everything so literally,' he advised. 'After all, this a marriage, not a traffic court.'

I never said it was going to be a subtle story, but it is a true one. And it illustrates just about as well as anything the role of economics in determining who holds the balance of marital power. Where husbands retain economic dominance, money remains a pretext on which we justify other forms of inequality. Where husbands do not, we find another pretext. The distribution of economic resources in marriage, in other words, may be an important factor in power allocation—and therefore in the maintenance of the service mentality which is the foundation of wifework—but there is surprisingly little evidence to suggest that it is the critical or most decisive factor.

The fact is, women serve men in marriage, and women and men both acknowledge the husband to be 'head of the household' regardless of who earns what relative to whom. When in 1999 marital studies expert Susan Rosenbluth and colleagues asked couples what they believed to be the 'essential aspects of marital equality', neither males nor females mentioned earnings at all.[7] Sociologist Veronica Jaris Tichenor studied decision-making patterns among couples in which wives were the top earners, worked in higher-prestige occupations, or both. To her surprise, she found that the balance of decision-making power in such couples rested exactly where it does in others: with the husband. What's more, these 'status-reversal' couples usually found that the occupational power gap created difficulties in the marriage, and much energy was expended trying to disguise, minimise or deny it.[8]

Indeed, it is almost a given in the literature that 'wife independence'—far from heralding a new era of marital democratisation—merely increases the relationship's instability. Sociologist Hiromi Ono predicts matter of factly that 'when wives control more resources, marital dissolution should increase in part because the level of wives' economic independence from their husbands also increases'—a startlingly cynical point of view which assumes that women will only remain within marriage if they have to. Needless to say, we do not often encounter the reverse argument: that the economic independence of *men* weakens marital stability. On the contrary, this form of inequality is so taken for granted in the literature it is rarely remarked upon. Consider, for example, the observation by Ono that 'as young women enter marriage with a higher level of career investment and commitment, they and their spouses may have difficulty escaping the problems of status inconsistency and conflicting career demands within marriage'.[9] Try that sentence replacing 'young women' with 'young men' and you'll see how euphemistic terms like 'status inconsistency' and 'conflicting career demands' really are. The issue is not inequality or inconsistency at all; it's inequality or inconsistency that goes against the prevailing grain of male privilege.

Nevertheless, the substance of these observations is as unassailable as it is dispiriting. The research shows clearly that wives who earn more than their husbands really are a risk factor for divorce. And so are wives who are more highly educated. Even controlling for all other variables, the higher the wife's educational level at first marriage, the greater the

risk of marital dissolution. (The problem, according to one commen-
tator, is that educational attainments increase the 'opportunity costs' in
becoming in housewife!) For husbands, it's just the opposite. Research
across a wide spectrum shows that when the economic performance of
husbands improves, as measured by higher real income, marital dissolution decreases.[10] Although it strains credulity, a number of observers
have attempted to 'explain' this finding by pointing to the couple's
enhanced capacity 'to purchase stress-reducing goods and services' that
'may improve the family's lifestyle'—as if a husband's earnings had
purchase power, and a wife's didn't![11]

Study after study has shown that economic clout may consolidate a
husband's power base, but it does not create it. A woman's economic
clout can and usually does create problems in a marriage by eroding or
at least threatening that power base. But in and of itself, her financial
contribution is highly unlikely to dismantle it outright. One interesting
study looked at the marriages of pre- and post-retirement couples in an
effort to determine the relationship between husband's earnings and his
perceived power in the relationship. Contrary to researcher's expectations, there were no differences at all in the two groups.[12] Sociologist
Pat O'Connor looked at marital power and its relationship to economics
from a different perspective. Would wives who were financially dependent on their husbands perceive themselves to be 'powerless' in the
relationship? she wondered. The answer was that a third did—but two-
thirds did not.[13] Clearly, there is some link between money and power
in marriage. It's just a lot weaker than many of us—including most feminists and virtually all Marxists—once thought.

Power relations in marriage seem to be mediated more strongly by
what sociologists call 'norms regarding gender roles' than they are
by crude dollars and cents. Israeli sociologist Liat Kulik cites extensive
cross-cultural evidence that where patriarchal values are strongly held,
the impact of resources on marital power is limited. 'In these social
contexts,' writes Kulik, 'the wife is expected to accept her husband's

decisions even when she possesses considerable resources'.[14]

Where more egalitarian views are held, however, one should expect something of a market economy effect between resources and power in marriage—a freer and fairer rate of exchange. Janice Steil's study of dual-income earner couples provided some support for this notion—but only among married couples who were childless. Reports Steil, 'The more a woman without children earned relative to her husband, the less responsibility she had for the house and the greater her say in marital decisions.' But for married women with children, Steil found no such effect. Relative to their husband's earnings, the financial contributions made by these women 'were unrelated to any of the responsibility or influence variables' the study examined.[15] Looking at her results overall, Steil concluded that 'how much one earned was unrelated to the amount of influence one had'. The single most important predictor of marital power in her study was 'perceived career importance'. Wives consistently rated their husbands' careers as more important than their own. Needless to say, such findings in no way 'explain' the phenomenon of husband dominance. On the contrary, they simply provide further evidence that it exists.

In one typical study, for example, it was found that husbands who earned more than wives rated their own careers as more important; yet, where wives' income was higher, *neither* partner rated her career as more important.[16] Predictably enough, this business of 'career importance' became a pressing issue in my first marriage, at the point I started earning more. My career as an academic was dismissed as 'just teaching'. I found this patronising. But to be honest I didn't fundamentally disagree with it, or at least not openly. His was the 'real' job. In my second marriage, my paid work—which had dwindled to part-time after the birth of my children—was downgraded still further. My husband consistently referred to my research as 'your hobby'.

The surprisingly weak relationship between earnings and power is one of the most grievous disappointments of end-of-the-century feminism. Equal opportunity for women in the workplace was supposed to change everything. It hasn't. 'Everything'—most emphatically including the construction of gender roles within marriage—has proved to be almost nightmarishly resilient. The 'Revolving Door Model' of social change, with its commonsensical assumption that, as women took on more paid work, men would compensate by taking on more unpaid work, and wifework as we know it would cease to exist, has been thoroughly discredited by study after study. Yet it is one of those comforting myths that we seem unable to renounce, a kind of theoretical transitional object, like a teddy bear or a scrap of blanket we cling to in the darkness. The mantras we repeat to ourselves today—that 'social change happens slowly' and 'we've come a long way, really'—are the same ones our mothers and grandmothers were repeating forty, fifty, even sixty years ago.

Earning money is one thing, and it's a thing readily accomplished these days by both males and females. 'Being the provider' is another, however. Being a provider is not simply having a job, it's taking on an entire role—a role freighted with psychological meaning and, in all probability, underpinned by evolutionary imperatives. The provider role, it seems, is so central a feature of adult male identity that without it (or without at least the illusion of it) the prospects of maintaining a lifelong heterosexual relationship are exceedingly dim. If there is such a thing as 'husbandwork', in other words, this is it.

The perceptions both men and women continue to hold about the sanctity of male employment may be the real 'bottom line'—or one of them, anyway. The idea that men fulfil their obligation to the marriage, and to the family at large, through paid work—and anything else is a bonus—is still widely, if covertly, held. Israeli sociologist Orly Benjamin observes that the husband's employment continues to function as the pivot around which family relationships almost irresistibly revolve. 'Her' work is still perceived as optional, a 'choice' rather than a necessity. 'His' work, by contrast, is 'non-negotiable, it is a constraint on the family's priorities and a goal to which the family must devote all of its resources'.[17] In some ways, this dynamic becomes even more visible when a relationship breaks up.

One man I know whose wife deserted him and his two young sons was thrilled to be awarded interim custody of his children. A year later, he reluctantly ceded custody back to his ex-wife. 'Working the kind of hours I do, it just isn't possible to provide good-quality care for the boys,' he explained to his friends. It was a horribly difficult decision, but everyone was sympathetic, including his lawyers. After all, the man's career was at stake. Today, he sees that decision as the worst one he ever made. At the time, he believed he 'had no choice' but to protect the integrity of his business, and the high-profile professional identity that went along with it. He considered hiring a full-time, live-in nanny. But, by his own admission, he never considered working part-time, or finding a job that was more flexible and less demanding. Nor, it is important to note, did anybody else he knew. In time, it was the unexpected deprivations of alternate weekend parenting that forced him to re-evaluate these utterly taken-for-granted priorities. This man is now attempting to negotiate a joint custody arrangement, and today he *does* work part-time by choice, a decision that has been greeted by his mostly male colleagues with a combination of suspicion and disbelief.

It should be needless to say, but obviously isn't, that a woman who relinquished her children because they interfered with her paid work would be vilified as a monster. Yet a man can do so with the full sympathy and support of his community. We not only do not judge him; we feel sorry for him. Among the many things this tells us is that reports of the death of the 'provider role' in the contemporary family script have been greatly exaggerated. Not even divorce can wither it, nor the procrustean provisions of the Family Court.

The provider role enslaves men still. Yet, in crucial respects, it also continues to set them free. Being a provider, observes Janice Steil, continues to entitle a husband 'to put his career above his wife's, free him from a number of responsibilities at home, entitle him to a position of greater influence, and allow him to perceive the time he devotes to his paid work as an expression of family caring. Traditionally, it has also allowed husbands to feel entitled to their wives' undivided support.'[18] A woman's paid work, by contrast, continues to be seen as a potential threat to her ability to care for her family—regardless of how much pay for how little work.

It's important to recognise that we all collude in this belief, females as well as males, whether consciously or not. A number of recent studies, for example, have found that the higher a husband's salary the better he feels about himself as both a partner and a parent. The greater a woman's earnings relative to her husband's the *worse* she says she feels about herself as a wife.[19] In one study conducted in 1992 among professional dual-career couples, virtually every last participant agreed that it would be 'easier' if the wife's career was less successful than the husband's. When wives were asked to explain why, three main reasons emerged: 1) his work was more important to his sense of self; 2) she needed him to be successful, possibly to fulfil her own fantasies about how a 'real man' conducts himself; and 3) she feared she'd be blamed if he *wasn't* successful![20]

Another bewildering aspect of the problem is that—if recent sociological research is to be believed—not only most men but also most women (at least the ones who stay married, which admittedly makes for a rather slim majority) appear to like it this way. Or so they tell researchers. Ken Dempsey, who has conducted extensive research on married women's perceptions of fairness, believes that 'probably only a small minority of women have been pressing their husbands for substantial change'.[21] This is not the same as saying that women don't desire change, or that they don't complain privately about the lack of change. But it's still an intriguing finding—or a totally outrageous one.

Although it is a possibility rarely canvassed by sociologists, I suspect one reason for wives' puzzling acquiescence has to do with the utterly rational (albeit politically incorrect) judgment that a flawed relationship is better than no relationship at all—and that no relationship at all may be precisely what a wife will be left with after 'pressing her husband for substantial change'. As Dempsey has observed, 'Women may set aside their egalitarian ideals if pursuing these ideals puts at risk other outcomes from their marriage that they value more highly'—like peace, for example.[22] Although I am not aware of any academic research on this, my own acquaintance (not to mention my own life!) is full of examples of women who start off marriage fighting the good fight, and end up beating their swords into ploughshares, or, more commonly, into perambulators. The challenges and rewards of motherhood are in some respects a compensation for the disappointments of marriage—and in other ways a distraction from them. The transition to parenthood, as we have seen, will not necessarily draw a couple closer together. Almost inevitably it will strengthen their commitment to coupledom.

It is my (utterly untested) hypothesis that motherhood profoundly increases a woman's conservatism, encouraging her to 'play it safe' for the sake of her children in all kinds of unanticipated ways. Consider the staunch Labor voter who enrols her daughter in a snooty private school, or the feminist who regretfully but resolutely refuses her toddler son's request for pink sneakers. For me, the penny dropped the day I realised I was subtly discouraging my son's friendship with the child of a single mother. The fact that I was a single mother myself did not make this revelation any easier to accept.

A more conservative stance towards marriage itself is often part of this package. The presence of children almost inevitably raises the stakes, making compromise more acceptable and inequities easier to rationalise. Even more fundamentally, I suspect, a woman's desire to protect and nurture her young deepens even further 'the deep institutional taboo against direct confrontation' marriage traditionally imposes on wives.[23] Even if this were not the case, the presence of children provides a distraction from relationship problems—even though it also increases the gap between His marriage and Hers. Particularly in the early years of parenting, many women find they haven't the energy to devote to pressing their claims further—or even maintaining the ones they've got. It's not for nothing that the famous 'seven year itch'—a high point for divorce—coincides so beautifully with the entrance of the first child into primary school.

The question why men don't press for change within marriage has failed to attract much attention in the research community. I suppose the answer is too obvious even for academics! Men don't seek change to the status quo because the status quo has been good to them. Husbands don't actively seek more equality in marriage for the same reason that managers don't lobby for sales jobs, doctors don't aspire to become nurses, and queen bees don't facilitate workers' strikes. In no other social structure imaginable would the holders of power be expected to agitate for change. Why should marriage be any different? Of course, in cases where a man's marriage fails, he may be powerfully motivated to ponder questions of equity. There is some evidence to suggest that by a man's second or subsequent marriage he will be much more likely to give true mutuality a try. And if he does, researchers point out, he may find a number of unexpected positive outcomes—including relief from the achievement and performance anxieties associated with 'breadwinning', better intimacy and more freedom of expression and experience.[24] The irony is that equality probably *is* a better deal for men, too: psychologically, emotionally and spiritually. Unfortunately, inequality ain't bad either—and no man has to lift a finger to achieve it.

sleeping with the enemy

'What would happen if one woman told the truth
about her life? The world would split open.'
Muriel Rukeyser

Taking responsibility for abolishing wifework is also wifework. But it is wifework of a different kind altogether—a kind diametrically opposed to our normal understanding of the job description 'wife'. For, although the job of wife entails substantial responsibilities for unpaid physical labour, even more fundamental to the wifely role is labour expended in tending *relationships*. In almost all marriages, wives are the Relationship Managers, responsible not only for taking the emotional temperature of her husband (and proceeding accordingly) but for the marriage itself and for extended family relationships created by the marriage (in-laws, former spouses, stepchildren, etc.).

The role of Relationship Manager extends to extra-familial relationships as well, with wives typically responsible for organising the family's social calendar in everything from playdates to dinner parties. Wives remember and are usually responsible for commemorating birthdays, anniversaries, graduations and other special events that occur within the family and the wider social circle. They are responsible, too, for the follow-up to such events (RSVPs, thank-you cards and other forms of acknowledgment). One friend of mine, a newlywed, ran into unexpected in-law trouble when she forgot to send her husband's mother a birthday card. 'She didn't get angry at her *son* for forgetting her birthday,' she fumed. 'She got angry at *me*!' It's a familiar story. The suggestion that such work is actually *work* would, I suspect, be regarded by most men and probably many women as well as cold-blooded at best. It's one more example of wifework which is so taken for granted it is mistaken for something women 'are' rather than something they 'do'.

Filling the role of Relationship Manager is often a pleasure, sometimes a pain, and almost always a big responsibility that goes unheralded—by women as much as by men, in my experience. At a deeper level, however, the Relationship Manager role—a role most women enact so automatically it seems less a collection of learned responses than a matter of instinct or reflex—lies at the very core of our social construction of femininity. It is perhaps a woman's pre-eminent job, in other words, to maintain and mend relationships, to smooth things over when the going gets rough. The taboo against direct confrontation in marriage is an exclusively female taboo; even when it is more honoured in the breach, it remains an enormously powerful one. One result is that women who do agitate for change within their marriages—regardless of the outcome—often feel guilty and vaguely 'unfeminine'. Another consequence is that women may find it easier to leave their husbands, and keep a sense of feminine identity intact, than to confront them and risk losing that identity. This dynamic may explain why so many women talk about their marriage problems to their girlfriends, rather than to their husbands; and why so many men are gobsmacked to find their marriages exploding in their faces when 'everything seemed fine'.

At another level, the result of the taboo on direct confrontation may be the persistence of wifework itself, aka the 'stalled revolution'. Women who say what they want, and say it plainly, may work wonders in the office, but they still run the risk of wreaking havoc at home. What is applauded as an 'assertive' style of communication on the job or in the classroom becomes 'bulldozing' in the family room. Far from smoothing things over, such behaviour seems to plough them up. It does not feel like 'managing the relationship'; it feels like blowing the relationship to bits. It feels, in other words, like the antithesis of what women are in marriage *for*.

We all want to think we are beyond this. Yet studies are still being conducted that show, for example, that wives are three times more likely to ask questions of husbands than husbands are of wives, and that wives try to initiate conversation more and succeed less, while husbands try less but seldom fail.[1] Few men may openly boast that they are the kings of their castles, but husbands remain the agenda setters in the marital conversation. In a study published in 1998, researchers James Honeycutt and Renee Brown found support for the 'superiority theory of humour' in marriage. Translation: husbands tell the jokes, and wives 'reinforce' the jokes by laughing at them.[2] To put the whole thing into more socio-logical language, a 'woman's role as change agent conflicts with her role as nurturer and relationship maintainer'—and a man's role as change agent conflicts with his role as beneficiary of the status quo.[3] When it comes to producing lasting, structural change within marriage, women are disabled and men disinclined. No wonder we're stuck.

Yet this is not the whole story either. Other observers believe we've seen so little revolution and so much stalling for the simple reason that social change is *always* slow to happen. Sometimes referred to as the 'lagged adaptation hypothesis', this theory suggests that there is a fixed threshold of social change for any single generation, beyond which it is simply impossible to go. As your grandmother might have put it, the apple doesn't fall far from the tree. Enough successive falls over enough generations will mean substantial ground eventually gets covered, but it all takes a tiresome amount of time. The lagged adaptation hypoth-esis has what sociologists call enormous intuitive appeal. (In other words, it seems to make sense.) Problem is, there are countless instances in which this 'law' of social change has been spectacularly violated. 'Change, including gendered change, has often been rapid, sometimes beyond all predictions,' observes Anthony McMahon. 'Some traditions collapse overnight.'[4] McMahon cites the rise of the dual-career marriage as an obvious example. One thinks too of the 180-degree swing of the pendulum with respect to child-care philosophy (from the 'children should be seen and not heard' school in which many of our parents were reared to the militantly 'child-centred' family of today), or fashions favouring bottle- or breastfeeding, or 'natural' versus medicalised child-birth. In the late 1940s, television was a novelty in most American homes. Within less than four decades, American children were spending more time watching television than doing any other activity, besides sleeping. In our own lifetime, we've seen lots of things collapse overnight: from the Berlin Wall to the social cachet of smoking cigarettes. Why wifework has not been one of them still needs explaining, and the reminder that Rome was not built in a day is hardly a compelling sociological argument.

Another explanation that's been put forward to explain why wives are still laughing at the jokes, rather than telling them, is that the status quo might be unequal, but it's not unjust. According to this theory, the traditional role structure of marriage persists because it represents a highly rational solution to the problem of resource allocation. Arguments that run along these lines suggest that men really 'should' work longer hours for pay because men earn higher wages, and women really 'should' perform more unpaid work because they're better housekeepers. As Michael Bittman has observed, the rational allocation model would be extremely persuasive if only it could be proved that 'it took a man six minutes to boil an egg that a woman could boil in three'.[5] In the absence of such proof, this theory—widely cited in the literature—can be safely consigned to the too-easy basket, the resting place for any argument that advances debate no further than its own first principles.

Ken Dempsey believes that in marriage, as in life generally, people don't really expect equality. What they do expect is equity, or rewards that are commensurate with contributions. In marriage, both partners underrate the wife's contribution while overvaluing that of the husband. As a result, married men and women have a very different take on what Dempsey calls the 'psychology of entitlement' (and what Arlie Hochschild in *The Managed Heart* called 'the economy of gratitude').

Husbands believe they are entitled to a lot, and are satisfied with no less. Wives believe they are entitled to little, and are uncomfortable with any more, unless they become ex-wives, in which case the tables are often turned with a palpable vengeance. Writes Dempsey, 'The fewer resources a person brings to a relationship, or the lesser value she places on those resources, the lower her expectations of the relationship.'[6] Women who feel, or who are made to feel, that they contribute little to the marriage will inevitably suffer from a depleted sense of entitlement. Instead of feeling angry or resentful towards their partners, and pressing them for change, they will instead feel gratitude—even a sense of indebtedness. Obviously, the problems here stem from how we define and assign value to resources, paid and unpaid, material and reproductive. Most interesting of all, to me, is that in our society the unique biological capital a woman brings to marriage—her ability to bear children—is regarded as negligible, if not an outright liability. And yet, from an evolutionary point of view, the reproductive resources of females should constitute a hugely powerful bargaining chip in human sexual politics.

Women who show they are able to compete with men on their own terms—that is to say, through professional achievement—may actually find it hinders their chances for producing change within their marriages. Steven Nock believes that the more equality women achieve in the workforce, the *less* likely husbands are to give up the perks of office associated with being a married man. By way of evidence, he cites studies that show unemployed men married to employed women perform less unpaid work, rather than more. The reason, Nock argues, is not that men are horrifyingly lazy. It's that they're horrifyingly fragile—or their sense of masculinity is, anyway. According to this argument, men avoid housework and other forms of wifework for the same reason schoolboys avoid wearing pink shorts and flowered T-shirts: because doing so makes them feel like girls. Why the performance of paid work does not make women feel like boys is a good question—which analysts like Nock explain with reference to the relative robustness of feminine gender identity. Underlying this argument is the assumption that manhood is 'problematic', as anthropologist David Gilmore puts it, and that growing up male inevitably produces a psychic wound that never quite heals over.[7]

Part of the problem, it has been proposed, is that females experience a visible and unambiguous rite of passage to womanhood with the onset of menstruation. Boys, by contrast, are never quite certain when—or whether—the transition to manhood has been achieved. As a result of all this, men 'must continually prove and demonstrate their masculinity, whereas women do not need to constantly justify their claims to femininity'.[8] Maintaining rigid divisions between His work and Hers within marriage is one such 'proof and demonstration' of a husband's masculinity.

Critics of this theory point out that to describe femininity as unproblematic simply because girls menstruate and most women bear children is a huge oversimplification. They also point out that focusing on the so-called male wound as the 'real problem' distracts from the equally real problem that wives are being exploited by their husbands. I agree entirely with the spirit of these criticisms. At the same time, however, it seems to me that the gender anxiety theory contains some irrefutable, though inconvenient, truths about why wifework is still central to how we 'do' marriage. There is no doubt in my mind that many men do approach life with an 'us–them' mentality towards gender, to a much greater degree than women do. Gendered 'shades of grey'—as represented by male homosexuality (but not female homosexuality, interestingly), or by unemployed men, or by women who are voluntarily childless, or, God forbid, celibate—provoke a good deal more anxiety in most males than they do in most females, for example.[9]

Today, despite the persistence of wifework, the rigid 'us–them' division of labour that characterised most marriages even a couple of generations ago has eroded in a number of important ways. This is evident in the image update of fatherhood. One thinks of the multitudinous popular photographs—there's one at my hairdresser's and one at my GP's—of bare-chested, heavily muscled (i.e., hypermasculine) men cuddling naked newborn babies. Unwritten caption: IF A BIG GUY LIKE THIS CAN HOLD A BABY AND STILL NOT TURN INTO A GIRL, WHO KNOWS? MAYBE YOU CAN TOO. My own father boasts that he never changed a nappy and never pushed a pram. These days, fathers boast that they always do. I suspect both are gross exaggerations—yet at the same time each is a faithful reflection of a set of prevailing social norms. To some degree, cooking is another area which is now seen as acceptably masculine—whether owing more to the popularity of sexy celebrity chefs or of feminist rhetoric, it is impossible to say. The participation of married men in cooking rose significantly throughout the late seventies and early eighties, although it has plateaued ever since. We have already seen that men's participation in parenting, while it has expanded, especially during the infancy and preschool stage, is still dwarfed by that of their wives. Ditto cooking. It's no longer a 'girl thing' to whip up a stir fry, or even a soup-to-nuts dinner party. But husbands are still only doing a fraction of the cooking that wives do.

The gender-anxiety argument may be a necessary part of the answer, but it is not a sufficient one. The more tiresome and less public wife-work tasks—from laundry and 'tidying' to relationship management and conjugal sex work—remain tarred by the feminine brush. Yet one suspects that a public-service campaign featuring semi-clad Iron Men doing the vacuuming, or beer-swilling lads de-moulding the shower stall, would take us only so far. Assuring men that they can perform 'women's work' and emerge with their masculinity intact is perhaps a necessary first step. But it's a long way from acknowledging that one 'can' participate to accepting that one has an equal obligation to do so; it's the distance between 'helping out' with family life, and living it.

The Sleeping with the Enemy argument (as I like to think of it) suggests that gender roles within marriage have proved so resistant to change not simply because the arrangement suits men better—but because it may suit women better as well. We have already encountered the notion of 'gatekeeping', which suggests that women may consciously or unconsciously discourage husbands from infiltrating the wifely domain. This theory suggests that women too experience gender anxiety when traditional roles break down, adopting a sort of siege mentality with respect to what they see as 'their' power base: especially, the running of the home and the care of children. Although I reject entirely the notion that 'women are their own worst enemies'—a particularly ill-informed case of victim-blaming under the circumstances—there may be several sizeable grains of truth here. My own experience and observation, as well as a thorough reading of the research, suggest strongly that there is a degree of collusion in many marriages. Some women do enjoy the power and control that is the flip-side of the wifework imperative, perhaps particularly with reference to parenting. And there are other women, strange as it may seem to some, who just like the work itself.

Ken Dempsey's research found that it wasn't just men who had trouble seeing wifework as 'work'. Lots of women did too. To many, the performance of these tasks was very much 'an expression of love and affection' they were happy about making.[10] The biggest complaint these wives had was not the unequal distribution of labour, but the perception that their efforts were not appreciated or acknowledged by their husbands. In other cases, women did not complain about performing wifework as long as they felt there were sufficient trade-offs. Dempsey found that women were particularly likely to describe their situation as fair when they perceived their husbands to be 'good with the kids', when they felt they had sufficient opportunity for leisure, and when they experienced their husbands as 'warm and loving'. Other research has supported these findings. And so, of course, do the voices one hears in kitchens and cafes and schoolyards throughout the land. 'No marriage is perfect,' they say—and there's nothing to argue with there. 'It's all about give and take.' Yet this still doesn't explain why wives are so much more likely to be doing the giving and their husbands the taking.

The strategies women use to rationalise the inequities of wifework have been extensively documented. One of the most common is selective husband comparison, whereby women in unequal marriages compare their lot to that of women in even more unequal marriages. Often, the point of comparison is a woman's own family of origin: a starting point virtually guaranteed to make even the most troubled modern marriage come out smelling like an orange blossom. Men often do the same. My second husband frequently justified his own lack of participation in our family's life by observing that he 'earned a good living, never went to the pub and didn't screw around'. This struck me as something of an anachronism coming from a middle-class professional in the 1990s. Yet a mere generation previously, such a track record would have qualified an Australian working-class husband as a bonafide gem, one of those 'good men' which legend has it are so notoriously 'hard to find' in any age.

A number of observers have pointed out that such comparisons tend to be exclusively intra-gender. One informant in a recent study explained, 'When I think how much more helpful my husband is to me than my father was to my Mum I reckon I'm pretty well off.'[11] The fact that she refrained from comparing her husband's 'helpfulness' to her own 'helpfulness' is typical. Even within relatively egalitarian marriages, direct comparisons between His contribution and Hers are almost regarded as a reductio ad absurdum—a logical trick or fallacy.

'From now on,' my friend Jane announced to her husband recently, 'I'm going to be available to help you with the housework and cooking any time you feel you need it. Please don't hesitate to ask.'

At first Ted was puzzled. 'What are you talking about?' he asked.

'I'm only making the same offer to you that you've been making to me for years,' Jane explained. 'It seems to make you feel like you're "sharing" the load. So I thought I'd give it a try myself.'

Ted looked hurt. 'Very funny,' he said with a sniff.

For many women, the simple answer may be that they would rather live with wifework than without it—in the belief that living without it would mean living without marriage, and possibly without men, altogether. Although it is not a subject academics can easily canvass with surveys and observations and questionnaires, it seems to me that so many women are willing to settle for the wifework contract not because they believe it's fair, but because deep down they don't believe there's an alternative. Choosing to remain married, they may ultimately and not at all unwisely decide, is choosing to compromise. Yet where lies the line between compromise and surrender? Between relinquishing the ideal of perfection on the one hand, and losing one's integrity on the other? As journalist Danielle Crittenden so memorably phrased it, what price is too high for keeping 'a warm husband in one's bed'?[12]

surrendered judgments

'Most individuals who rebel against marriage and
monogamy are angry and unhappy people who
understandably rationalize their objections...They
need therapeutic help so that they can mature and
derive genuine pleasure from living.' Herbert Strean

Almost all of us describe our marriages as equal. The evidence
indicates that nine out of ten of us are lying. Even more demoralising, it suggests that most of us are far more likely to expend our
energy making excuses than making changes. Acknowledging the
disjuncture between the ideal of equal partnership and the reality of
wifework is painful—humiliating even. Yet, without that acknowledgment, how can we expect to move forward in the way we live our
married lives?

We have looked closely at some of the reasons for the persistence of
wifework. Now we will consider its expendability. Is marriage without
wifework a contradiction in terms? Or marriage without gender? Or
gender without injustice? Is marriage good for anything, or for anyone?
Is it necessary at all? Do women need to discard the idea of a happy
marriage as a hopeless oxymoron? And, if not, what exactly would need
to change—and how?

At the moment, if the research is to be believed, happy marriages do
indeed exist—but they are largely the result of two people dedicated to
lying, obfuscation and fantasy. Consider, for example, the study
conducted by Sandra Murray, a psychologist from the University of

Buffalo, who showed that successful marriages are built on 'stories' that partners tell themselves (and the world) about each other—marital tall tales that exaggerate good qualities while minimising the bad. What can't be denied outright is reframed in a more positive light. (Does he spend more time interacting with the reticulation than he does with his children? That's because he's such a dedicated gardener! Does she continually bicker with his parents? That's because she's so loyal and cares so deeply.) The capacity of a couple for mutual self-delusion, Murray's research suggests, may be the truest indicator of their chances for marital success. Confirms journalist Bettina Arndt, 'Contented couples collude to see the best in each other.'[1]

And what's the harm in that? After all, whoever said honesty was the best policy obviously lived alone, and liked it that way. According to Murray and her colleagues John Holmes of the University of Waterloo, Canada and Dale Griffin of the University of Sussex, couples who maintain what they call 'positive illusions' are well placed to avoid major conflict, build trust and overlook transgressions and imperfections. It's a sentiment echoed by sociologist Lynn Jamieson, who notes wryly that a couple's 'true collaborative effort' is likely to revolve around 'a shared repertoire of cover stories, taboos and self-dishonesty'.[2]

To illustrate the point, Bettina Arndt cites an academic analysis of the TV program 'The Simpsons' that grapples with the urgent cultural conundrum of why Marge continues to stay with Homer, 'her nearly irredeemable slob of a husband'. 'Marge clearly recognises the imperfections in Homer,' writes Arndt, 'but his faults pale under the steady gaze of her loyalty and affection. The lesson is that slight perfections can be found…even in those we believe most imperfect.'[3]

Leaving aside for a moment the mystery of what a 'slight perfection' might refer to, one is compelled to ask whether this business of maintaining positive illusions might be another form of unpaid labour whose distribution in marriage is suspiciously uneven. More wifework, but at a deeper level. Do we watch TV programs that depict *wives* who, despite being 'nearly irredeemable slobs' (not to mention moral imbeciles), are nevertheless viewed through 'the steady gaze of loyalty and affection' by *husbands*? I can't think of any. To put it another way, exactly how 'mutual' is the mutual self-delusion uncovered by Sandra Murray and colleagues? Do husbands maintain an equal number of 'positive illusions' about their wives as wives do about their husbands? Or is the collusion of the average husband more simply a matter of choosing to embrace his wife's idealised image of him?

One can't help but wonder. Especially when you consider—as Arndt herself points out—that it is the disillusionment of women which constitutes the 'greatest threat to modern marriage'. It is women's 'positive illusions' that typically come crashing down when a marriage breaks up, not those of their husbands. It may be that the only truly dangerous positive illusion in which a man can indulge is the one that confuses the performance of wifework with the existence of genuine commitment, unswerving love or even heartfelt affection. If it has ever seemed to you that most men are more shocked by the break-up of their marriages than women are, the evidence suggests you are a very acute observer. Family Court counsellor Peter Jordan found in a recent study that most men are caught totally unawares when their wives announce that it's over. 'It was like being hit in the head by a piece of two-by-four,' remembered one informant.[4]

It's a remarkably common reaction. Of course, wives are not the only ones who depart a marriage abruptly, for reasons almost totally unforeseen by their partners. Statistically, however, the experience of an emotional hit-and-run when a marriage ends is much more likely to afflict men than it is women—and researchers believe it is an important reason why separated men are six times more likely to commit suicide than men who remain within marriage, and twelve times more likely to do so than separated women.[5]

Women, it seems, are less and less able, or less and less willing, to sustain the required level of positive illusions about their marriages generally and about their men in particular. What my mother used to call 'making the best of a bad show' is easy when you have no choice. These days, women do have choice. And they *are* increasingly disillusioned about marriage—whether they have ever experienced being a wife or not. According to data from the 1993 General Social Survey in the US, today's young women are significantly less likely to value marriage highly than young men are.[6] Only 66 per cent of never-married women under the age of thirty described getting married as 'important for their lives' compared to three-quarters of comparable young men— a finding that a mere generation ago would have been unthinkable. According to a recent article on 'Post Feminist Brides' in the *Sydney Morning Herald*, young women don't even squabble over the bride's bouquet any more. 'Instead it glides through the air with a reluctantly gathered crowd of single females parting as if avoiding a meteor as it lands untouched on the dance floor.'[7]

Among women who have experienced marriage that sense of disillusionment is even greater. Even in marriages which survive the long haul, women are less satisfied overall than men. A twenty-year longitudinal study of stable marriages in a culturally diverse sample found that, in the early years of marriage, only 63 per cent of wives remembered feeling satisfied by the relationship, compared with nearly 80 per cent of husbands. During the years of active child-rearing, the 'happiness gap' widened even further. Although roughly three-quarters of husbands reported marital satisfaction during this period, only half of wives did.[8] This study was conducted retrospectively. That is, participants were asked to recall past feeling states—a considerably less threatening task, one suspects, than revealing present emotional realities.

Nevertheless, there are still plenty of women who will go to any lengths to preserve the illusion of a happy marriage, even if it means capitulating to a wifely ideal that makes Marge Simpson look like a lesbian separatist. Or so, at least, the publicity for the so-called Surrendered Wives movement would have us believe. A neo-traditionalist fringe group dedicated to the proposition that, in the words of thirty-two-year-old founder Laura Doyle, 'you defer to your husband's thinking unless it hurts you physically', the Surrendered Wives have resolved the gender contradictions between public and private life by drawing a large dotted line down the middle. The idea, according to Doyle, 'is to go to work and boss everybody about until the glass ceilings break and true economic equality is achieved, but then to leave that spirit at work and come home a woman'.[9]

'Coming home a woman' apparently entails exactly the kind of positive reframing researchers have found to be so essential to maintaining a successful marriage. Surrendered Wife Landra Buchanan, for example, a twenty-eight-year-old office manager, has come to see her former complaints about her husband's slovenliness as evidence of her own 'control issues'. Today she concentrates on 'thinking of the glass as half-full instead of half-empty'. Her husband may have his faults, but 'he holds the door open and clears the dishes'. And that's not all. 'Once in a while, he'll realise he's been neglecting me and he'll buy me a whole new outfit and have it laying on the bed, or bring me flowers.'[10] Doyle's book, *Surrendered Wives: A Woman's Spiritual Guide to True Intimacy with a Man*, advises wannabe doormats to accentuate the gratitude and eliminate the 'attitude'. 'So in that moment when you're thinking he never helps out, and he's such a baby, instead you have to say, "OK, he works hard to support the family and he did load the dishwasher last night."'[11]

As a self-confessed former control freak, Laura Doyle has no illusions about who's really calling the shots in her surrendered marriage—which is why she advises, 'For best results, do not discuss what you learn from the book with your husband.' Her husband John, a pudgy computer programmer, concurs. 'If you go to see a magician, you don't really want to see how the tricks are done,' he observes. 'You just want to enjoy the results'—the performance, he might almost have said.[12]

It's absurd, of course. And yet the 'magic' that Surrendered Wives (and their husbands) report is also real. Surrendering actually 'works', in the sense that it reduces conflict and clarifies roles and responsibilities. And if that seems hard to believe, you need to go back to chapter one and start reading this book all over again. Surrendering closes an untold number of pesky open options in a marriage, from who takes out the rubbish to who takes out the mortgage. It also produces impressive results in the bedroom. 'The first rule for a great sex life is to be respectful and wear something sheer and lacy,' Doyle advises.[13] Surrendering not only overtly empowers men, it prevents women from taking on the role of Mum to their husband's Little Boy—an erotic kiss of death to which so many pseudo-egalitarian marriages succumb. Doyle may have a few screws loose, but she's a lot shrewder than the hype would suggest. She is, after all, a former advertising executive. 'Most men aren't interested in having sex with their mothers,' she notes dryly, 'and that is who we remind them of when we are forever controlling them and telling them what to do.'[14]

Marital therapy guru John Gottman, best-selling author of *The Seven Principles for Making Marriage Work*, dismisses Laura Doyle as a 'dinosaur'. Indeed, Gottman's own research suggests that one of the major secrets for marital success is, on the contrary, something more akin to husband surrender. 'Go ahead!' the engaging rabbi's son urges his marital therapy clientele. 'Give in to her!' Nevertheless, there is an insistent ring of truth about Doyle's neo-traditionalist counterattack that is impossible to dismiss. 'It seems to me that these people have simply empowered women to get divorced, become single mothers, get married again and leave the next man, too, because he is no good,' she argues.[15] It's backlash with a vengeance, sure. But name-calling won't make the argument go away. Surrendering will never become a mainstream way of life; even Doyle herself concedes that. But there's a rational message in all that star-spangled lunacy nonetheless. And it has to do with desperate times calling for desperate measures.

Either marriage has failed our generation, or our generation has failed marriage. As journalist Amy Dickinson points out, we're not even that good at divorce, looking at our rates of remarriage.[16] Laura Doyle is no social scientist. But you don't have to be to recognise that we've got a genuine crisis on our hands, and that to date the solutions proposed have fallen tragically short of the mark. Doyle is right that, despite the enormous tensions that inhere within most marriages today, neither men nor women are as a rule 'empowered' by divorce, and children are almost inevitably harmed by it. Doyle is also correct about the downside of the de facto lifestyle, according to a variety of credentialled and objective observers. If you've ever been tempted to ask yourself whether anything could be worse than marriage, this research suggests, you really need to try serial monogamy. Accurate also is Doyle's suggestion that the 'solution' to a bad marriage is normally not simply divorce. It is remarriage, or 're-partnering' as the social scientists now call it. Finally, she is correct in her assumption that the risk of divorce in second and subsequent marriages is even higher than it is in first unions. The odds that a second marriage will 'take' are slim indeed. And if children are involved, we're talking about a bona fide long shot. Maybe, just maybe, seeing the glass as half full isn't as dumb as it sounds. And if a *great* marriage is an unachievable goal, what's wrong with having a 'good enough' marriage?

It was psychoanalyst Donald Winnicott who introduced the concept of 'good enough mothering'—the idea that children don't really need perfect parents, only adequate ones, and that the margin for error is probably far wider than we fear. Mistakes, unhappiness, anger, ambivalence—they're all part of the parenting package, Winnicott argued. When it comes to child-rearing, love doesn't exactly conquer all; on the other hand, it probably conquers more than we think it does. The idea of 'good enough mothering' has proved a welcome antidote to the anxiety produced by earlier psychoanalytic theories, which seemed to blame Mum for everything from bed-wetting to autism. There is something so comforting and commonsensical about the idea that enough really is as good as a feast—better, in some ways, because it is so much more likely to be achieved. As in child-rearing, so in marriage itself? The idea of a 'good enough marriage' has been taken to extremes by Laura Doyle and her sister surrenderees. Yet it's still an idea worth exploring.

It seems to me that we do need to ask *less* of marriage. At the same time—and this is where I decisively part company with Doyle & Co— we need to ask *more* of husbands. To be sure, a willingness to compromise, to 'settle', if you will, is essential for both partners. The hard part is figuring out where to give ground, and where to stand firm. What is, or should be, non-negotiable in a marriage?

We have already observed that the institution of marriage arose originally as a solution to the intricate problems of human dependency. It was never an ideal solution. Throughout most of the history of our species, however, it has proved the best available compromise for the largest number of individuals. Today, we are accustomed to think of marriage in terms of its two most obvious stakeholders: the husband and the wife. In fact, until extremely recently, the primary stakeholder in monogamy has been neither of these, but the product of both: the offspring of the couple. In a very real sense, children are what marriage is 'for', biologically, socially and (for those who think in such terms) morally. And this is so because the dependency needs of males and females stem almost entirely from their relative reproductive assets and liabilities. Simply put, males have needed females firstly in order to produce offspring and secondly in order to ensure the survival of those offspring. Females have needed male protection and provisioning only as a consequence of the intense physical demands of continuous pregnancy, birth and lactation. What all the evolutionary imperatives come down to is that the chief beneficiary of monogamy is the child. Everything beyond the survival of the offspring is a symptom of monogamy, not a cause—and that includes sexual passion, economic security, companionship, the building of family alliances and all the other good reasons men and women believe they choose to marry.

Can men live happily and productively outside of stable monogamous relationships? Well, some can, of course. But, for the vast majority, marriage affords a kind of protection to health and happiness that no other way of life seems able to offer. Marriage also continues to protect women, but to a much lesser degree. What tips the balance—perhaps the only thing tipping the balance—is children. The truly awful news of the post-no-fault divorce era—and it is news we have tried our damnedest to deny—is that marriage is good for kids. No one really understands exactly why at the moment, but all the evidence suggests—indeed it pretty much hollers—that even a tense, or empty, or conflicted marriage between biological parents is probably better for children than even the most perfect divorce. Your grandparents didn't need any 'evidence' to convince them of this truth. They believed it in their bones. Maybe your parents did too. I know mine did. Yet somewhere between the baby and the boom the idea of 'staying together for the sake of the children' became as thoroughly discredited as antenatal X-rays, or asbestos draperies, or aluminium siding. By the time of the first no-fault divorce laws of the 1970s, it was something people didn't *do* anymore. By the 1980s, men and women—but perhaps particularly women—began to justify not marriage but divorce itself on the grounds of 'the best interests of the child'. Again, there are undeniably cases in which divorce really does serve the needs of children best, cases of entrenched physical or sexual abuse, or what the divorce courts used to call 'mental cruelty'. No one disputes that. But conflict per se? Even unhappiness per se? Today, the best evidence tells us the damage to children from such normal dysfunctions of marital life is negligible compared with the almost certain impact of divorce.

Today, this is news. Such big news that it was recently featured on the front page of the *New York Times Book Review* under the banner headline 'Bye-Bye Splitsville'. The lead article was a review of marital studies guru Judith Wallerstein's *The Unexpected Legacy of Divorce: A 25 Year Landmark Study*. What was 'unexpected' was the finding that divorce makes a substantial and persistent difference to the lives of the children caught in its crossfire. It turns out that children are not nearly as resilient as we were all assuring ourselves a mere ten or even five years ago. On the contrary, even twenty-five years post-divorce, the aftershocks for offspring are still considerable. Indeed, Wallerstein's findings suggest that the impact is felt most keenly when children grow up and attempt to forge intimate relationships.

Wallerstein's reading of the literature emphasises the psychological disadvantages suffered by the children of divorce. Children from divorced and remarried families, she has found, 'experience more depressions, have more learning difficulties and suffer from more problems with peers than children from intact families' (p. xxiii). Wallerstein's respondents were apparently unanimous in the hope that their own children would experience a different, and better, sort of childhood. She reflects, 'Not one ever said, "I want my children to live in two nests"' (p. xxv)—an observation both simple and devastating.

According to the latest Australian data, children whose parents have divorced end up with about a year's less education than children in intact families—an effect only partially accounted for by socio-economic factors. Research carried out by Princeton University sociologist Sara McLanahan, co-author of *Growing Up with a Single Parent*, has found that loss of income accounts for only half the educational risk. The other half is explained by 'inadequate parental guidance and attention and the lack of ties to community resources'.[17] Lack of parental supervision in single-parent families has also been suggested as a reason that kids from those families are so much more likely to be involved in juvenile crime than children who live with two parents (22 per cent compared to 8 per cent, according to one Australian study). Less easy to quantify, but equally serious, are more subtle effects of altered family dynamics—for example, post-separation role reversals which find school-aged children 'parenting' their grieving elders, or self-esteem issues tied up with children's sense of responsibility for a break-up.

In the US today, 28 per cent of all children live in single-parent households, with 84 per cent of them female-headed. The proportion of children in the US living with single fathers, though it has doubled in the two decades since 1980, still stands at only 4 per cent. In Great Britain, it is estimated that some 2.8 million children live in one-parent families, which today account for approximately one-quarter of all households. In 1971, the figure was only 8 per cent of families. In the UK, as in the US and Australia, the vast majority of one-parent families are headed by women. Of all British families with dependent children, only 1.8 per cent are today headed by single Dads.[18] In Australia today, almost one-quarter of all children live in single-parent families, 80 per cent of them female-headed.[19] Three-quarters of all Australian single mothers receive welfare support to supplement the often minimal child-support payments from fathers (46 per cent of men registered to pay child support claim annual earnings of less than $16,000).

Not surprisingly, children in lone-parent families are twice as likely to live in poverty as those in intact families—a disadvantage so exhaustively documented in the sociological literature that no sane observer could dispute it.[20] The impact of poverty on the children of divorce is enormous. Yet experts and lay people alike continue to dismiss it as a red herring—or, to use more sociological language, a confounding variable. The 'real' problem, such observers argue, is not the loss of two parents; it is the loss of two incomes. What nonsense. The economic consequences of marital breakdown are every bit as real as the emotional consequences—and to pretend otherwise is to fall victim to the same hopelessly romantic myth that teaches us marriage is 'really' about love, not money. Marriage is really about love *and* money. (More accurately, marriage is really about the exchange of resources, both reproductive and material.) Divorce is too.

At cocktail parties and book-club meetings and around the dinner table, the question of the impact of divorce on children remains a hotly disputed issue, with a fundamentalist fringe on either side maintaining, respectively, that it makes no difference at all ('the kids haven't even noticed he's gone!') or that it will destroy civilisation as we know it. The truth, as are most truths, is located somewhere in the middle. Divorce does make a difference for children, and we are only just beginning to look at how much and for how long. As divorced mother and children's author Susanne Gervay told journalist Bettina Arndt, 'What's hardest is that no one acknowledges how hard it is on them. Divorce is now seen as socially acceptable so no one is prepared to talk about what it does to children. And the children are left feeling no one understands what they are going through.'[21]

In many cases, the grown-ups are too busy licking their own wounds to notice. We offer each other glib reassurances: 'I've been a single mother all their lives, really', or 'Kids are so resilient!' or—a favourite among weekend fathers—that old chestnut about 'quality time' being 'the main thing'. Of course kids survive divorce. (But is survival really our highest aspiration for them?) And, in many cases, a divorce 'for the sake of the children' really is a brave and positive step. But those are the exceptions. For most children, growing up within even a deeply flawed marriage is preferable to growing up with divorce. And if you don't believe me, I suggest you ask your kids.

I know from experience what a bitter pill this is to swallow. Like most, I learned too late to do anything about it. And by that I don't mean that I've come to believe my marriage was really OK, or that it was wrong not to suffer through it for the sake of my children. But I do mean that I would have done things differently, perhaps even very differently, if I'd had any notion of the enormity of the undertaking. I'd have tried to pour my energy into seeking help and negotiating changes, rather than in proving that I could manage fine on my own. If I'd known more about what the birth of three children in four years can do to even the best relationship I might have been less frightened of the chaos, and more accepting of the conflict. (Maybe it's a bit like childbirth itself. Knowing that the pain is *supposed* to be outrageous may make it just bearable.) If I'd had any notion how irreplaceable are the bonds of blood—how impossible it is to substitute, divert or suspend them at another's convenience—maybe I would have gone slower. Maybe my husband would have too. Who knows?

A childless woman who looks at her marriage and asks herself, 'What's in this for *me*?' is in one place. A woman who has had children and asks herself the same question is in a different place—or ought to be. When children are involved, the future of marriage is an issue of urgent social importance. When they are not, it isn't. What goes on between two adults in an intimate relationship is nobody's business but their own. What goes on in families is everybody's business.

As presently constituted, marriage represents a poor bargain for any woman who does not see motherhood as part of her life plan. For such women, becoming a wife will almost certainly entail more responsibilities—and more sheer work—than it offers privileges or perks. No matter what commitment to 'equal sharing' she or her partner professes, marriage will almost guarantee that genuine equality will elude them both. In all likelihood, he will continue to perform as a kind of closet breadwinner, and she as a closet housewife. The question 'Who needs it?' is a very, very good one. For such women, a committed, cohabiting relationship generally offers a more attractive deal. Although cohabiting women also run the risk of succumbing to the wifework imperative—with many becoming wives in all but name—she will have a much better chance of resisting it if she remains outside of marriage than within it.

For women who do intend having children, the wifework entailed will be even more arduous, and the inequalities within marriage even more pronounced. And yet the protective benefits of marriage for the children produced by such women will tip the scales considerably (although not necessarily decisively) towards matrimony. It is quite possible to have children outside of marriage; indeed, nearly 30 per cent of the time, that's exactly what we are doing. In 1987, cohabiting couple families formed only one in thirty British families with dependent children. By 1998, the proportion had increased to one in twelve. At the moment, such families represent only about 5 per cent of the total—but demographers point to the 'sustained and significant growth' in de facto families, relative to other family types.[22] Premarital cohabitation in the US is also 'blurring the boundaries of "marriage"', according to social scientists Marcia Carlson and Sheldon Danziger. According to 1990 Census data, 2.2 million American children live in de facto families, and nearly a third of such families exist below the poverty line.[23] In 1996, 270,000 Australian children lived with parents in a de facto relationship—twice as many as a decade earlier.[24] Yet, as far as the welfare of children is concerned, cohabitation is a surprisingly poor substitute for legal marriage.

A study by Robert Whelan of the UK-based Family Education Trust found that children living with unmarried biological parents were twenty times more likely to become victims of child abuse, while those living with a mother and her de facto boyfriend were thirty-three times more at risk.[25] Cohabitations are more unstable generally, and those involving children break up at four to five times the rate of married families. Cohabiting partners are also less likely to pool their financial resources.[26] Most women having children in de facto relationships are not movie stars; they are under twenty-five, poor and poorly educated. When relationships break up, cohabiting fathers pay less child support and are less likely to keep in contact with their children than married fathers. Are there individual cohabiting relationships that are stable, committed, safe and solvent places for the nurture of children? Of course there are—just as, heaven knows, there are plenty of toxic marriages. But considered overall, the evidence is unmistakable. Where children are concerned, the 'for better, for worse' issue couldn't be clearer. Marriage is better, cohabitation is worse.

Women who desire children have an intrinsic motivation to marry and to remain married. They have something big to gain, and something precious to lose. Men who desire children do also. But then again, as we have seen repeatedly, men have a great deal to gain from marriage whether children are involved or not. Marriage is good for men. Marriage protects men. Marriage, to use Dalma Heyn's metaphor, *welcomes* men. It is reasonable to assume that the institution of marriage will be kept alive by those who have most to gain from it: and that means women who have, or intend to have, children, and all men. The next question is, how?

chapter 17

whose wife is it, anyway?

'A rabbi was trying to resolve a marital dispute. He
listened carefully to the story told by the first spouse.
When it was finished, he shook his head sadly. "You
are absolutely right," he agreed. Then he listened
carefully to the other spouse's story. Once again, he
shook his head. "You are absolutely right," he agreed.'
old Talmudic story

At first glance, the idea of entrusting men with the responsibility
for reconstructing marriage seems a bit like entrusting a child to
trade his lollipop for a bowl of green vegetables. I think of the scene
from *Gone with the Wind* where Rhett Butler tries to win the twice-
widowed Scarlett as his bride. 'Did you ever think of marrying for fun?'
he proposes with a leer. 'Marriage? Fun?' Scarlett practically sputters.
'Fiddledee-dee! Fun for men, you mean!' We are so accustomed to
thinking of marriage as something women *need* to do, a favour that men
might or might not bestow, that we have not yet assimilated how decisively the balance of power has shifted, how far the 'economy of gratitude'
has been redistributed between the genders. If the institution is to survive,
marriage will have to become 'fun for the woman' as well, in ways entirely
unprecedented in human history. If men cannot manage that, then it will
increasingly be the case that women cannot manage marriage.

'Quite simply,' writes Steven Nock, 'marriage must be redefined to
reflect the greater gender equality found everywhere else, *or women will*

not marry.[1] Having a wife and children is today a privilege that a man must earn—or forgo. Marriage is better for offspring than cohabiting with a male partner. But it may not be better, or even as good, as some other alternative: cohabiting with groups of women, for example, or with older female kin. Indeed, the more fragile marriage becomes, the more likely it is that another, more stable arrangement may prove more adaptive.

Making marriage fun for wives—or more fun, anyway—will mean an end to wifework as an imperative to service the needs of men. But it will not (alas!) mean that something resembling husbandwork will arise to take its place. Seriously, I know of no woman who has ever argued that it should. Contrary to what many contemporary husbands may fear, women become 'control freaks' only by default, growing hyper-responsible as a compensation for the relative mindlessness of their men. What women really want is co-operation. Not each and every task split down the middle with a ruler and a calculator, but a genuine sharing of both labour and leisure that casts both partners as adults with equal status and entitlements. It's not fun to scrub the toilet. It's not fun to do the washing up, to change the sheets or de-crumb the toaster. It's even less fun to pretend women do these tasks simply because they are more proficient at them—as if proficiency had nothing at all to do with habit, expectation or necessity. It's not fun to pretend you're in an equal relationship when you know damn well you're responsible for three times as much scut work as your partner, for only a fraction of the kudos. There is nothing we can do to make housework fun, exactly. But there are any number of things we can do to make it less dreary and burdensome.

Couples who can afford to hire it out may think they've solved the problem already. But outsourcing will take even the most affluent of us only so far. Are you going to outsource feeding the dog, as well as walking it; driving the car, as well as cleaning it; taking the kids on holiday, as well as before- and after-school care? What about having sex with your husband? When *that* gets to be too much of a chore, who ya gonna call? Women who try to buy their way out of wifework—and even those who to a large extent succeed—do not necessarily end up with better, let alone more equal marriages. For one thing, at the first fiscal crisis, it is they and not their husbands who will be accused of extravagance. It is wives who will be pressured to sack the help and roll up their sleeves and get on with it.

For many middle-class couples, outsourcing tasks like lawn-mowing, ironing and heavy housecleaning has gone from being a form of conspicuous consumption to a way of life. Interestingly, it is among the leisured classes—a kingdom still peopled by male breadwinners and their stay-at-home wives—that one encounters women essentially free of domestic burdens. Yet these 'ladies who lunch' do not enjoy more equal marriages at all. In my observation, they seem particularly bound by the imperative to service and maintain their husband's needs—including the need to be seen to be wealthy enough to afford a wife whose value is almost aggressively non-productive. Like a Ming vase, she is expensive, beautiful and utterly pointless. Her function is not to have a function.

Becoming the manageress of the household work, rather than the drudge who performs it, is a promotion in name only. Marriages in which most of the unpaid domestic burden is hired out will always be a tiny minority, anyway—and for couples with children, an even tinier one. Throwing money at a problem is very rarely a satisfactory solution over the long term. I think of the truly staggering number of marriages I know which were supposed to be 'saved' by moving to a new house, or adding a second storey or a new bathroom. If only life were that simple! Usually, such devices represent a strategy for deferring a resolution rather than negotiating one.

The practice of husbands 'helping' around the house is no more a solution either. Any man who insists that this is good enough should be immediately downgraded to 'helping' with his wife's sex life as well. And 'helping' with the kids is somehow even more chilling. (Subtext: 'Father' is less a parent than he is a male au pair.) Men who are invited, or allowed, to 'help' invariably manage to help themselves to whatever tasks are the least arduous and time-consuming. There's nothing shocking in that. So would a woman, if she were given the choice. Men should not be permitted to pick and choose the most attractive/intermittent/creative/noticeable household tasks. Nor should they be supervised/criticised/coached (beyond whatever initial training period may be necessary to ensure a satisfactory result) or derided/nagged/fulsomely praised. The need for 'ownership' of tasks is critical—not only in ensuring the job gets done, but in safeguarding whatever small gratifications housework can provide.

The need for specialisation is perhaps even more critical. Housework is not exactly an art and not quite a 'craft' either, but it's hardly unskilled labour. Maybe it really is true that 'any idiot can do the laundry', but I've got a whole drawer of splotchy pink bras and underpants that says some idiots do it better than others. There's stuff to learn—in most cases more than you'd think—about doing even the most basic of basics. Vacuuming, say, or making a bed. There are even tricks to 'tidying up'—most of which I've learned from watching my cleaning lady! As in other forms of productive labour, the name of the game is working smarter, not harder—or, heaven forbid, slower. Most women, I think it's fair to say, have picked up some of this know-how by osmosis, through observing their mothers (and other cleaning ladies) in action. But the biggest learning curve is traversed by the doing. Men who are not put in charge of a specific area of housework—doing all the family laundry, say, or looking after grocery shopping and meals preparation—never get the opportunity to acquire specialist knowledge. They remain callow apprentices, klutzy helpers who rarely develop the requisite expertise to do any household task well or thoroughly. The predictable result is that, over time, such men will perform less work not more. The 'help' they offer is simply not worth the bother—and both parties know it. 'It's easier to do it myself,' women say with a sigh and a roll of the eyeballs. At one level, it's a perfectly understandable response. Yet by so doing, wives add yet another chore to the long list already awaiting them: diggers of their own graves.

So what is the secret to getting men to shoulder their fair share? Well, the first bit of bad news is that there is no secret. There's no magic formula or bulleted list of tips and tricks. It's important to bear in mind that men, too, are struggling to forge new directions. Their journey into manhood, at this moment in our social history, has been strikingly different from that of their own fathers. As a result, many feel they have arrived at adulthood without a compass, exactly as their wives have done. We have seen that many women feel ambivalent about the 'shoulds' of wifework—'I should iron his shirts', 'I should fold his underwear', 'I should offer unconditional emotional support, no matter what'—because even if they no longer believe this stuff with their conscious, adult minds, they may have imbibed it pre-consciously and unconsciously in their families of origin. Well, men too are grappling with an identity crisis. On the one hand, there's the role of husbandhood they probably grew up with: 'I shouldn't have to worry about housework if I'm earning a good living'; 'I should be entitled to uninterrupted leisure time'; 'I should provide for my family no matter what'. On the other, there's the role they have been told they must now assimilate: 'I should be an equal partner and an equal parent'; 'I should share my feelings openly'; 'I should value family time over time spent on the job'. The problem of 'knowing' that something is right, but still 'feeling' that it's wrong afflicts men every bit as much as it does women.

For spouses struggling to balance gender roles in marriage, the reality is that the going will almost certainly be tough. In many if not most cases, the war against wifework will prove ultimately unwinnable in adult relationships today. Yet I am passionately convinced that we need to keep on struggling anyway. Who was it who said that lost causes are the only ones worth fighting for? I believe it's important to battle these most intimate of injustices for the same reason that I believe we must battle to preserve marriage itself: for the sake of our children. Despite notable and increasingly numerous exceptions, most marriages already formed are unlikely to achieve the goal of genuine symmetry. Yet even the highly imperfect unions we model for our children represent a significant advance on those that were modelled for us. We have moved forward—whether we've gotten there by marching in a straight line or through blind stumbling isn't really that important. I thought of this yesterday when I arrived at school to pick up my children. The first thing I saw was a Dad—a tall, important-looking bloke—with a flowered nappy bag slung over his shoulder and a preschooler dancing around his feet. Another man sat on a bench holding his squirmy toddler son on his lap. I looked just in time to see him give the boy a big unselfconscious kiss. Things like that give you hope. And we need hope.

Achieving a more equitable distribution of unpaid labour is an important way marriage can be made more fun for wives—but it's not the only way. Remember the research that showed clearly that wives who felt cared for emotionally were far more likely to describe their marriages as 'fair'? And that was irrespective of who was doing what around the house. Obviously, getting the emotional division of labour right is at least as critical to the well-being of wives as achieving more tangible forms of equity. Women who feel that their husbands are emotionally 'on the take' report low levels of marital satisfaction. And why not? The unconditional, unrelenting giving demanded by many husbands may tap into women's strong maternal instincts. But what could be less fun than functioning as Mummy to a grown man? This sort of emotional role structure remains remarkably widespread in marriages today. I am convinced it contributes significantly to women's disenchantment generally, and to the sexual frustrations of both husbands and wives. In this I agree 100 per cent with Surrendered Wife Laura Doyle.

If marriage is to be made more fun for women, it's got to be made sexier too. The flair for sex work demonstrated by nearly all men during courtship needs to be carried over in the marriage bed as well—whether that wooing behaviour is translated into a willingness to engage in extended foreplay or to perform extended oral sex. We have also observed that the well documented 'sexual reluctance' of many wives may be in part a definitional difficulty—a result of defining sexuality within marriage with exclusive reference to the preferences and rhythms of husbandly desire. As a result, our energies have tended to be channelled into coaxing wives to conform to a male sexual standard. It's an assumption we have all internalised—which is why so many wives feel not simply anxious about sex, but actually guilty. The pressure to 'submit' comes as much from within as from without.

To reverse this injustice by placing wives' sexual needs ahead of those of their husbands is not the answer either—although it is not without appeal! Apart from the daunting practical difficulties involved, such a role reversal would not solve the problem of inequality but merely displace it. What we require instead is a genuine re-examination of the basis of sexual relating in marriage, so that women get more of what they need, when and how they need it. And if that means men get less of what they need, so be it. We need to be brave about this one. The myth of male sexuality which teaches us that men 'must' be satisfied—with an implied 'or else'—remains a powerful undercurrent in our gender politics at large. It's high time that the idea of 'nuptial rights', formerly the basis for regarding 'wife rape' as a legal contradiction in terms, was made to work both ways: to recognise and respect the sexual rhythms of wives as well as those of husbands.

How we accomplish all this is of course the real question, and one to which I am not at all sure of an answer. Yet, at the risk of fudging furiously, I do believe a shift in consciousness is a necessary precondition for achieving any lasting change between partners. Women who have never considered the integrity of their own sexuality as a primary force rather than a reactive response to that of a male partner are unlikely even to imagine alternatives, let alone to succeed in bringing them into being.

Yet the problem of sexuality and marriage goes much deeper, if you'll forgive a bad pun, than who does what to whom. Research indicates that sexual incompatibility is very rarely cited as the reason for marital break-ups: only about 2 per cent according to a 1999 survey by the Australian Institute of Family Studies. On the other hand, infidelity—which many would define as the ultimate in sexual incompatibility—accounted for one in five break-ups. In fact, after 'communication problems' (27 per cent), infidelity ranked equal second with generalised 'drifting apart' (21 per cent) as the main reason respondents gave for their marriages ending.[2] Clearly, there are a lot of sexually dissatisfied married people out there. Equally clearly, the desire for more, better or just plain different sex is a formidable factor in the breakdown of contemporary marriage. It's one of the problems social commentators are least likely to discuss—undoubtedly because it is among the least amenable to changes in social policy or procedure. Marriage counsellors can have a go at teaching couples how to 'communicate' better. But I've yet to see a handbook for couples who need to get better at fidelity.

The challenge of staying satisfied by a single sexual partner over the course of a lifetime is a problem that has dogged monogamy forever. Patriarchal cultures have given rise to numerous ingenious solutions to this in-built threat to family stability. Not at all surprisingly, they have been exclusively focused on the satisfaction of male erotic needs. Such solutions have ranged from the extreme of legal polygamy to more covertly sanctioned sexual safety valves like prostitutes, concubines, mistresses and (as in contemporary Japan) 'sex wives'. We tend to forget that the rise in divorce statistics has been paralleled by an equally precipitous decline in such covert relationships. The Hillary Clintons of the world notwithstanding, wives who, in another time and place, would have turned a blind eye to an infidelity, are today increasingly unwilling to do so. Let's face it. They are no longer compelled to by social or economic necessity.

Infidelities committed by wives, on the other hand, have rarely been afforded the same tolerance by husbands. It is only in the last fifty years that infidelity has ceased to be regarded as an airtight legal defence for wife murder. Obviously, women have been unfaithful to their husbands since time immemorial. Indeed, recent research suggests that such infidelities probably represent an important, albeit vestigial, strategy of sexual selection. Research conducted by evolutionary anthropologist David Buss, for example, found that women who cheat on their husbands do so when they are most likely to conceive, but have sex with their spouses when they are least likely to do so.[3] The imperative to acquire better genes through a variety of partners is still very much a part of the animal nature of our species—whether we are male or female. The difference is that, today, when sexual fatigue sets in within the original relationship, females are independent enough to sever it outright. Let a more attractive pair of genes (as it were) present itself, and she's outta there.

My impression—and it really is just that, I have no hard data on this one at all—is that men are a lot less likely to end a relationship over their own infidelity. And the reason, I suspect, is that once the sexual adventure is over—whether for the afternoon, or for all time—a man wants to go home again. And home is where his wife and children and associated comforts and services are. Home, you might say, is where the wifework is. For a woman, of course, all of this is different. A woman is like a turtle. She carries her home on her back. She carries her children there too. The wife rarely loses her home when a marriage ends in the same way that her husband will. I don't simply mean that she is likely to be awarded ownership of the family house, but that she will remain the homemaker in every sense of that term. For a man, divorce is not simply the loss of a woman, his wife. It is the loss of *home*—family, hot meals, clean underwear, ironed shirts, a tidy house, routine, structure, a social identity and a reason to go to work every morning. Compared to all that, sex with the proper stranger—or even an improper one—seems decidedly anticlimactic.

Men are more protective, more conservative about marriage—sex or no sex—because it gives them so very much. Women have become more cavalier, more adventuresome, more critical, more willing to pursue risk, because for them marriage represents just the opposite kind of bargain. The way marriage is currently structured and carried out, they have a point. For many women, husbands really are expendable. The fallacy for wives lies in assuming that fathers are too. Partly because we are now encouraged to regard marriage as an arrangement between two adults, instead of a device for the rearing of children, it is easy to underestimate how big a hole in the home an absentee father will leave. Even if his role seemed purely ceremonial to her, even if she 'felt like a single mother already', nine chances out of ten the children felt differently. To them, he was as much at the heart of family life as she was, no matter how much he did or didn't 'participate'. If there's one thing children teach you, it's that it's not always what you do that matters. It's who you are.

The question of how to achieve fidelity within marriage is the wrong question. Rather, we need to address the issue of how to manage sexuality within marriage. The risk of infidelity will always be there; so too will the reality. We can take steps to reduce its likelihood; but we will never, ever be able to prevent it happening, even within the 'best' of marriages. Sex isn't terribly amenable to discipline, as most of us have learned to our amazement, grief or horror. There is no doubt that the average marriage bed is a highly unerotic space for women, and a somewhat less unerotic space for men. To an extent, that's the nature of the beast. Familiarity, routine, competing needs and stresses all take their toll in time—a remarkably fast time—on marital sexuality. 'Keeping the magic alive,' as they say, is one of the most challenging of all relationship tasks, and the least likely to be attended to in those critical 'crunch' years of early parenting. Yet taking a technical approach to marital sexuality, finding tips and tricks to help us keep on keeping on, is perhaps itself part of the problem.

I suspect our expectations about sexual gratification within marriage are way out of line with what most normal human beings can be expected to deliver. Sure, there are couples who manage to make the earth move, and keep it moving for a lifetime, never straying, always inventive, ever attentive. But all the evidence suggests that the shining example such couples set are highly exceptional. Anomalous, even. To brand marriages that fall short of such a standard as failures is worse than cruel. It's counterproductive. Whether extra-maritally or intra-murally, we need to put sex in its place. Past the age of raging adolescent hormones, sex doesn't really deserve to reign at the centre of our lives. It's an important driving force in the creation of family life. If we allow it to become the decisive one, its potential for destruction will be assured.

In a broader sense, it is ironic that our expectations of marriage appear to have risen almost as precipitously as the divorce rate itself. Ironic, but not coincidental. The ideal of the companionate marriage—a marriage between friends, equals, soulmates, lovers—proposes a marriage that exists, like art, for its own sake. Sociologist Anthony Giddens has termed this new ideal the 'pure relationship'. The 'impossible relationship' would probably be accurate.

Writes Giddens, 'A pure relationship is one in which external criteria have become dissolved: the relationship exists solely for whatever rewards that relationship can deliver'.[4] Interestingly, these statements are echoed almost word for word by the editors of *The New Republic*, in an article supporting the establishment of homosexual marriage. Marriage, they argue, is 'a situation where a social relation is entered into for its own sake, for what can be derived by each person from a sustained association with another; and which is continued only in so far as it is thought by both parties to deliver enough satisfaction for each individual to stay within it'.[5] Such postmodern definitions emphasise marriage as a two-way street, not an 'intersection' in which other parties—i.e., offspring and extended family members, for starters—are important stakeholders. They underscore too the totally voluntary nature of the connection.

Under such terms and conditions, marriage has a contingent shelf life: it is only good until further notice.[6] Any relationship that does not deliver intimacy, equality and mutuality at the recommended dosages and intervals has passed its use-by date.

The change from marriage-as-an-institution to marriage-as-a-relationship, notes Australian social critic Hugh Mackay, virtually guarantees a revolving-door approach to family life. 'Under the new contract, we cannot help but feel that "the relationship" is on permanent trial', Mackay writes. As a result, 'glitches that might once have been tolerated as part of married life—from a tiff over money to darker periods of mutual loathing—can feel like potentially fatal flaws'.[7] The concept of the pure relationship has raised the marriage stakes to heights so lofty only the tiniest minority of mere mortals could ever achieve them. At the same time, it has also sold marriage far, far too cheaply. It is incredibly naive, yet such assumptions about what marriage ought to be are precisely those that have most profoundly infiltrated our popular imagination. They have been accepted, without reservation, by the majority of young and young-ish (i.e., baby boomer and below) people today. I used to be one of them. I am no longer. Today, I find it extraordinary that anybody could have ever expected anything *but* a massive breakdown of family life with such principles to guide us. Indeed, the only real surprise is not that half of all marriages fail, but that half survive.

The reality, according to people who have 'succeeded' at marriage and those who study them, could not be further away from the ideals of the pure relationship. Sociologist Lawrence Kurdek, for example, looked at 500 couples over a ten-year period in an effort to determine 'the trajectory of change in marital quality'. What he found was absolutely astonishing…to anyone who hadn't been married for ten years. Kurdek's findings have established that the quality of marriage for both spouses sinks rapidly after they say 'I do', and continues downward throughout the next four years. Finally the couple reaches a plateau of discontent.

That lasts about three years. Next, they experience yet another precipitous plummet into marital misery, which starts at around the infamous seven-year mark and doesn't finish until about year ten. These second-tier declines are even steeper when children are present. From that point on, Kurdek surmises, things start to look up. Then again, how would he know? His study stopped after ten years. Kurdek's findings are corroborated by numerous other researchers. Notes Howard Markman, head of the Center for Marital and Family Studies at the University of Denver, 'problems early in marriage worsen over time'.[8] Even the best marriages 'don't see the dawn of mutuality—that easy flow of support and mutuality—before ten to 15 years', according to Dr Liberty Kovacs, head of the Center for Marriage and Family Therapy in Sacramento, California.[9]

Depressing? Well, I suppose that all depends on your perspective. Lawrence Kurdek, for one, is 'actually rather hopeful' about his findings on marital quality. 'We have to build into marriage the idea that there will be lots of change,' he explains.[10] I would add that it's not just the change we've got to acknowledge, but its direction: downward. For me, the parallel with childbirth is an obvious one. If you haven't been prepared for the pain, you will not only find it unendurable—you'll feel frightened, betrayed, depressed and inferior. If you have been prepared, you may still find the pain unendurable. But you increase the odds that you'll go the distance, and you'll not compound the misery with fear and self-flagellation. Simply knowing that 'this is the way it's supposed to be' can make all the difference in the world to pain management, whether in childbirth or any other labour of love. At the very least, the best information we have at our disposal suggests that even a 'good' marriage will test to the limit partners' capacity to defer gratification. Couples who stagger through the first years of marriage—hell, even the first decade—thinking resentfully 'It shouldn't have to be this hard' can think again. As a matter of fact, it *does* have to be that hard.

Marriage entails a sort of base level of unhappiness that couples need to learn to anticipate and accept. In other words, there is only so much fun to go around. So when we speak of 'making marriage more fun for women' we need to remember that we're looking to achieve a better *balance*—a closer ratio of playfulness to sobriety, of pleasure to service.

For both parties, however, marriage today seems like harder work than ever. Did our parents, for example—who never seemed to worry about having a Relationship—really agonise the way modern couples do? Was married life really and truly simpler then, or were we too young to notice the complexities? The answer is almost certainly a bit of both. Marriages made a generation ago, according to recent research, actually *were* less conflictual than today's. A study of two generations conducted by Stacy Rogers and Paul Amato found the younger group had significantly lower levels of interaction and higher levels of struggle and problems—yet in this case the two groups were only twelve years apart. According to their analysis of data from the General Social Survey, the number of people reporting 'very happy marriages' declined gradually but significantly from 1973 to 1988.[11] This is even more worrying when you consider that during the same period the divorce rate was skyrocketing—thus removing the really awful marriages from the total pool (or so one would have thought). Perhaps 'happiness', in the final analysis, is simply a reflection of the fit between expectation and reality.

We all expect more of marriage than our parents ever did. But the generation gap yawns particularly wide for women. I think of my mother's response when my second marriage ended. 'But he's the father of your children!' she cried. 'And he earns so much money!' For her, nothing short of sustained physical abuse would have constituted acceptable grounds for divorce under those circumstances. If a man was a good provider, didn't sleep around and loved his children—even if he rarely caught a glimpse of them!—then that was enough. For most women today, needless to say, it would not be. I also think most men would have higher expectations of themselves as husbands than such a brief checklist would suggest. Yet perhaps not *much* higher. Among many other observers, sociologist David De Vaus believes the 'gender gap' in marriage is still uncomfortably wide. 'Over the last quarter-century the women's movement has successfully challenged many aspects of traditional gender roles. There have been significant changes in the aspirations, expectations and behaviour of many women,' he notes. 'But we do not know whether men have been changing at the same rate or even in the same direction.'[12]

De Vaus' own research indicates they haven't. He found that men were more inclined than women to think mothers of young children should stay home, and believed full-time work for women generally was bad for families. More men than women endorsed the breadwinner role for husbands and saw themselves as protectors. The men in De Vaus' study were also more 'couple-minded' than women. They were more likely to believe that married couples should do most things together. They were more inclined to believe that married people were happier than single people. They believed more strongly that 'the really important relationships' were those in the home. Men not only opposed single parenting more often than women did, but they were also more inclined to stress the value of having children. And finally—perhaps the least surprising finding of all—they were more opposed to divorce.

It's not that men haven't changed at all over the last quarter-century. It's simply that they haven't changed as fast, or as far, as women have. Yet it would also be a mistake to overestimate (as many, many of us have done) the degree to which women themselves have 'evolved' over the same period. As we have seen throughout this book, there remains a huge gap between what women say they believe about marriage, and how they actually behave as wives. There are plenty of contradictions between the words and the deeds of husbands too. Yet overall I suspect there is more synchrony of belief and action among married men than among married women. The result is that men are less conflicted about marriage than women are. They are far less likely to see 'what the fuss is all about'—in many cases, right up until the moment they are asked to leave.

Understanding how and why this chaotic and contradictory state of affairs has arisen is a crucial first step towards resolution. Assigning blame, on the other hand, will only take us further and further away from that goal. Is feminism to 'blame' for the crisis in modern marriage? That's what the neo-traditionalists would have us believe, from Laura Doyle and the Surrendered Wives to social critics like Danielle Crittenden, author of *What Our Mothers Didn't Tell Us*. In a way, of course, they're right. Without the equality that women have achieved in public life, there would be no crisis about the degree of inequality they still labour under in their private lives. It's a bit like blaming black unemployment on the abolition of slavery. Alternatively, we can blame 'society' for what's gone wrong with marriage today—for 'giving us', as we often say, gender roles that are no longer adequate to the task. Well, there's a lot of truth here as well. We do not exist apart from 'society' and its 'rules', the vast majority of which we have inherited, not created. Yet 'society' is no more a static entity than 'personality' or 'intelligence' or 'marriage' itself, for that matter. The 'society made me do it' argument often amounts to a cop-out. 'Don't ask little *me* to change,' it simpers. 'I'm just following orders.'

To blame individual men and women for these difficulties, particularly the individual men and women we happen to love, seems equally futile. Women who express their unhappiness with the wifely role through husband-bashing generally achieve very little anyway. They are dismissed as 'attacking' or 'controlling' and too often end up by accepting that their discontents are 'their own problem'. Wives who lecture their husbands about equality and mutuality in marriage usually discover, to their frustration, that they are only consolidating the role structure that casts women as the disgruntled grown-ups and men as the cheeky little boys. Blaming women themselves is, if anything, even less appropriate. The argument that 'women are their own worst enemies' is a very popular one—particularly, I have noticed, among women who enjoy the privilege of unusual professional or financial success. To be sure, most women do collude in the maintenance of the structures that constrain them, but it is collusion at a very deep level of consciousness and inheritance. Blaming women for their collusion in wifework is a bit like blaming poverty on the poor. Of course wives are their own worst enemies. When self-sacrifice in the service of others is exactly what the social construction of 'wife' requires, how could it be otherwise?

There's a scene in John Steinbeck's *The Grapes of Wrath* in which a dustbowl farmer's land is about to be repossessed. Half-crazed with worry, he explains that his family will starve without their land. 'Don't go blaming me,' the man with the writ interrupts irritably. 'It ain't my fault. All I know is I got my orders.' But who do the orders come from? the farmer wants to know. 'It ain't nobody, it's a company,' he is told. Doesn't the company have a president? the farmer persists. 'Oh, son, it ain't his fault,' comes the reply. 'The bank tells him what to do.' And so it goes, till the farmer, in exasperation, cries, 'Well who *do* I shoot?' 'Brother, I don't know,' admits the bureaucrat. The fact that there is no clear culprit, Steinbeck seems to be saying, is an essential part of the tragedy.

Who should we shoot for wifework? There's nobody and nothing to blame; and yet responsibility for the crisis belongs to all of us. The first order of business is to recognise our complicity, without beating ourselves up or anybody else up either. For men and women alike, the challenge is to understand our past behaviour, and to take responsibility for producing change for the future—which is our children's future, and our grandchildren's.

Marriage will not die, even if we try to kill it. But it can and it must adapt to the adaptations of its environment. And a new balance between the 'enduring vulnerabilities' of both male and female participants will have to be found. It may well be that, in the next generation, marriage will cease to be the default option for achieving adult status in our society. Indeed, the two clearest demographic trends of the next fifty years forecast rising rates of cohabitation and falling rates of fertility—a combination of circumstances strongly favouring the return of marriage to its original function: as a social nest for the bearing and rearing of children. People who don't intend to have children—a larger and larger segment of post-industrial society—simply won't bother with marriage. People who do will be left to hammer out an arrangement that offers 'good enough' rewards to *all* stakeholders.

One thing is certain. Marriage must be made to serve wives at least as much as wives serve marriage, if women are to be induced to participate in it. At the same time, having a wife and children must be seen by men for the enormous privilege that it is: the pearl of great price for which no sacrifice is too great. Yet the insight itself is not enough. As we have seen repeatedly, our beliefs and values about marriage and family life are one thing, our behaviour quite another. When our words and our deeds are no longer two but one—as partners in marriage are meant to be—we'll know we have succeeded.

notes

1: the job description

1 Julie Macken, 'The Mystery of Why Women Marry', *Australian Financial Review*, 28–29 August 1999, p. 32.

2 Dalma Heyn, *Marriage Shock*, Villard Books, New York, 1997.

3 Joan Chandler, *Women without Husbands*, Macmillan Education, London, 1991, p. 7.

4 Arlie Russell Hochschild, *The Time Bind*, Henry Holt, New York, 1997, p. 210.

5 Naomi Miller, *Single Parents by Choice*, Plenum Books, New York, 1992, p. 1.

6 Jessie Bernard, *The Future of Marriage*, 2nd edn, Yale University Press, New Haven, 1982, p. 5.

7 Irene Wolcott & Jody Hughes, 'Towards Understanding the Reasons for Divorce' in Australian Institute of Family Studies working paper no. 20, June 1999.

8 Carol Tavris, *The Mismeasure of Woman*, Simon & Schuster, New York, 1992.

9 Janice Steil, *Marital Equality*, Sage Publications, Thousand Oaks, California, 1997, pp. 15–16.

10 Julian Hafner, *The End of Marriage*, Random House, London, 1993.

11 Heyn, *Marriage Shock*.

12 ibid, p. 11.

13 quoted in Hara Estroff Marano, 'The Reinvention of Marriage' in *Psychology Today*, January–February 1992, p. 48.

14 Natalie Angier, 'Men: Are Women Better Off with Them or without Them?', *New York Times*, 21 June 1998.

15 Steil, *Marital Equality*.

16 US Census data, quoted in Eric Schmitt, 'For First Time, Nuclear Families Drop Below 25% of Households', *New York Times*, 14 May 2001.

17 Steven Nock, 'The Problem with Marriage', in *Society*, vol. 36 (5), 1999, p. 20.

18 Sarah Blaffer Hrdy, *Mother Nature*, Chatto & Windus, London, 1999, p. 232.

19 Steil, *Marital Equality*.

20 Hiromi Ono, 'Historical Time and US Marital Dissolution' in *Social Forces*, vol. 77 (3), 1999, p. 969.

21 Nock, *Society*, p. 20.

22 Linda Waite, 'The Importance of Marriage Is Being Overlooked' in *USA Today*, 127, 2644, 1999, p. 46; Nock, 'The Problem with Marriage'; Steil, *Marital Equality*; Hafner, *The End of Marriage*.

23 Steven Nock, *Marriage in Men's Lives*, Oxford University Press, New York, 1998, p. 15.

24 Mary Bowler, 'Women's Earnings: An Overview', Monthly Labor Review Online, vol. 122 (12), December 1999.

25 Equal Pay Task Force, 'Just Pay: The Report of the Equal Pay Task Force', EOC, 2001.

26 Ken Dempsey, 'Women's Perceptions of Fairness and the Persistence of an Unequal Division of Housework', *Family Matters*, Spring–Summer 1997, p. 15.

27 Dorothy Smith, *The Everyday World as Problematic*, Northeastern University Press, Boston, 1987, p. 33.

28 Dale Spender ed., *Weddings and Wives*, Penguin, Ringwood, 1994, p. 56.

29 cited in Anthony McMahon, *Taking Care of Men*, Cambridge University Press, Cambridge, 1999.

30 Judith Wallerstein & Sandra Blakeslee, *The Good Marriage*, Houghton Mifflin, New York, 1995, p. 70.

31 Steil, *Marital Equality*, p. 80.

32 quoted in McMahon, *Taking Care of Men*, p. 2.

33 Germaine Greer, *The Whole Woman*, Transworld, London, 1999, p. 244.

2: of marriage, metamorphosis and rotten eggs

1 Susan Rosenbluth, Janice Steil & Juliet Whitcomb, 'Marital Equality: What Does It Mean?' in *Journal of Family Issues*, May 1998, p. 227.

2 Michael Bittman & Jocelyn Pixley, *The Double Life of the Family*, Allen & Unwin, Sydney, 1997, p. 146.

3 McMahon, *Taking Care of Men*, p. 16.

4 Stephanie Dowrick, *Intimacy and Solitude*, Reed Books, Auckland, 1991, p. 107.

3: meet the wife

1 cited in Hrdy, *Mother Nature*, p. 216.

2 ibid, p. 228.

3 Nock, *Marriage in Men's Lives*, p. 32.

4 Hrdy, *Mother Nature*, p. 223.

5 Douglas T. Kenrick, Melanie R. Trost & Virgil L. Sheets, 'Power, Harassment, and Trophy Mates: The Feminist Advantages of an Evolutionary Perspective' in *Sex, Power, Conflict*, David Buss & Neil Malamuth eds, Oxford University Press, New York, 1996, pp. 42–43.

6 ibid, p. 44.

4: the monogamy trade-off

1 cited in Hrdy, *Mother Nature*, p. 229.

5: why do we do it to ourselves?

1 Macken, *Australian Financial Review*, p. 32.

2 Jason Fields & Lynne M. Casper, 'American Families and Living Arrangements: Population Characteristics', Current Population Reports, June 2001.

3 US Department of Commerce press release, 'Married Adults Still in the Majority', Census Bureau Reports, 7 January 1999.

4 ABS figures, 2001.

5 Amara Bachu, 'Trends in Marital Status of US Women at First Birth: 1930 to 1994', US Bureau of the Census, Population Division, working paper no. 20, March 1998.

6 Martha Albertson Fineman, *The Neutered Mother and the Sexual Family*, Routledge, New York, 1995, p. 76.

7 Barbara Dafoe Whitehead, *The Divorce Culture*, Vintage Books, New York, 1998, p. 149.

8 Bachu, 'Trends in Marital Status of US Women at First Birth: 1930 to 1994'.

9 'In Brief', *Population Trends 100*, Office for National Statistics (UK), Summer 2000.

10 Tamar Lewin, 'Child Well-being Improves, US Says', *New York Times*, 19 July 2001.

11 John Haskey, 'One-Parent Families and their Dependent Children', *Population Trends 91*, ONS (UK), Spring 1998.

12 Australian Bureau of Statistics, 1997 Births Australia, 3301, 12 November 1998.

13 John Fox & David Pearce, 'Twenty-five Years of Population Trends', *Population Trends 100*, ONS (UK).

14 *Australian*, 2 August 2000, p. 1.

15 Whitehead, *The Divorce Culture*, p. 149.

16 Deborah Orr, 'New Rights the Best Gifts for Fathers', *Independent*, 15 June 2001.

17 Whitehead, *The Divorce Culture*, p. 145.

18 ibid, p. 146.

19 ibid, p. 146.

20 John Stapleton, 'An Ordinary Decent Father Can Make a World of Difference', *Weekend Australian*, 5–6 August 2000, p. 27.

21 Patricia Cohen, 'Daddy Dearest: Do You Really Matter?', *New York Times*, Arts & Ideas, 11 July 1998.

22 Stapleton, *Weekend Australian*.

23 Cohen, *New York Times*.

24 Stapleton, *Weekend Australian*.

25 ibid.

26 Cherry Norton, 'New Fathers Get Better Jobs and Work Harder', *Independent*, 9 May 2000.

27 'Parents Hit the Career Bump', *Independent on Sunday*, 2 April 2000.

28 Cherry Norton, 'Ministers Join Bid to Give Fathers More Support', *Independent*, 18 November 1999.

29 Yvonne Roberts, 'Fathers Are Doing It for Themselves', *Independent*, 6 December 1999.

30 Deborah Orr, 'Caring Fathers Get a Raw Deal', *Independent*, 16 June 2000.

31 Lorna Duckworth, 'New Place for Fathers in Maternity Wards', *Independent*, 16 June 2001.

32 Deborah Orr, 'Men and Women Can't Be Equal', *Independent*, 12 September 2000.

33 Norton, *Independent*, 9 May 2000.

6: rising expectations and diminishing returns

1 Andrea Carson, 'Female Pay Scales Fail to Keep Up', *Age*, 12 May 2000, p. 3.

2 Sylvia Ann Hewlett, 'Have a Child, and Experience the Wage Gap', *New York Times*, 16 May 2000.

3 Frances Drever, Katie Fisher, Joanna Brown & Jenny Clark, 'Social Inequalities, 2000 Edition', ONS (UK), 2000.

4 Australian Bureau of Statistics, 'Employee Earnings and Hours, Australia, 6306.0, 25 March 1999.

5 ibid.

6 Spender, *Weddings and Wives*, p. 41.

7 Hrdy, *Mother Nature*, p. 346.

8 Katharine Graham, *Personal History*, Orion, London, 1998, p. 417.

9 cited in Michele Lonsdale, *Liberating Women*, Cambridge University Press, Cambridge, 1991, p. 20.

10 *Australian Women's Weekly*, 25 August 1954, p. 21.

11 Abigail Trafford, Patricia A. Avery, Jeannye Thornton, Joseph Carey & Joseph L. Galloway, 'She's Come a Long Way—or Has She?', US News and World Report, vol. 97, p. 44 (8), 6 August 1984.

12 Philip N. Cohen & Suzanne M. Bianchi, 'Marriage, Children, and Women's Employment: What Do We Know?', *Monthly Labor Review*, December 1999.

13 Walter Licht & Jonathan Grossman, 'How the Workplace Has Changed in 75 Years', *Monthly Labor Review*, vol. 111, no. 2, p. 19 (7), February 1988.

14 Steil, *Marital Equality*, p. 48.

15 Daphne Spain & Suzanne Bianchi, *Balancing Act: Motherhood, Marriage and Employment among American Women*, Russell Sage Foundation, New York, 1996, pp. 152–53.

16 cited in Bittman & Pixley, *The Double Life of the Family*, p. 52.

17 Hafner, *The End of Marriage*, p. 188.

18 ibid, p. 188.

19 ibid, p. 194.

20 Greer, *The Whole Woman*, p. 251.

21 Bittman & Pixley, *The Double Life of the Family*, p. 52.

22 Waite, *USA Today*.

23 Steil, *Marital Equality*, p. 80.

24 cited in Chandler, *Women without Husbands*, pp. 50–51.

25 Greer, *The Whole Woman*, p. 247.

26 cited in Miriam Johnson, *Strong Mothers, Weak Wives*, University of California Press, Berkeley, 1988.

7: mars and venus scrub the toilet

1 Spain & Bianchi, *Balancing Act*, p. 171.

2 McMahon, *Taking Care of Men*, p. 15.

3 Chandler, *Women without Husbands*, pp. 121–22.

4 cited in McMahon, *Taking Care of Men*.

5 cited in Nock, *Marriage in Men's Lives*, p. 39.

6 cited in Bittman & Pixley, *The Double Life of the Family*, p. 111.

7 ibid, p. 105.

8 Nock, *Marriage in Men's Lives*, pp. 86–87.

9 Suzanne Bianchi, Melissa A. Milkie, Liana C. Sayer & John P. Robinson, 'Is Anyone Doing the Housework? Trends in the Gender Division of Household Labor', *Social Forces*, vol. 79, i. 1, p. 91, September 2000.

10 Bittman & Pixley, *The Double Life of the Family*.

11 cited in Jo Lindsay, 'Diversity But Not Equality: Domestic Labour in Cohabiting Relationships' in *Australian Journal of Social Issues*, August 1999, p. 267.

12 Rebecca Abrams, *The Playful Self*, Fourth Estate, London, 1997.

13 Ken Dempsey, 'Attempting to Explain Women's Perceptions of Their Fairness of the Division of Housework' in *Journal of Family Studies*, April 1999, pp. 3–24.

14 Greer, *The Whole Woman*, p. 119.

15 Abrams, *The Playful Self*, p. 17.

16 Bittman & Pixley, *The Double Life of the Family*.

17 *Australian Women's Weekly*, 21 January 1958, p. 19.

18 Dowrick, *Intimacy and Solitude*, p. 17.

19 Dempsey, *Journal of Family Studies*.

20 quoted in McMahon, *Taking Care of Men*, p. 4.

21 *Australian Women's Weekly*, 18 March 1959, reproduced in Lonsdale, *Liberating Women*, pp. 13–15.

8: believing in pyjamas

1 Camille Sweeney, 'The Truth about Sex—At Any Given Moment' in *New York Times Magazine*, 16 May 1999.

2 Steil, *Marital Equality*, p. 97.

3 ibid.

4 ibid, p. 40.

5 cited in Hochschild, *The Time Bind*, p. 184.

6 Steil, *Marital Equality*, p. 52.

7 Bittman & Pixley, *The Double Life of the Family*, pp. 149–50.

8 Nock, *Society*.

9 McMahon, *Taking Care of Men*, p. 67.

10 Bittman & Pixley, *The Double Life of the Family*.

11 ibid.

12 Greer, *The Whole Woman*, p. 57.

13 ibid, p. 62.

14 McMahon, *Taking Care of Men*, p. 47.

15 Chandler, *Women without Husbands*, p. 227.

16 Greer, *The Whole Woman*, pp. 133–34.

17 Nock, *Marriage in Men's Lives*, p. 86.

18 Bittman & Pixley, *The Double Life of the Family*, p. 165.

19 ibid, p. 167.

20 ibid, p. 165.

21 ibid, p. 158.

22 cited in McMahon, *Taking Care of Men*, p. 18.

23 Steil, *Marital Equality*, p. 34.

24 Rosenbluth et al., 'Marital Equality'.

25 Bittman & Pixley, *The Double Life of the Family*, p. 47.

26 Dempsey, *Journal of Family Studies*, p. 4.

27 Bittman & Pixley, *The Double Life of the Family*, p. 157.

28 Susan Maushart, 'Mother Knows Best: Australian Women Learn to Mother', International Year of the Family research report, Family and Children's Services, Western Australia, 1996.

29 Spain & Bianchi, *Balancing Act*, p. 171.

30 Steil, *Marital Equality*, pp. 107–8.

31 Dempsey, *Journal of Family Studies*.

9: and baby makes two and a half

1 Henry Weir, 'Dad's Dilemma—Family vs. Career' in *Family Circle*, August 2000, p. 22.

2 Alice Lesch Kelly, *New York Times*, 13 June 1999.

3 ibid.

4 ibid.

5 Carolyn Pape Cowan & Philip Cowan, *When Partners Become Parents*, Basic Books, New York, 1992, p. 109.

6 quoted in Terri Apter, *Why Women Don't Have Wives*, Macmillan, London, 1985, p. 98.

7 Wallerstein & Blakeslee, *The Good Marriage*, p. 24.

8 Cowan & Cowan, *When Partners Become Parents*.

9 cited in Robert Emery & Michele Tuer, 'Parenting and the Marital Relationship' in *Parenting: An Ecological Perspective*, Tom Luster & Lynn Okagaki eds, Lawrence Erlbaum Associates Inc., Hillsdale, NJ, 1993.

10 J. Belsky, M. Lang & M. Rovine, 'Stability and Change across the Transition to Parenthood: A Second Study' in *Journal of Personality and Social Psychology*, vol. 50, 1985, pp 517–22.

11 Rosenbluth et al., *Journal of Family Issues*.

12 Steil, *Marital Equality*, p. 18.

13 Nock, *Society*.

14 ABS 3101, 1999.

15 Bernard, *The Future of Marriage*.

16 'Marriages in England and Wales during 1999, *Population Trends 103*, ONS (UK).

17 John Haskey, 'Cohabitation in Great Britain: Past, Present and Future Trends—and Attitudes, *Population Trends 104*, ONS (UK).

18 'Fertility, Family Planning and Women's Health: New Data from the 1995 National Survey of Family Growth', US Department of Health and Human Services, series 23, no. 19, May 1997.

19 Stephanie J. Ventura, Joyce A. Martin, Sally C. Curtin & T. J. Mathews, 'Births: Final Data for 1997', National Vital Statistics Reports, vol. 47, no. 18, 29 April 1999.

20 'Birth Statistics, Review of the Registrar General on Births and Patterns of Family-building in England and Wales, 1999', series FM1, no. 28, London Stationery Office.

21 ABS 3301, 1999.

10: equality go bye-byes

1 John P. Robinson & Geoffrey Godbey, *Time for Life: The Surprising Ways Americans Use Their Time*, Pennsylvania State University Press, University Park, 1997, p. 104.

2 cited in McMahon, *Taking Care of Men*, p. 13.

3 Michael Bittman, *Juggling Time: How Australian Families Use Time*, Commonwealth of Australia, Canberra, 1991.

4 quoted in Nicole Martin, 'Caring Fathers Help Children to Thrive', *Daily Telegraph*, 13 June 2001.

5 Bittman & Pixley, *The Double Life of the Family*.

6 ibid, p. 21.

7 David Demo, Katherine R. Allen & Mark A. Fine eds, *Handbook of Family Diversity*, Oxford University Press, New York, 2000, p. 89.

8 McMahon, *Taking Care of Men*, p. 72.

9 ibid, p. 81.

10 Grace Baruch & Rosalind Barnett, 1986, cited in Steil, *Marital Equality*, pp. 51–52.

11 Demo et al., *Handbook of Family Diversity*, p. 93.

12 Elizabeth Ozer, 'The Impact of Childcare Responsibility and Self Efficacy on the Psychological Health of Professional Working Mothers' in *Psychology of Women Quarterly*, September 1995, pp. 315–35.

13 Nicole Martin, 'Working Mothers Are Stressed and Exhausted', *Daily Telegraph*, 13 June 2001.

14 Demo et al., *Handbook of Family Diversity*, p. 89.

15 Lucy Ward & Peter May, 'Daddy's Home . . .', *Guardian*, 16 June 1999.

16 Cherry Norton, 'UK Parents Spend Most "Quality" Time with Children', *Independent*, 27 October 2000.

17 Ward & May, *Guardian*, 16 June 1999.

18 'Recent Changes in Unpaid Work', ABS occasional paper, 4154.0, 1995.

19 ibid.

20 Demo et al., *Handbook of Family Diversity*, pp. 89–90.

21 Catherine M. Lee & Linda Duxbury, 'Employed Parents' Support from Partners, Employers and Friends', *Journal of Social Psychology*, vol. 138, no. 3, p. 303 (20), June 1998.

22 William T. Bailey, 'A Longitudinal Study of Fathers' Involvement with Young Children: Infancy to Age 5 Years', *Journal of Genetic Psychology*, vol. 155, no. 3, p. 331 (9), September 1994.

23 Tamar Lewin, 'Men Assuming Bigger Share at Home, New Survey Shows', *New York Times*, 15 April 1998.

24 Pleck, 1985, cited in Anna Dienhart, *Reshaping Fatherhood: The Social Construction of Shared Parenting*, Sage, Thousand Oaks, 1998.

25 Charles Hoffman & Michelle Moon, 'Women's Characteristics and Gender Role Attitudes: Support for Father Involvement with Children' in *Journal of Genetic Psychology*, December 1999, pp. 411–18.

26 Sarah Allen & Alan Hawkins, 'Maternal Gatekeeping: Mothers' Beliefs and Behaviors That Inhibit Greater Father Involvement in Family Work' in *Journal of Marriage and the Family*, February 1999, pp. 199–212.

27 June Ellestad & Jan Stets, 'Jealousy and Parenting: Predicting Emotions

from Identity Theory' in *Sociological Perspectives*, Fall 1998, pp. 639–68.

28 Dienhart, *Reshaping Fatherhood*, p. 176.

29 ibid, p. 180.

30 Paula Caplan, *Don't Blame Mother: Mending the Mother–Daughter Relationship*, Harper & Row, New York, 1989.

31 Dorothy Dinnerstein, *The Rocking of the Cradle and the Ruling of the World*, Women's Press, London, 1987.

11: the wifely art of emotional caregiving

1 Pepper Schwartz, *Peer Marriage*, Free Press, New York, 1994, p. 3.

2 Jean Duncombe & Dennis Marsden, '"Workaholics" and "Whingeing Women": Theorising Intimacy and Emotion Work' in *Sociological Review*, vol. 43, 1995, pp. 150–69.

3 cited in McMahon, *Taking Care of Men*, p. 26.

4 Duncombe & Marsden, *Sociological Review*.

5 Steil, *Marital Equality*.

6 quoted in McMahon, *Taking Care of Men*, p. 196.

7 Schwartz, *Peer Marriage*, p. 23.

8 ibid, p. 22.

9 quoted in Heyn, *Marriage Shock*, p. 173.

10 ibid, p. 174.

11 Wolcott & Hughes, 'Towards Understanding the Reasons for Divorce'.

12 Tavris, *The Mismeasure of Woman*, p. 265 (emphasis retained).

13 Hafner, *The End of Marriage*, p. 94.

14 McMahon, *Taking Care of Men*, p. 197.

12: giving, receiving...getting depressed

1 Susan Donath, 'Pipe and Slippers or Kitchen Sink?' paper presented at the seventh Australian Institute of Family Studies conference, Sydney, July 2000.

2 Janeen Baxter, *Work at Home: The Domestic Division of Labour*, University of Queensland Press, St Lucia, 1993.

3 cited in McMahon, *Taking Care of Men*.

4 Cherry Norton, 'Forecasts of Leisure Society Fail to Materialise', *Independent on Sunday*, 4 October 1998.

5 Abrams, *The Playful Self*, p. 97.

6 Hochschild, *The Time Bind*, pp. 39–40.

7 Greer, *The Whole Woman*, p. 121.

8 M. Deborah Bialeschki & Sarah Michener, 'Re-Entering Leisure: Transition within the Role of Motherhood' in *Journal of Leisure Research*, Winter 1994, p. 57.

9 Valeria Freysinger, 'Leisure with Children and Parental Satisfaction' in *Journal of Leisure Research*, Summer 1994, p. 212.

10 Bialeschki & Michener, *Journal of Leisure Research*.

11 Karla Henderson, 'One Size Doesn't Fit All: The Meaning of Women's Leisure' in *Journal of Leisure Research*, Summer 1996, p. 139.

12 cited in Henderson, *Journal of Leisure Research*.

13 Rebecca Erickson, 'Reconceptualizing Family Work: The Effect of Emotion Work on Perceptions of Marital Quality' in *Journal of Marriage and the Family*, November 1993, p. 888.

14 ibid, p. 890.

15 quoted in Tavris, *The Mismeasure of Woman*, p. 203.

16 A. S. Byatt, *The Virgin in the Garden* in *The Virgin in the Garden/Still Life*, Chatto & Windus, London, 1991, p. 112.

17 cited in Abrams, *The Playful Self*.

18 Erickson, *Journal of Marriage and the Family*.

19 Tim Reid, 'Professor Finds Key to Lasting Happiness', *Sunday Telegraph*, 4 October 1998.

20 Travers & Richardson, 1993, cited in McMahon, *Taking Care of Men*, p. 83.

21 cited in Blaine J. Fowers, 'Psychology and the Good Marriage: Social Theory as Practice' in *American Behavioral Scientist*, January 1998, p. 516.

22 ibid.

23 cited in Steil, *Marital Equality*, pp. 7–8.

24 Claire Rabin & Ofrit Shapira-Berman, 'Egalitarianism and Marital Happiness: Israeli Husbands and Wives on a Collision Course' in *American Journal of Family Therapy*, Winter 1997, p. 319.

25 Steil, *Marital Equality*, p. 80.

26 ibid.

27 cited in McMahon, *Taking Care of Men*, p. 83.

28 Pepper Schwartz, 'Modernizing Marriage' in *Psychology Today*, September–October 1994, p. 54.

29 Ronald F. Levant, 'The Crisis of Connection between Men and Women' in *Journal of Men's Studies*, August 1996, p. 1.

30 Hafner, *The End of Marriage*, p. 29.

31 quoted in Marano, *Psychology Today*, p. 48.

32 Orly Benjamin, 'Therapeutic Discourse, Power and Change: Emotion and Negotiation in Marital Conversations' in *Sociology*, November 1998, p. 771.

33 quoted in 'Studies Show Men Do Better in Marriage than Women' in *Jet*, 12 May 1997, p. 18.

34 quoted in Heyn, *Marriage Shock*, p. 131.

35 Elizabeth Costello, 'Married with Children: Predictors of Mental and Physical Health in Middle-Aged Women' in *Psychiatry: Interpersonal and Biological Processes*, August 1991, p. 292.

36 Roni Beth Tower & Stanislav Kasl, 'Gender, Marital Closeness, and Depressive Symptoms in Elderly Couples' in *Journals of Gerontology*, Series B, May 1996, p. 115.

37 Steil, *Marital Equality*, p. 84.

38 Heather A. Turner & R. Jay Turner, 'Gender, Social Status and Emotional Reliance' in *Journal of Health and Social Behavior*, December 1999, p. 360.

39 'Study: Bad Relationships Affect Women More' in *Mental Health Weekly*, 1 May 2000, p. 8.

40 Marilyn McKean Skaff, John Finney & Rudolf Moos, 'Gender Differences in Problem Drinking and Depression' in *American Journal of Community Psychology*, February 1999, p. 25.

41 ibid.

42 Tavris, *The Mismeasure of Woman*, p. 260.

43 *Jet*, 12 May 1997.

13: not tonight, darling

1 John Harlow, 'Till Death—or the 30-Month Itch—Do Us Part', *Australian*, 26 July 1999, p. 1.

2 Vaughn Call, Susan Sprecher & Pepper Schwartz, 'The Incidence and Frequency of Marital Sex in a National Sample' in *Journal of Marriage and the Family*, August 1995, p. 639.

3 ibid, p. 649.

4 ibid, p. 639.

5 ibid.

6 Schwartz, *Peer Marriage*, p. 81.

7 Cowan & Cowan, *When Partners Become Parents*, p. 106.

8 ibid.

 9 ibid, p. 87.

10 Heyn, *Marriage Shock*, p. 106.

11 quoted in Heyn, *Marriage Shock*, p. 221.

12 Waite, *USA Today Magazine*, p. 46.

13 cited in Sally Dallos & Rudi Dallos, *Couples, Sex and Power: The Politics of Desire*, Open University Press, Buckingham, 1997, p. 150.

14 Jean Duncombe & Dennis Marsden, 'Whose Orgasm Is It, Anyway? "Sex Work" in Long-Term Heterosexual Couple Relationships' in *Sexual Cultures: Communities, Values and Intimacy*, Jeffrey Weeks & Janet Holland eds, St Martin's Press, New York, 1996.

15 Christine Delphy & Diane Leonard, *Familiar Exploitation: A New Analysis of Marriage in Contemporary Western Society*, Polity, Cambridge, 1992, p. 22.

16 Dallos & Dallos, *Couples, Sex and Power*, p. 75.

17 Delphy & Leonard, *Familiar Exploitation*, p. 240.

18 quoted in Susie Orbach, 'Women, Men and Intimacy' in *Rethinking Marriage: Public and Private Perspectives*, Christopher Clulow ed., H. Karnac Ltd, London, 1993, p. 114.

19 Dallos & Dallos, *Couples, Sex and Power*, p. 52.

20 Schwartz, *Peer Marriage*, p. 101.

21 ibid, p. 83.

22 cited in Duncombe & Marsden, 'Whose Orgasm Is It, Anyway?' p. 225.

23 ibid.

24 ibid, p. 230.

25 ibid, p. 230.

26 ibid, p. 234.

27 Dallos & Dallos, *Couples, Sex and Power*, p. 145.

28 ibid, p. 144.

29 Duncombe & Marsden, 'Whose Orgasm Is It, Anyway?', p. 226.

30 Schwartz, *Peer Marriage*, p. 91.

31 Duncombe & Marsden, 'Whose Orgasm Is It, Anyway?', p. 226.

32 Paul Brown, 'Sexuality and the Couple' in Clulow, *Rethinking Marriage*, p. 102.

33 Duncombe & Marsden, 'Whose Orgasm Is It, Anyway?', p. 226.

34 cited in Dallos & Dallos, *Couples, Sex and Power*, pp. 133–34.

35 ibid, p. 139.

36 Natalie Angier, *Woman: An Intimate Geography*, Virago Press, London, 1999.

37 cited in Karen Milliner, 'Why Women Walk', *Sunday Times* (Perth, Western Australia), 9 January 2000, p. 39.

38 Natalie Angier, 'Finding Trouble in Paradise: Do Women Really Prefer Cuddling over "The Act"?' in *Time*, 28 January 1985, p. 76.

39 Dallos & Dallos, *Couples, Sex and Power*, p. 103.

14: excuses, excuses

1 Wallerstein & Blakeslee, *The Good Marriage*, p. 3.

2 cited in Bettina Arndt, 'Castles in the Air', *Sydney Morning Herald*, 28 October 2000, p. 8.

3 De Vaus, *Family Matters*.

4 Julia Hartley-Brewer, 'Brave New Age Dawns for Single Women', *Guardian*, 18 October 1999.

5 Drever et al., 'Social Inequalities, 2000 Edition'.

6 Ken Dempsey, *Family Matters*.

7 Susan Rosenbluth et al., *Journal of Family Issues*, p. 227.

8 Veronica Jaris Tichenor, 'Status and Income as Gendered Resources: The Case of Marital Power' in *Journal of Marriage and the Family*, August 1999, p. 638.

9 Ono, *Social Forces*, p. 969.

10 ibid.

11 ibid.

12 Liat Kulik & Haia Zuckerman Bareli, 'Continuity and Discontinuity in Attitudes toward Marital Power Relations: Pre-retired vs. Retired Husbands' in *Ageing and Society*, September 1997, p. 571.

13 Pat O'Connor, 'Women's Experience of Power within Marriage: An Inexplicable Phenomenon?' in *Sociological Review*, November 1991, p. 823.

14 Liat Kulik, 'Marital Power Relations, Resources and Gender Role Ideology: A Multivariate Model for Assessing Effects' in *Journal of Comparative Family Studies*, Spring 1999, p.189.

15 Steil, *Marital Equality*, pp. 29–30.

16 cited in Pamela Regan & Susan Sprecher, 'Gender Differences in the Value of Contributions to Intimate Relationships' in *Sex Roles: A Journal of Research*, August 1995, p. 221.

17 Benjamin, *Sociology*.

18 Steil, *Marital Equality*, p. 49.

19 ibid, p. 53.

20 ibid.

21 Dempsey, *Family Matters*, p. 16.

22 Dempsey, *Journal of Family Studies*, p. 7.

23 Benjamin, *Sociology*.

24 Steil, *Marital Equality*.

15: sleeping with the enemy

1 cited in Steil, *Marital Equality*.

2 James Honeycutt & Renee Brown, 'Did You Hear the One about: Typological and Spousal Differences in the Planning of Jokes and Sense of Humor in Marriage' in *Communication Quarterly*, Summer 1998, p. 342.

3 Steil, *Marital Equality*, p. 102.

4 McMahon, *Taking Care of Men*, p. 161.

5 quoted in ibid, p. 163.

6 Dempsey, *Journal of Family Studies*, p. 6.

7 Nock, *Marriage in Men's Lives*, p. 44.

8 ibid.

9 De Vaus, *Family Matters*.

10 Dempsey, *Family Matters*, p. 16.

11 ibid, p. 18.

12 Danielle Crittenden & Jennifer Pozner, 'Is Early Marriage the Best Choice for American Women?' in *Insight on the News*, vol. 15 (7), 1999, p. 24.

16: surrendered judgments

1 Bettina Arndt, 'Castles in the Air'.

2 Lynn Jamieson, 'Intimacy Transformed? A Critical Look at the "Pure Relationship"' in *Sociology*, August 1999, p. 477.

3 Arndt, 'Castles in the Air'.

4 ibid.

5 *West Australian*, 21 November 2000.

6 cited in Nock, *Society*.

7 Clare Payne, 'Post-Feminist Brides Still Want to Be Princess for a Day', *Sydney Morning Herald*, 3 May 2000.

8 Richard Mackey & Bernard O'Brien, 'Adaptation in Lasting Marriages' in

Families in Society: The Journal of Contemporary Human Services, vol. 80 (6), November 1999.

9 Charles Laurence, 'The Shrew Who Wants Taming', *West Australian*, 28 January 2000, p. 17.

10 Susan Carpenter, 'From Feminist to Doormat' in *Marie Claire* (Australia), November 2000, p. 91.

11 ibid.

12 ibid.

13 Laurence, *West Australian*.

14 ibid.

15 ibid.

16 Amy Dickinson, 'Positive Illusions: From "I Do" to the Seven-Year Itch: A New Study Shows That Marriage (Surprise) Is Hard Work' in *Time*, 27 September 1999, p. 112.

17 cited in Bettina Arndt, 'Silent Witness to Male Suicide', *Sydney Morning Herald*, 9 December 1999.

18 Haskey, *Population Trends 91*.

19 Australian Bureau of Statistics, 'Household and Family Projections, Australia', 3236.0, 28 October 1999.

20 Arndt, 'Silent Witness to Male Suicide'.

21 ibid.

22 Haskey, *Population Trends 104*.

23 Marcia Carlson & Sheldon Danziger, 'Cohabitation and the Measurement of Child Poverty', Poverty Measurement working papers, US Bureau of the Census.

24 Bettina Arndt, 'Double or Nothing', *Sydney Morning Herald*, 2 December 1999.

25 cited in ibid.

26 Jennifer Barber & William Axinn, 'Gender Role Attitudes and Marriage among Young Women' in *Sociological Quarterly*, Winter 1998, p. 11.

17: whose wife is it, anyway?

1 Nock, *Society*, (my emphasis).

2 Wolcott & Hughes, 'Towards Understanding the Reasons for Divorce'.

3 David Buss, *The Dangerous Passion*, Bloomsbury Publishing, London, 2000.

4 quoted in Jamieson, *Sociology*.

5 'Separate But Equal?', *The New Republic*, 10 January 2000, p. 9.

6 Jamieson, *Sociology*.

7 Hugh Mackay, 'Playing the Marriage Game', *West Australian*, 19 September 2000, p. 17.

8 quoted in Marano, *Psychology Today*.

9 ibid.

10 quoted in Dickinson, *Time*.

11 Stacy Rogers & Paul Amato, 'Is Marital Quality Declining? The Evidence from Two Generations' in *Social Forces*, March 1997, p. 1089.

12 De Vaus, *Family Matters*.

bibliography

books

Abrams, Rebecca, *The Playful Self*, Fourth Estate, London, 1997.

Angier, Natalie, *Woman: An Intimate Geography*, Virago Press, London, 1999.

Apter, Terri, *Why Women Don't Have Wives*, Macmillan, London, 1985.

Baxter, Janeen, *Work at Home: The Domestic Division of Labour*, University of Queensland Press, St Lucia, 1993.

Berk, Sarah Fenstermaker, *The Gender Factory*, Plenum Press, New York, 1985.

Bernard, Jessie, *The Future of Marriage*, 2nd edn, Yale University Press, New Haven, 1982.

Bittman, Michael, *Juggling Time: How Australian Families Use Time*, Office of the Status of Women, Department of the Prime Minister and Cabinet, Canberra, 1991.

Bittman, Michael & Pixley, Jocelyn, *The Double Life of the Family*, Allen & Unwin, Sydney, 1997.

Bolen, Jean Shinoda, *Goddesses in Everywoman: A New Psychology of Women*, Harper & Row, New York, 1984.

Buss, David M., *The Dangerous Passion*, Bloomsbury Publishing, London, 2000.

Buss, David M. & Malamuth, Neil M. eds, *Sex, Power, Conflict: Evolutionary and Feminist Perspectives*, Oxford University Press, New York, 1996.

Byatt, A. S., *The Virgin in the Garden/Still Life*, Chatto & Windus, London, 1991.

Caplan, Paula, *Don't Blame Mother: Mending the Mother–Daughter Relationship*, Harper & Row, New York, 1989.

Chandler, Joan, *Women without Husbands*, Macmillan Education, London, 1992.

Cherlin, Andrew J., *Public and Private Families: A Reader*, McGraw Hill, New York, 1997.

Chodorow, Nancy J., *Feminism and Psychoanalytic Theory*, Yale University Press, New Haven, 1989.

Clulow, Christopher ed., *Rethinking Marriage: Public and Private Perspectives*, H. Karnac Ltd, London, 1993.

Coontz, Stephanie, *The Way We Never Were: American Families and the Nostalgia Trap*, Basic Books, New York, 1992.

Cowan, Carolyn Pape & Cowan, Philip, *When Partners Become Parents*, Basic Books, New York, 1992.

Dallos, Sally & Dallos, Rudi, *Couples, Sex and Power: The Politics of Desire*, Open University Press, Buckingham, 1997.

Delphy, Christine & Leonard, Diana, *Familiar Exploitation: A New Analysis of Marriage in Contemporary Western Society*, Polity, Cambridge, 1992.

Demo, David, Allen, Katherine R. & Fine, Mark A. eds, *Handbook of Family Diversity*, Oxford University Press, New York, 2000.

Dienhart, Anna, *Reshaping Fatherhood: The Social Construction of Shared Parenting*, Sage, Thousand Oaks, California, 1998.

Dinnerstein, Dorothy, *The Rocking of the Cradle and the Ruling of the World*, Women's Press, London, 1987.

Dowrick, Stephanie, *Intimacy and Solitude*, Reed Books, Auckland, 1991.

Dryden, Caroline, *Being Married, Doing Gender*, Routledge, London, 1999.

Elkind, David, *Ties That Stress: The New Family Imbalance*, Harvard University Press, Cambridge, 1994.

Fineman, Martha Albertson, *The Neutered Mother and the Sexual Family*, Routledge, New York, 1995.

Funder, Kathleen, Harrison, Margaret & Weston, Ruth, *Settling Down: Pathways of Parents after Divorce*, Australian Institute of Family Studies, Melbourne, 1993.

Giddens, Anthony, *The Transformation of Intimacy: Sexuality, Love and Eroticism in Modern Societies*, Polity, Cambridge, 1992.

Goffman, Erving, *Gender Advertisements*, Harvard University Press, Cambridge, 1979.

Goldscheider, Frances & Waite, Linda, *New Families, No Families: The Transformation of the American Home*, University of California Press, Berkeley, 1991.

Gottman, John, *Why Marriages Succeed or Fail*, Simon & Schuster, New York, 1994.

Graham, Katharine, *Personal History*, Orion, London, 1988.

Green, Eileen, Hebron, Sandra & Woodward, Diana, *Women's Leisure, What Leisure?*, Macmillan, London, 1990.

Greer, Germaine, *The Whole Woman*, Transworld, London, 1999.

Hafner, Julian, *The End of Marriage*, Random House, London, 1993.

Hays, Sharon, *The Cultural Contradictions of Motherhood*, Yale University Press, New Haven, 1996.

Heyn, Dalma, *Marriage Shock*, Villard Books, New York, 1997.

Hochschild, Arlie Russell, *The Time Bind*, Henry Holt, New York, 1997.

Hrdy, Sarah Blaffer, *Mother Nature*, Chatto & Windus, London, 1999.

Johnson, Miriam, *Strong Mothers, Weak Wives*, University of California Press, Berkeley, 1988.

LaChance, Carol Wallas, *The Way of the Mother*, Element Inc., Rockport, 1991.

Laing, R. D., *The Politics of the Family and Other Essays*, Pantheon Books, New York, 1969.

Lasch, Christopher, *Women and the Common Life: Love, Marriage and Feminism*, Elisabeth Lasch-Quinn ed., W. W. Norton & Co., New York, 1997.

Lonsdale, Michele, *Liberating Women*, Cambridge University Press, Cambridge, 1991.

Lopata, Helena Znaniecka, *Circles and Settings: Role Changes of American Women*, State University of New York Press, Albany, 1994.

Luster, Tom & Okagaki, Lynn eds, *Parenting: An Ecological Perspective*, Lawrence Erlbaum Associates Inc., Hillsdale, 1993.

Mackay, Hugh, *Reinventing Australia: The Mind and Mood of Australia in the '90s*, Angus & Robertson, Sydney, 1993.

Mackay, Hugh, *The Family: '90s Style*, Mackay Research, Sydney, 1991.

McDonald, Peter, *Families in Australia*, Australian Institute of Family Studies, Melbourne, 1995.

McKenna, Elizabeth Perle, *When Work Doesn't Work Anymore*, Delacorte Press, New York, 1997.

McLanahan, Sara & Sandefur, Gary, *Growing up with a Single Parent: What Hurts, What Helps?*, Harvard University Press, Cambridge, 1994.

McMahon, Anthony, *Taking Care of Men*, Cambridge University Press, Cambridge, 1999.

Miller, Naomi, *Single Parents by Choice: A Growing Trend in Family Life*, Plenum Books, New York, 1992.

Nock, Steven L., *Marriage in Men's Lives*, Oxford University Press, New York, 1998.

Peters, Joan K., *When Mothers Work: Loving Our Children without Sacrificing Ourselves*, Addison-Wesley, Reading, 1997.

Popenoe, David, *Life without Father*, Simon & Schuster, New York, 1996.

Robinson, John P. & Godbey, Geoffrey, *Time for Life: The Surprising Ways Americans Use Their Time*, Pennsylvania State University Press, University Park, 1997.

Schwartz, Pepper, *Peer Marriage*, Free Press, New York, 1994.

Shelton, Beth, *Men, Women, and Time*, Greenwood Press, New York, 1992.

Skolnick, Arlene, *Embattled Paradise: The American Family in an Age of Uncertainty*, Basic Books, New York, 1991.

Smith, Dorothy, *The Everyday World as Problematic*, Northeastern University Press, Boston, 1987.

Spain, Daphne & Bianchi, Suzanne, *Balancing Act: Motherhood, Marriage and Employment among American Women*, Russell Sage Foundation, New York, 1996.

Spender, Dale ed., *Weddings and Wives*, Penguin, Ringwood, 1994.

Steil, Janice M., *Marital Equality*, Sage Publications, Thousand Oaks, 1997.

Tavris, Carol, *The Mismeasure of Woman*, Simon & Schuster, New York, 1992.

Travers, Peter & Richardson, Sue, *Living Decently: Material Well-Being in Australia*, Oxford University Press, Melbourne, 1993.

Wallerstein, Judith & Blakeslee, Sandra, *The Good Marriage*, Houghton Mifflin, New York, 1995.

Wallerstein, Judith, Lewis, Julia & Blakeslee, Sandra, *The Unexpected Legacy of Divorce*, Hyperion, New York, 2000.

Waite, Linda & Gallagher, Maggie, *The Case for Marriage*, Doubleday, New York, 2000.

Weeks, Jeffrey & Holland, Janet eds, *Sexual Cultures: Communities, Values and Intimacy*, St Martin's Press, New York, 1996.

Whitehead, Barbara Dafoe, *The Divorce Culture*, Vintage Books, New York, 1998.

journals

Allen, Sarah & Hawkins, Alan, 'Maternal Gatekeeping: Mothers' Beliefs and Behaviors That Inhibit Greater Father Involvement in Family Work', *Journal of Marriage and the Family*, February 1999, p. 199.

Australian Bureau of Statistics, 'Household and Family Projections, Australia', 3236.0, 28 October 1999.

'Recent Changes in Unpaid Work', occasional paper, 4154.0, 1995.

'1997 Births Australia', 3310.0, 12 November 1998.

'Employee Earnings and Hours, Australia', 6306.0, 25 March 1999.

'Labour Force (PR) Participation Rate', 6291.0.40.001, 15 June 2000.

Bachu, Amara, 'Trends in Marital Status of US Women at First Birth: 1930 to 1994', US Bureau of the Census, Population Division, working paper no. 20, March 1998.

Bailey, William T., 'A Longitudinal Study of Fathers' Involvement with Young Children: Infancy to Age 5 Years', *Journal of Genetic Psychology*, vol. 155, no. 3, September 1994, p. 331 (9).

Barber, Jennifer & Axinn, William, 'Gender Role Attitudes and Marriage among Young Women', *Sociological Quarterly*, Winter 1998, p. 11.

Barnett, Rosalind C. & Shen, Yu-Chu, 'Gender, High- and Low-Schedule-Control Housework Tasks, and Psychological Distress: A Study of Dual-Earner Couples', *Journal of Family Issues*, vol. 18 (4), July 1997, pp. 403–28.

Barris, Beverly H., 'Employed Mothers: The Impact of Class and Marital Status on the Prioritizing of Family and Work', *Social Science Quarterly*, vol. 72 (1), March 1991, pp. 50–66.

Bartle-Haring, Suzanne & Echelberger Strimple, Richelle, 'Association of Identity and Intimacy: An Exploration of Gender and Sex-Role Orientation', *Psychological Reports*, December 1996, p. 1255.

Baxter, Janeen & Western, Mark, 'Satisfaction with Housework: Examining the Paradox', *Sociology*, February 1998, p. 101.

Belsky, J., Lang, M. & Rovine, M., 'Stability and Change across the Transition to Parenthood: A Second Study', *Journal of Personality and Social Psychology* vol. 50, 1985, pp. 517–22.

Benjamin, Orly, 'Therapeutic Discourse, Power and Change: Emotion and Negotiation in Marital Conversations', *Sociology*, November 1998, p. 771.

Bialeschki, M. Deborah & Michener, Sarah, 'Re-Entering Leisure: Transition within the Role of Motherhood', *Journal of Leisure Research*, Winter 1994, p. 57.

Bianchi, Suzanne, Milkie, Melissa A., Sayer, Liana C. & Robinson, John P., 'Is Anyone Doing the Housework? Trends in the Gender Division of Household Labor', *Social Forces*, vol. 79, i. 1, September 2000, p. 91.

Blain, J., 'Discourses of Agency and Domestic Labour: Family Discourse and Gendered Practice in Dual-Earner Families', *Journal of Family Issues*, vol. 15 (4), 1994, pp. 515–49.

Blossfeld, Hans-Peter & Huinink, Johannes, 'Human Capital Investments or Norms of Role Transition? How Women's Schooling and Career Affect the Process of Family Formation', *American Journal of Sociology*, vol. 97, 1991, pp. 143–68.

Bowler, Mary, 'Women's Earnings: An Overview', Monthly Labor Review Online, vol. 122 (12), December 1999.

Brines, J., 'Economic Dependency, Gender, and the Division of Labor at Home', *American Journal of Sociology*, vol. 100 (3), 1994, pp. 652–88.

Bromberger, Joyce & Matthews, Karen, 'Employment Status and Depressive Symptoms in Middle-Aged Women: A Longitudinal Investigation', *American Journal of Public Health*, February 1994, p. 202.

Byers, Sandra & Heinlein, Larry, 'Predicting Initiations and Refusals of Sexual Activities in Married and Cohabiting Heterosexual Couples', *Journal of Sex Research*, May 1989, p. 210.

Call, Vaughn, Sprecher, Susan & Schwartz, Pepper, 'The Incidence and Frequency of Marital Sex in a National Sample', *Journal of Marriage and the Family*, August 1995, p. 639.

Carlson, Marcia & Danziger, Sheldon, 'Cohabitation and the Measurement of Child Poverty', Poverty Measurement working papers, US Bureau of the Census.

Censer, Jane Turner, 'What Ever Happened to Family History?', *Comparative Studies in Society and History*, July 1991, p. 528.

Clarkberg, Marin, Stolzenberg, Ross & Waite, Linda, 'Attitudes, Values, and Entrance into Cohabitational Versus Marital Unions', *Social Forces*, December 1995, p. 609.

Cohen, Philip N. & Bianchi, Suzanne M., 'Marriage, Children, and Women's Employment: What Do We Know?', *Monthly Labor Review*, December 1999.

Coiro, Mary Jo & Emery, Robert, 'Do Marriage Problems Affect Fathering More Than Mothering? A Quantitative and Qualitative Review', *Clinical Child and Family Psychology Review*, March 1988, p. 23.

Costello, Elizabeth, 'Married with Children: Predictors of Mental and Physical Health in Middle-Aged Women', *Psychiatry: Interpersonal and Biological Processes*, August 1991, p. 292.

Craddock, Alan, 'Relationships between Marital Satisfaction and Privacy Preferences', *Journal of Comparative Family Studies*, Autumn 1994, p. 371.

Crispell, Diane, 'Why Men Take out the Garbage', *American Demographics* vol. 19 (11), November 1997, p. 35.

Dehle, Crystal & Weiss, Rober, 'Sex Differences in Prospective Associations between Marital Quality and Depressed Mood', *Journal of Marriage and the Family*, November 1998, p. 1002.

Dempsey, Ken, 'Women's Perceptions of Fairness and the Persistence of an Unequal Division of Housework', *Family Matters*, Spring–Summer 1997, p. 15.

Dempsey, Ken, 'Attempting to Explain Women's Perceptions of Their Fairness of the Division of Housework', *Journal of Family Studies*, April 1999, pp. 3–24.

De Vaus, David, 'Family Values in the Nineties: Gender Gap or Generation Gap?', *Family Matters*, Spring–Summer 1997.

Dimitrovsky, Lilly, Schapira-Beck, Ester & Itskowitz, Rivka, 'Locus of Control of Israeli Women during the Transition to Marriage', *Journal of Psychology*, September 1994, p. 537.

Dion, Karen & Dion, Kenneth, 'Individualistic and Collectivistic Perspectives on Gender and the Cultural Context of Love and Intimacy', *Journal of Social Issues*, Fall 1993, p. 53.

Donath, Susan, 'Pipe and Slippers or Kitchen Sink?', paper presented at the seventh Australian Institute of Family Studies conference, Sydney, July 2000.

Drever, Frances, Fisher, Katie, Brown, Joanna & Clark, Jenny, 'Social Inequalities, 2000 Edition', Office for National Statistics (UK).

Duncombe, Jean & Marsden, Dennis, '"Workaholics" and "Whingeing Women": Theorising Intimacy and Emotion Work', *Sociological Review*, vol. 43, 1995.

Ellestad, June & Stets, Jan, 'Jealousy and Parenting: Predicting Emotions from Identity Theory', *Sociological Perspectives*, Fall 1998, p. 639.

Equal Pay Task Force, 'Just Pay: The Report of the Equal Pay Task Force', 2001.

Erickson, Rebecca, 'Reconceptualizing Family Work: The Effect of Emotion Work on Perceptions of Marital Quality', *Journal of Marriage and the Family* vol. 55 (11), November 1993, pp. 888–900.

Fields, Jason & Casper, Lynne M., 'American Families and Living Arrangements: Population Characteristics', Current Population Reports, June 2001.

Fowers, Blaine J., 'Psychology and the Good Marriage: Social Theory as Practice', *American Behavioral Scientist*, January 1998, p. 516.

Fowers, B. J., Lyons, E. M. & Montel, K. H., 'Positive Illusions about Marriage: Self Enhancement or Relationship Enhancement?' *Journal of Family Psychology*, vol. 10, 1996, pp. 192–208.

Fox, John & Pearce, David, 'Twenty-Five Years of Population Trends', *Population Trends*, Summer 2000, p. 6.

Frazier, Shervert H., 'Psychotrends: Taking Stock of Tomorrow's Family and Sexuality', *Psychology Today*, January–February 1994, p. 32.

Freysinger, Valeria, 'Leisure with Children and Parental Satisfaction', *Journal of Leisure Research*, Summer 1994, p. 212.

Glass, Shirley & Wright, Thomas, 'Justifications for Extramarital Relationships: The Association between Attitudes, Behaviors, and Gender,' *Journal of Sex Research*, August 1992, p. 361.

Glendon, Mary Ann, 'Feminism and The Family', *Commonweal*, vol. CXXIV (3), 1997, pp. 11–15.

Godwyn, Mary, 'Co-Parenting and Gender Equality: A Reexamination of Nancy Chodorow's Contribution', Society for the Study of Social Problems, 1999.

Graff, E. J., 'What's Love Got to Do with It?', *Utne Reader*, May–June 1999, p. 65.

Greenstein, Theodore, 'Gender Ideology and Perceptions of the Fairness of the Division of Household Labor: Effects on Marital Quality', *Social Forces*, March 1996, p. 1029.

Gupta, Sanjiv, 'The Effects of Transitions in Marital Status on Men's Performance of Housework', *Journal of Marriage and the Family*, August 1999, p. 700.

Hakim, C., 'Five Feminist Myths about Women's Employment', *British Journal of Sociology*, vol. 46 (3), 1995, pp. 429–55.

Haskey, John, 'One-Parent Families and Their Dependent Children', *Population Trends 91*, Spring 1998.

Haskey, John, 'Cohabitation in Great Britain: Past, Present and Future Trends and Attitudes', *Population Trends 104*.

Hawkins, A., Marshall, C. & Meiners, K., 'Exploring Wives' Sense of Fairness about Family Work', *Journal of Family Issues*, vol. 16 (6), 1995, pp. 693–721.

Hayghe, Howard V., 'Developments in Women's Labor Force Participation', *Monthly Labor Review*, vol. 120 (9), September 1997, p. 41(6).

Heaton, Tim & Albrecht, Stan L., 'Stable Unhappy Marriages', *Journal of Marriage and the Family*, vol. 53, 1991, pp. 747–58.

Henderson, Karla, 'One Size Doesn't Fit All: The Meaning of Women's Leisure', *Journal of Leisure Research*, Summer 1996, p. 139.

Hilton, Jeanne & Devall, Esther, 'Comparison of Parenting and Children's Behavior in Single-Mother, Single-Father, and Intact Families', *Journal of Divorce and Remarriage*, 1998, p. 23.

Hoffman, Charles & Moon, Michelle, 'Women's Characteristics and Gender Role Attitudes: Support for Father Involvement with Children', *Journal of Genetic Psychology*, December 1999, p. 411.

Honeycutt, James & Brown, Renee, 'Did You Hear the One about: Typological and Spousal Differences in the Planning of Jokes and Sense of Humor in Marriage', *Communication Quarterly*, Summer 1998, p. 342.

Huston, Ted L. & Geis, Gilbert, 'In What Ways Do Gender-Related Attributes and Beliefs Affect Marriage?', *Journal of Social Issues*, Fall 1993, p. 87.

Jacobs, Steven, 'The Effects of Family Structure and Fathering Time on Child Behavior Problems and Reading Deficits', Dissertation Abstracts International Section A: Humanities and Social Sciences, May 1999, p. 3978.

Jamieson, Lynn, 'Intimacy Transformed? A Critical Look at the "Pure Relationship"', *Sociology*, August 1999, p. 477.

Kulik, Liat, 'Marital Power Relations, Resources and Gender Role Ideology: A Multivariate Model for Assessing Effects', *Journal of Comparative Family Studies*, Spring 1999, p.189.

Kulik, Liat & Bareli, Haia Zuckerman, 'Continuity and Discontinuity in Attitudes toward Marital Power Relations: Pre-Retired vs. Retired Husbands', *Ageing and Society*, September 1997, p. 571.

Lang-Takac, Esther & Osterwell, Zahava, 'Separateness and Connectedness: Differences between the Genders', *Sex Roles: A Journal of Research*, September 1992, p. 277.

Larson, Jeffry, Hammond, Clark & Harper, James, 'Perceived Inequity and Intimacy in Marriage', *Journal of Marital and Family Therapy*, October 1998, p. 487.

Lee, Catherine M. & Duxbury, Linda, 'Employed Parents' Support from Partners, Employers and Friends', *Journal of Social Psychology*, vol. 138, no. 3, June 1998, p. 303 (20).

Levant, Ronald F., 'The Crisis of Connection between Men and Women', *Journal of Men's Studies*, August 1996, p. 1.

Licht, Walter & Grossman, Jonathan, 'How the Workplace Has Changed in 75 Years', *Monthly Labor Review*, vol. 111, no. 2, February 1988, p. 19 (7).

Lindsay, Jo, 'Diversity But Not Equality: Domestic Labour in Cohabiting Relationships', *Australian Journal of Social Issues*, August 1999, p. 267.

London Stationery Office, 'Birth Statistics, Review of the Registrar General on Births and Patterns of Family-building in England and Wales, 1999', series FM1, no. 28.

Long, Patricia, 'Sex after Marriage? It's Boring, Too Many Couples Say', *Health*, May–June 1996, p. 42.

Mackey, Richard & O'Brien, Bernard, 'Adaptation in Lasting Marriages', *Families in Society: The Journal of Contemporary Human Services*, vol. 80 (6), November 1999.

Major, Brenda, 'Gender, Entitlement, and the Distribution of Family Labor', *Journal of Social Issues*, vol. 49 (3), Fall 1993, p. 141.

Manke, B., Seery, B., Crouter, A. & McHale, S., 'The Three Corners of Domestic Labor: Mother's, Father's and Children's Weekday and Weekend Housework', *Journal of Marriage and the Family*, vol. 56, 1994, pp. 657–68.

Marano, Hara Estroff, 'The Reinvention of Marriage', *Psychology Today*, January–February 1992, p. 48.

Mattingly, Marybeth, 'Gender, Parenting and Free Time', American Sociological Association, 2000.

Maushart, Susan, 'Mother Knows Best: Australian Women Learn to Mother', International Year of the Family research report, Family and Children's Services, Western Australia, 1996.

McKean Skaff, Marilyn, Finney, John & Moos, Rudolf, 'Gender Differences in Problem Drinking and Depression', *American Journal of Community Psychology*, February 1999, p. 25.

Mental Health Weekly, 'Study: Bad Relationships Affect Women More', 1 May 2000, p. 8.

Miller, Melody L. et al., 'Motherhood, Multiple Roles and Maternal Well Being', *Gender and Society*, vol. 5 (4), December 1991, pp. 565–82.

Mitchell, Susan, 'Who Does the Shopping?', *American Demographics*, vol. 18 (8), August 1996, p. 56.

Morokoff, Patricia & Gillilland, Ruth, 'Stress, Sexual Functioning, and Marital Satisfaction', *Journal of Sex Research*, February 1993, p. 43.

National Institute of Child Health & Human Development, Early Child Care Research Network, Rockville, MD, 'Factors Associated with Fathers' Caregiving Activities and Sensitivity with Young Children', *Journal of Family Psychology*, June 2000, p. 200.

Nock, Steven, 'The Problem with Marriage', *Society*, vol. 36 (5), 1999, p. 20.

O'Connor, Pat, 'Understanding Variation in Marital Sexual Pleasure: An Impossible Task?', *Sociological Review*, May 1995, p. 342.

O'Connor, Pat, 'Women's Experience of Power within Marriage: An Inexplicable Phenomenon?' *Sociological Review*, November 1991, p. 823.

Office for National Statistics (UK), 'Marriages in England and Wales during 1999', *Population Trends 103*.

'In Brief', *Population Trends 100*, Summer 2000.

Ono, Hiromi, 'Historical Time and US Marital Dissolution', *Social Forces*, vol. 77 (3), 1999, p. 969.

Oppenheimer, Valerie K., 'Women's Rising Employment and the Future of the Family in Industrial Societies', *Population and Development Review 20*, 1994, pp. 293–342.

Overall, Christine, 'Monogamy, Nonmonogamy, and Identity', *Hypatia*, Fall 1998, p. 1.

Ozer, Elizabeth, 'The Impact of Childcare Responsibility and Self Efficacy on the Psychological Health of Professional Working Mothers', *Psychology of Women Quarterly*, September 1995, p. 315.

Perry-Jenkins, Maureen, Seery, Brenda & Crouter, Ann, 'Linkages between Women's Provider-Role Attitudes, Psychological Well-Being, and Family Relationships', *Psychology of Women Quarterly*, September 1992, p. 311.

Pina, Darlene & Bengston, Vern, 'Division of Household Labor and the Well-Being of Retirement-Aged Wives', *Gerontologist*, June 1995, p. 308.

Press, Julie & Townsley, Eleanor, 'Wives' and Husbands' Housework Reporting: Gender, Class, and Social Desirability', *Gender and Society*, April 1998, p. 188.

Pyke, Karen, 'Women's Employment as a Gift or Burden: Marital Power across Marriage, Divorce, and Remarriage', *Gender and Society*, March 1994, p. 73.

Rabin, Claire & Shapira-Berman, Ofrit, 'Egalitarianism and Marital Happiness: Israeli Husbands and Wives on a Collision Course', *American Journal of Family Therapy*, Winter 1997, p. 319.

Regan, Pamela & Sprecher, Susan, 'Gender Differences in the Value of Contributions to Intimate Relationships', *Sex Roles: A Journal of Research*, August 1995, p. 221.

Riley, Pamela & Kiger, Gary, 'Moral Discourse on Domestic Labor: Gender, Power and Identity in Families', *Social Science Journal*, July 1999, p. 541.

Rogers, Stacy & Amato, Paul, 'Is Marital Quality Declining? The Evidence from Two Generations', *Social Forces*, March 1997, p. 1089.

Rosenbluth, Susan, Steil, Janice & Whitcomb, Juliet, 'Marital Equality: What Does It Mean?', *Journal of Family Issues*, May 1998, p. 227.

Schumm, Walter, Webb, Farrell & Bollman, Stephan, 'Gender and Marital Satisfaction: Data from the National Survey of Families and Households', *Psychological Reports*, August 1998, p. 319.

Schwartz, Pepper, 'Modernizing Marriage', *Psychology Today*, September–October 1994, p. 54.

Shachar, Rina, 'His and Her Marital Satisfaction: The Double Standard', *Sex Roles: A Journal of Research*, October 1991, p. 451.

Starrels, Marjorie, 'Husbands' Involvement in Female Gender-Typed Household Chores', *Sex Roles: A Journal of Research*, vol. 31 (7/8), October 1994, p. 473.

Stevens, Nan, 'Gender and Adaptation to Widowhood in Later Life', *Ageing and Society*, March 1995, p. 37.

Stringer, Gayle, 'Wife Rape: Understanding the Response of Survivors and Service Providers', *Journal of Interpersonal Violence*, February 1998, p. 167.

Thabes, Virginia, 'A Survey Analysis of Women's Long-term, Postdivorce Adjustment', *Journal of Divorce and Remarriage*, November–December 1997, p. 163.

Thompson, Linda, 'Conceptualizing Gender in Marriage', *Journal of Marriage and the Family*, vol. 55, 1993, pp. 557–69.

Tichenor, Veronica Jaris, 'Status and Income as Gendered Resources: The Case of Marital Power', *Journal of Marriage and the Family*, August 1999, p. 638.

Tingey, Holly, 'Juggling Multiple Roles: Perceptions of Working Mothers', *Social Science Journal*, vol. 32 (2), 1996, pp. 183–91.

Tower, Roni Beth & Kasl, Stanislav, 'Gender, Marital Closeness, and Depressive Symptoms in Elderly Couples', *Journals of Gerontology*, series B, May 1996, p. 115.

Trafford, Abigail, Avery, Patricia A., Thornton, Jeannye, Carey, Joseph & Galloway, Joseph L., 'She's Come a Long Way—or Has She?', *US News and World Report*, vol. 97, 6 August 1984, p. 44 (8).

Turner, Heather A. & Turner, R. Jay, 'Gender, Social Status and Emotional Reliance', *Journal of Health and Social Behavior*, December 1999, p. 360.

US Department of Commerce, 'Married Adults Still in the Majority', press release, Census Bureau Reports, 7 January 1999.

US Department of Health and Human Services, 'Fertility, Family Planning and Women's Health: New Data from the 1995 National Survey of Family Growth', series 23, no. 19, May 1997.

Van Berkel, Michel & De Graaf, Nan Dirk, 'By Virtue of Pleasantness? Housework and the Effects of Education Revisited', *Sociology*, November 1999, p. 785.

VanEvery, J., 'De/Reconstructing Gender: Women in Antisexist Living Arrangements', *Women's Studies International Forum*, vol. 18 (3), 1995, pp. 256–69.

Ventura, Stephanie J., Martin, Joyce A., Curtin, Sally C. & Matthews, T. J., 'Births: Final Data for 1997', National Vital Statistics Reports, vol. 47, no. 18, 29 April 1999.

Waldrop, Judith, 'Dirty Laundry and Clean Dishes', *American Demographics* vol. 12 (12), December 1990, p. 15.

Ward, R., 'Marital Happiness and Household Equity in Later Life', *Journal of Marriage and the Family*, vol. 55, 1993, pp. 427–38.

Wolcott, Irene & Hughes, Jody, 'Towards Understanding the Reasons for Divorce', Australian Institute of Family Studies working paper no. 20, June 1999.

Wood, Julia & Inman, Christopher, 'In a Different Mode: Masculine Styles of Communicating Closeness', *Journal of Applied Communication Research*, August 1993, p. 279.

newspapers and magazines

Angier, Natalie, 'Finding Trouble in Paradise: Do Women Really Prefer Cuddling over "The Act"?', *Time*, 28 January 1985, p. 76.

Angier, Natalie, 'Men: Are Women Better Off with Them or without Them?', *New York Times*, 21 June 1998.

Arndt, Bettina, 'Divide and Ruin', *Sydney Morning Herald*, 9 October 1999.

'Silent Witness to Male Suicide', *SMH*, 9 December 1999.

'Mothers Work: Raising Hell', *SMH*, 3 June 2000.

'For Better or Worth', *SMH*, 19 August 2000.

'Marriage Lite: The Facts about De Factos', *SMH*, 21 August 2000.

'Castles in the Air', *SMH*, 28 October 2000, p. 8.

Australian Women's Weekly, 25 August 1954; 18 March 1959 (reproduced in Lonsdale, *Liberating Women*, pp. 13–15); 21 January 1958.

Australian, 2 August 2000, p. 1.

Besharov, Douglas, 'Asking More from Matrimony', *New York Times*, 14 July 1999.

Breslin, Jimmy, 'By Love Depressed', *Esquire*, June 1995, p. 84.

Callahan, Sidney, 'Two by Two: The Case for Monogamy', *Commonweal*, 15 July 1994, p. 6.

Carpenter, Susan, 'From Feminist to Doormat', *Marie Claire* (Australia), November 2000, p. 91.

Carson, Andrea, 'Female Pay Scales Fail to Keep Up', *Age*, 12 May 2000, p. 3.

Cauchi, Steve, 'Is Marriage on the Rocks?', *Age*, 13 January 2001, p. 2.

Cherlin, Andrew J., 'By the Numbers', *New York Times Magazine*, 5 April 1998, p. 39.

Cohen, Patricia, 'Daddy Dearest: Do You Really Matter?', Arts & Ideas, *New York Times*, 11 July 1998.

Cosic, Miriam, 'Uncivil War', *Australian Magazine*, 21–22 August 1999, p. 15.

'Labour Relations', *Weekend Australian Review*, 18–19 September 1999, p. 8.

Crittenden, Danielle & Pozner, Jennifer, 'Is Early Marriage the Best Choice for American Women?' *Insight on the News* vol. 15 (7), 1999, p. 24.

Daley, Suzanne, 'French Couples Take Plunge That Falls Short of Marriage', *New York Times*, 18 April 2000.

DeClaire, Joan, 'Calling It Splits: A Psychologist Claims a Test Can Forecast Who Will Divorce and Who Won't', *People Weekly*, 19 October 1992, p. 131.

Dickinson, Amy, 'Positive Illusions: From "I Do" to the Seven-Year Itch: A New Study Shows That Marriage (Surprise) Is Hard Work', *Time*, 27 September 1999, p. 112.

Duckworth, Lorna, 'New Place for Fathers in Maternity Wards', *Independent*, 16 June 2001.

Gunn, Michelle & Crawford, Barclay, 'Motherhood Now a 30-Something Habit', *Australian*, 17 November 2000, p. 1.

Harlow, John, 'Till Death—or the 30-Month Itch—Do Us Part', *Australian*, 26 July 1999, p. 1.

Hartley-Brewer, Julia, 'Brave New Age Dawns for Single Women', *Guardian*, 18 October 1999.

Hewlett, Sylvia Ann, 'Have a Child, Experience the Wage Gap', *New York Times*, 16 May 2000.

Hitt, Jack, 'The Second Sexual Revolution', *New York Times Magazine*, 21 February 2000.

Independent on Sunday, 'Parents Hit the Career Bump', 2 April 2000.

Jet, 'Studies Show Men Do Better in Marriage Than Women', 12 May 1997, p. 18.

Kaplan, Morris, 'Joint Accounts But Love Overdrawn', *Australian*, 22 February 1999.

Kelly, Alice Lesch, *New York Times*, 13 June 1999.

Laurence, Charles, 'The Shrew Who Wants Taming', *West Australian*, 28 January 2000, p. 17.

Lewin, Tamar, 'Men Assuming Bigger Share at Home, New Survey Shows', *New York Times*, 15 April 1998.

Lewin, Tamar, 'Child Well-being Improves, US Says', *New York Times*, 19 July 2001.

Mackay, Hugh, 'Playing the Marriage Game', *West Australian*, 19 September 2000, p. 17.

Macken, Julie, 'The Mystery of Why Women Marry', *Australian Financial Review*, 28–29 August 1999, p. 32.

Malan, Andre. 'Live, Love But Let's Not Marry', *West Australian*, 15 February 2001, p. 21.

Martin, Nicole, 'Caring Fathers Help Children to Thrive', *Daily Telegraph*, 13 June 2001.

Martin Nicole, 'Working Mothers Are Stressed and Exhausted', *Daily Telegraph*, 13 June 2001.

Milliner, Karen, 'Why Women Walk', *Sunday Times* (Perth), 9 January 2000, p. 39.

Nagourney, Eric, 'Study Finds Families Bypassing Marriage', *New York Times*, 15 February 2000.

New York Times, 'Men: Say, "I Do," Then Obey', 2 February 1998.

'US Marriage Is Weakening, Study Reports', 4 July 1999.

Norton, Cherry, 'Forecasts of Leisure Society Fail to Materialise', *Independent on Sunday*, 4 October 1998.

Norton, Cherry, 'Ministers Join Bid to Give Fathers More Support', *Independent*, 18 November 1999.

Norton Cherry, 'New Fathers Get Better Jobs and Work Harder', *Independent*, 9 May 2000.

Norton, Cherry, 'UK Parents Spend Most "Quality" Time with Children', *Independent*, 27 October 2000.

Oderberg, David, 'Any Child Has a Right to a Father', *Australian*, 3 August 2000, p. 11.

Orenstein, Peggy, 'Almost Equal', *New York Times Magazine*, 5 April 1998, pp. 42–48.

Orr, Deborah, 'Caring Fathers Get a Raw Deal', *Independent*, 16 June 2000.

Orr, Deborah, 'Men and Women Can't Be Equal', *Independent*, 12 September 2000.

Orr, Deborah, 'New Rights the Best Gifts for Fathers', *Independent*, 15 June 2001.

Payne, Clare, 'Post-Feminist Brides Still Want to Be Princess for a Day', *Sydney Morning Herald*, 3 May 2000.

Reid, Tim, 'Professor Finds Key to Lasting Happiness', *Sunday Telegraph*, 4 October 1998.

Roberts, Yvonne, 'Fathers Are Doing It for Themselves', *Independent*, 16 June 2000.

Schmitt, Eric, 'For First Time, Nuclear Families Drop Below 25% of Households', *New York Times*, 14 May 2001.

Schrof, Joannie, 'A Lens on Matrimony', *US News and World Report*, 21 February 1994, p. 66.

Segell, Michael, 'The New Softness', *Esquire*, April 1996, p. 51.

Smiley, Jane, 'Money, Marriage and Monogamy', *Good Weekend*, 6 January 2001, p. 22.

Smith, Dinitia, 'The Opposites of Sex: The "Normal" and the Not', *New York Times*, 13 May 2000.

Stapleton, John, 'An Ordinary Decent Father Can Make a World of Difference', *Weekend Australian*, 5–6 August 2000, p. 27.

Sunday Age, 'Wedding Bells Lose Their (Ap)peal', 14 January 2001, p. 14.

Sweeney, Camille, 'The Truth about Sex—At Any Given Moment', *New York Times Magazine*, 16 May 1999.

USA Today Magazine, 'Women Still Chained to Housework', vol. 122 (2584), January 1994, p. 10.

Waite, Linda, 'The Importance of Marriage Is Being Overlooked', *USA Today Magazine*, vol. 127 (2644), 1999, p. 46.

Ward, Lucy & May, Peter, 'Daddy's Home . . .', *Guardian*, 16 June 1999.

Weinstein, Michael, 'A Man's Place', *New York Times Magazine*, 16 May 1999.

Weir, Henry, 'Dad's Dilemma—Family vs. Career', *Family Circle*, August 2000, p. 22.

West Australian, 'Support Urged for Fathers', 21 November 2000, p. 9.

Williamson, J., 'Having Your Baby and Eating It', *New Statesman*, 15 April 1988, pp. 44–45.

index

A note on the author

Susan Maushart was born in New York and emigrated to Australia in 1985. She is the author of two books: *Sort of a Place Like Home* published in 1994, and *The Mask of Motherhood* published to international acclaim in 1999. A senior research associate at Curtin University and a columnist for the Australian Magazine, Susan Maushart lives in Perth with her three children.